The Three Rooms in Valerie's Head

By **David Gaffney**
& **Dan Berry**

Fic
GAFFNEY
GN

APR '18

19.99

Published by Top Shelf Productions, PO Box 1282, Marietta, GA 30061-1282, USA. Top Shelf Productions is an imprint of IDW Publishing, a division of Idea and Design Works, LLC. Offices: 2765 Truxtun Road, San Diego, CA 92106. Top Shelf Productions®, the Top Shelf logo, Idea and Design Works®, and the IDW logo are registered trademarks of Idea and Design Works, LLC. All Rights Reserved. With the exception of small excerpts of artwork used for review purposes, none of the contents of this publication may be reprinted without the permission of IDW Publishing. IDW Publishing does not read or accept unsolicited submissions of ideas, stories, or artwork. Printed in Korea.

ISBN 978-1-60309-415-3

Editor-in-Chief: Chris Staros.

Designed by Dan Berry & Gilberto Lazcano.

Edited by Chris Staros & Zac Boone.

Visit our online catalog at topshelfcomix.com.

The authors would like to thank the Lakes International Comic Art Festival for commissioning this work, Arts Council England for supporting composer Sara Lowe's original music for the live performance, and Salt Publishing, who originally published parts of the text which appear here with their kind permission.

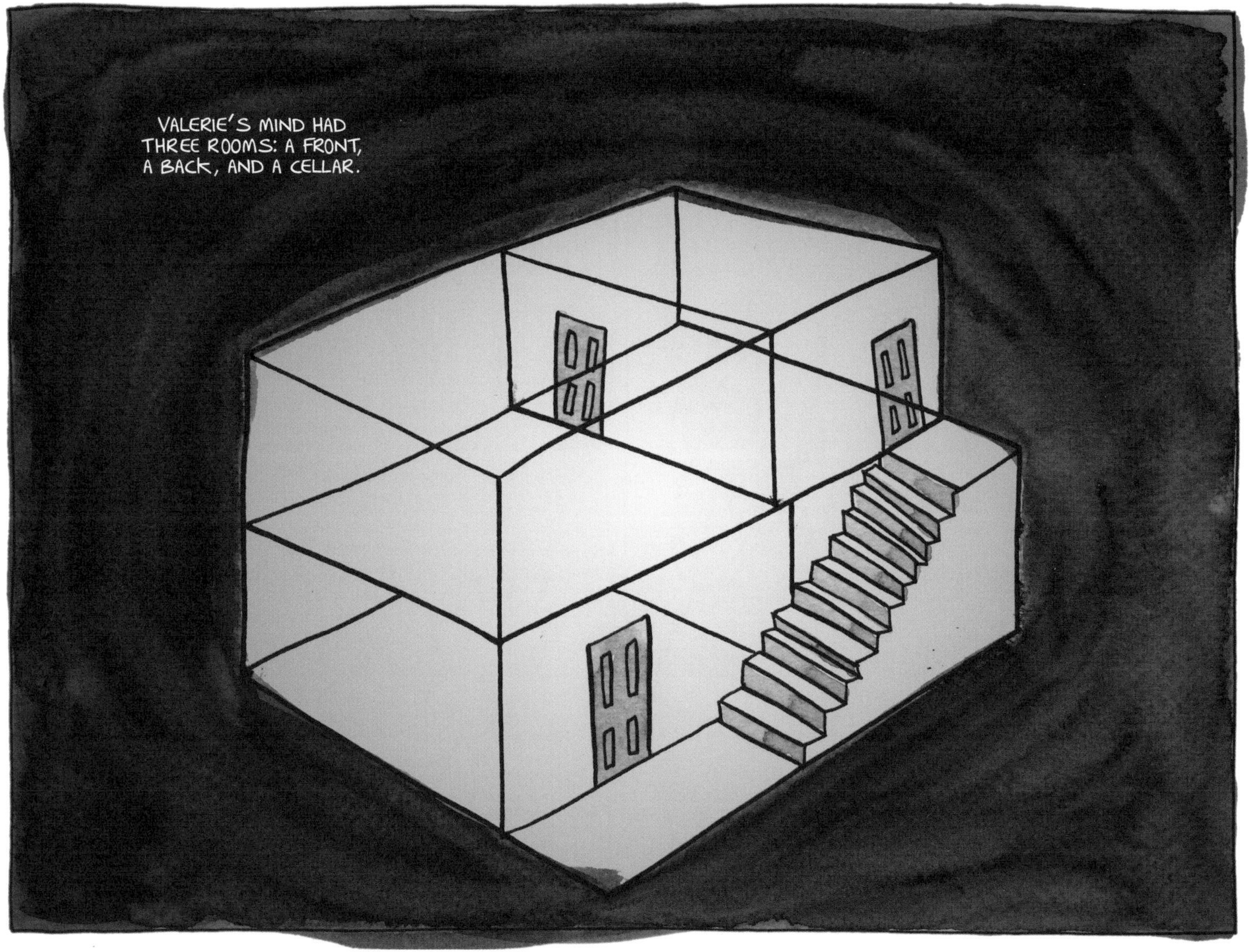
VALERIE'S MIND HAD THREE ROOMS: A FRONT, A BACK, AND A CELLAR.

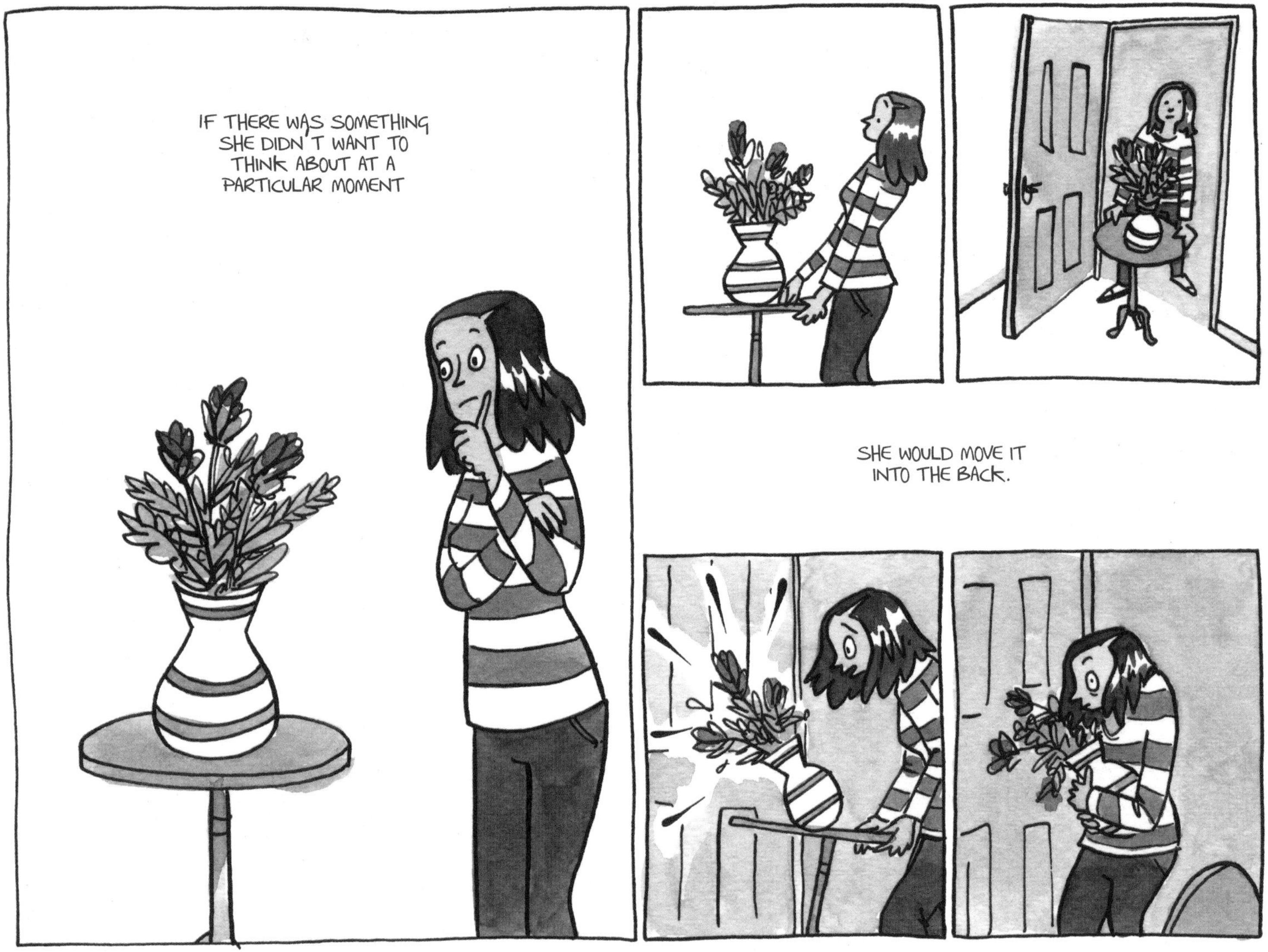
IF THERE WAS SOMETHING
SHE DIDN'T WANT TO
THINK ABOUT AT A
PARTICULAR MOMENT
SHE WOULD MOVE IT
INTO THE BACK.

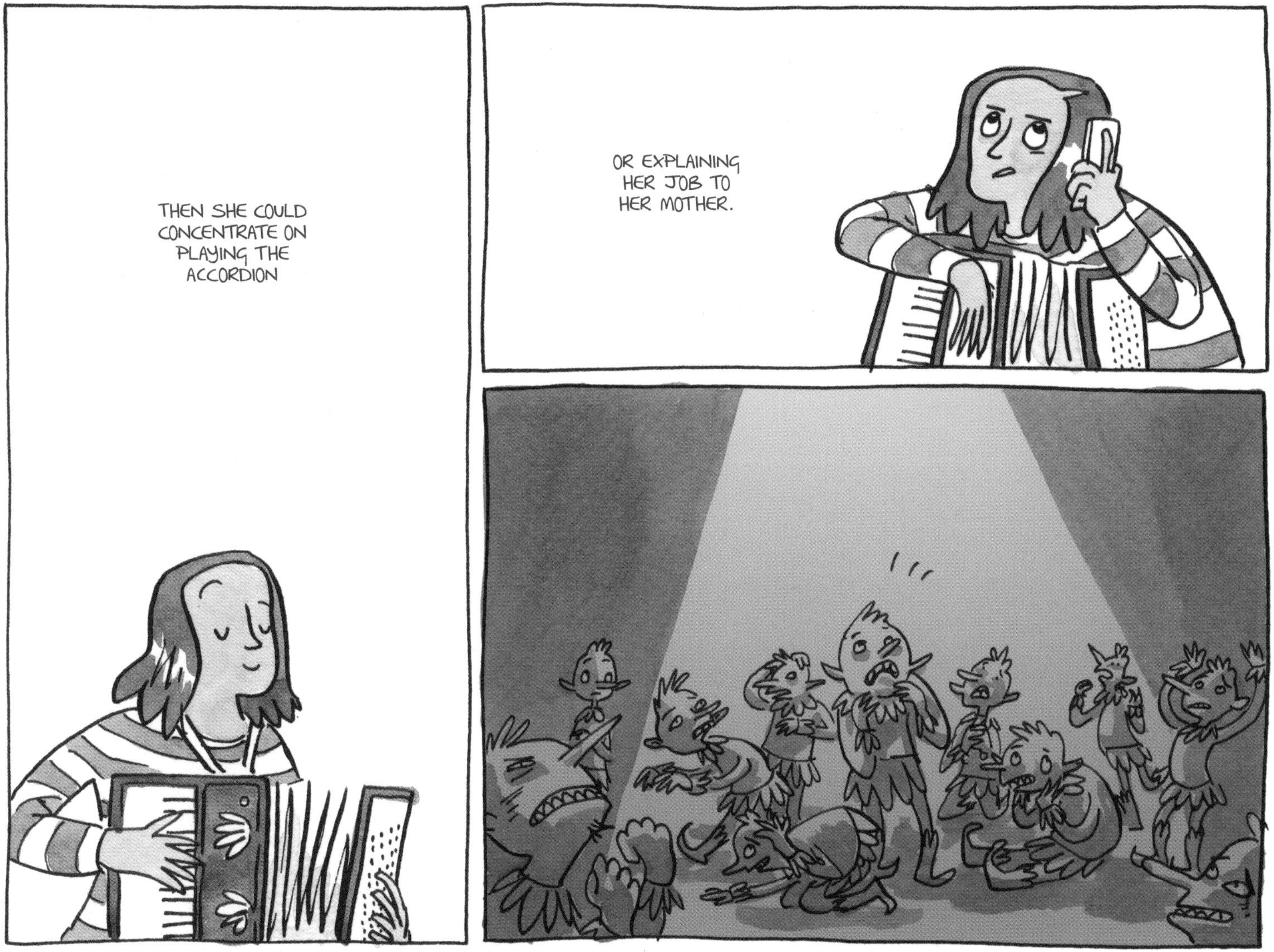
THEN SHE COULD CONCENTRATE ON PLAYING THE ACCORDION
OR EXPLAINING HER JOB TO HER MOTHER.

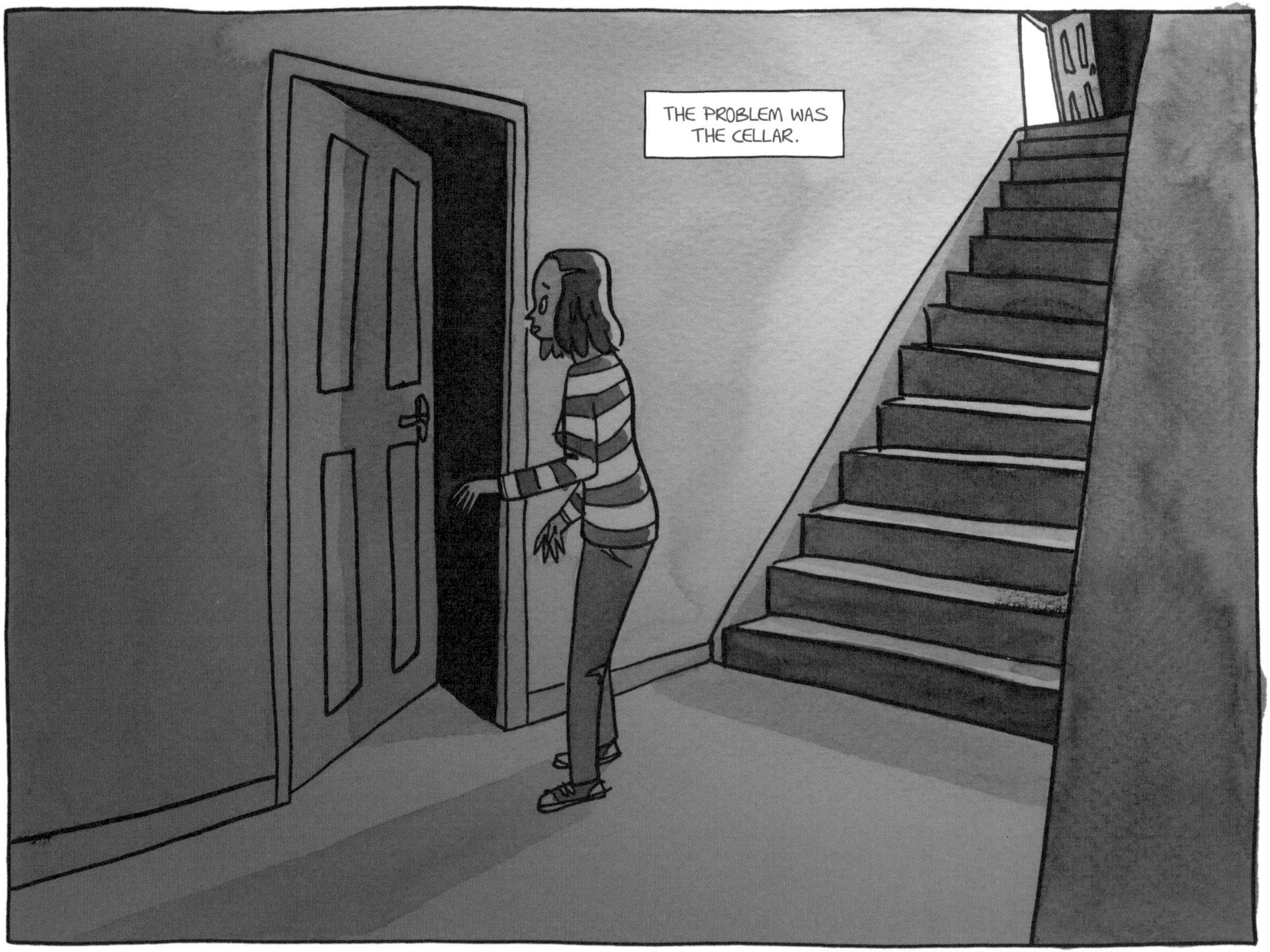
THE PROBLEM WAS THE CELLAR.

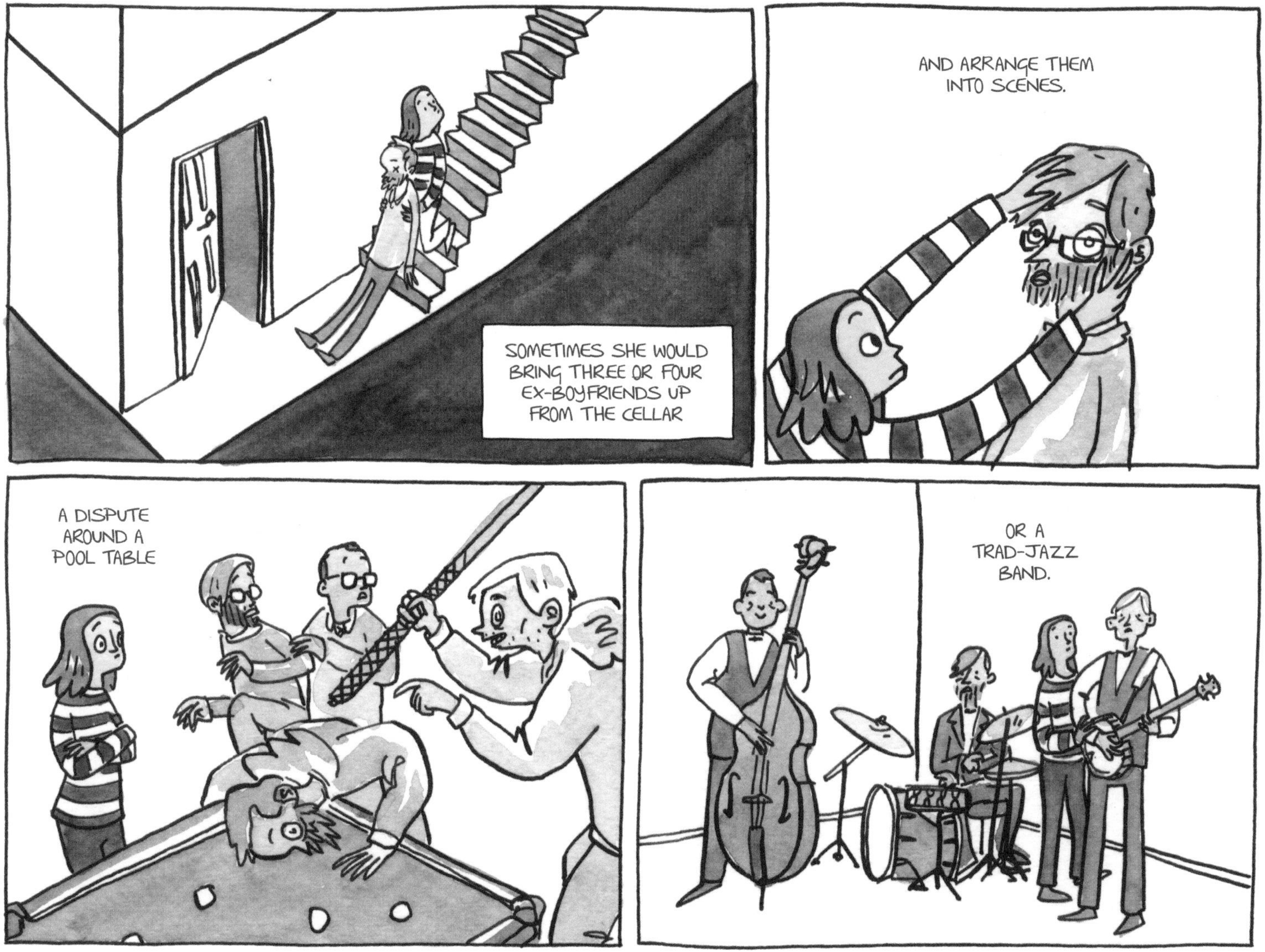
SOMETIMES SHE WOULD BRING THREE OR FOUR EX-BOYFRIENDS UP FROM THE CELLAR
AND ARRANGE THEM INTO SCENES.
A DISPUTE AROUND A POOL TABLE
OR A TRAD-JAZZ BAND.

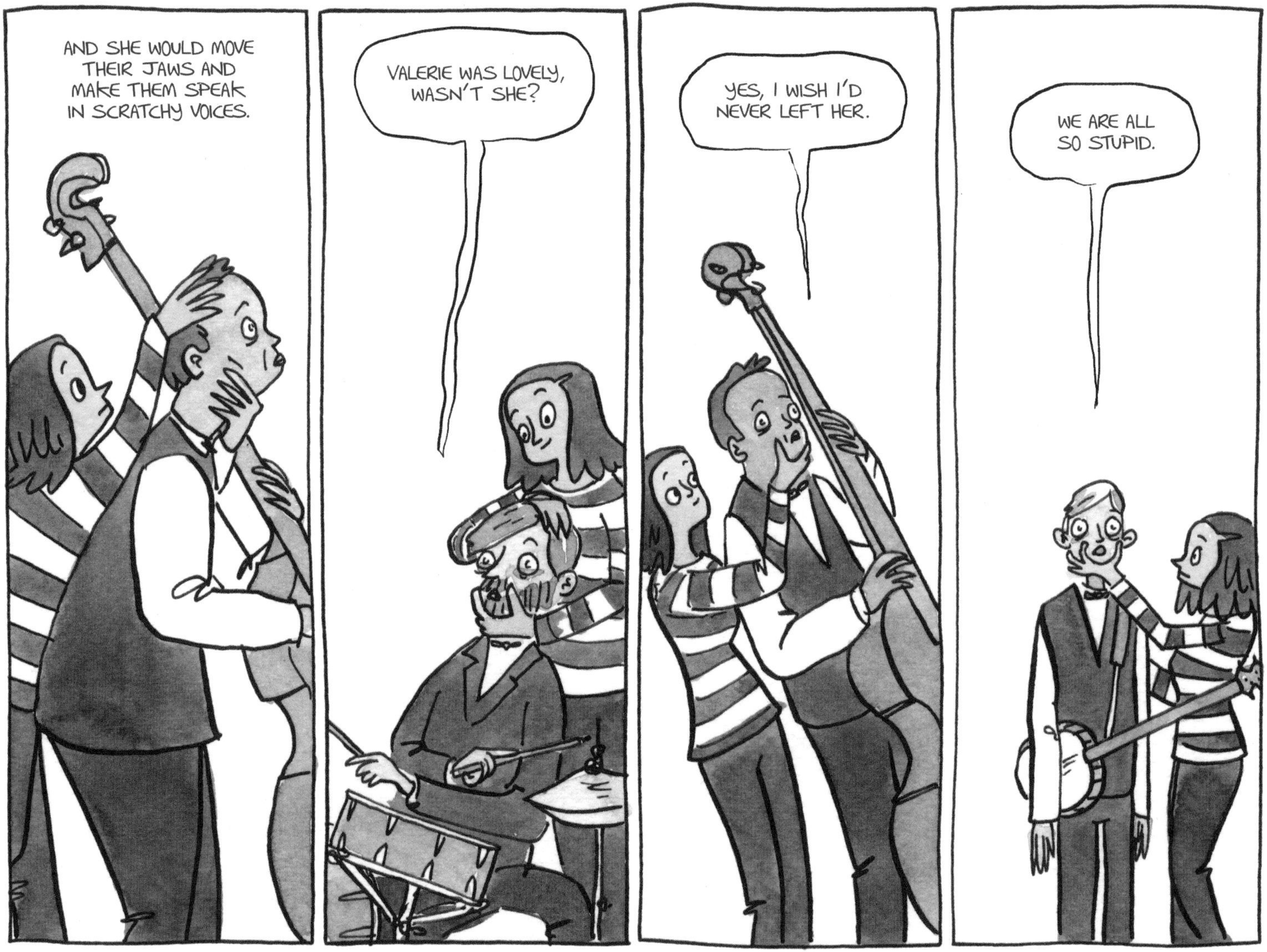
AND SHE WOULD MOVE THEIR JAWS AND MAKE THEM SPEAK IN SCRATCHY VOICES.
VALERIE WAS LOVELY, WASN'T SHE?
YES, I WISH I'D NEVER LEFT HER.
WE ARE ALL SO STUPID.

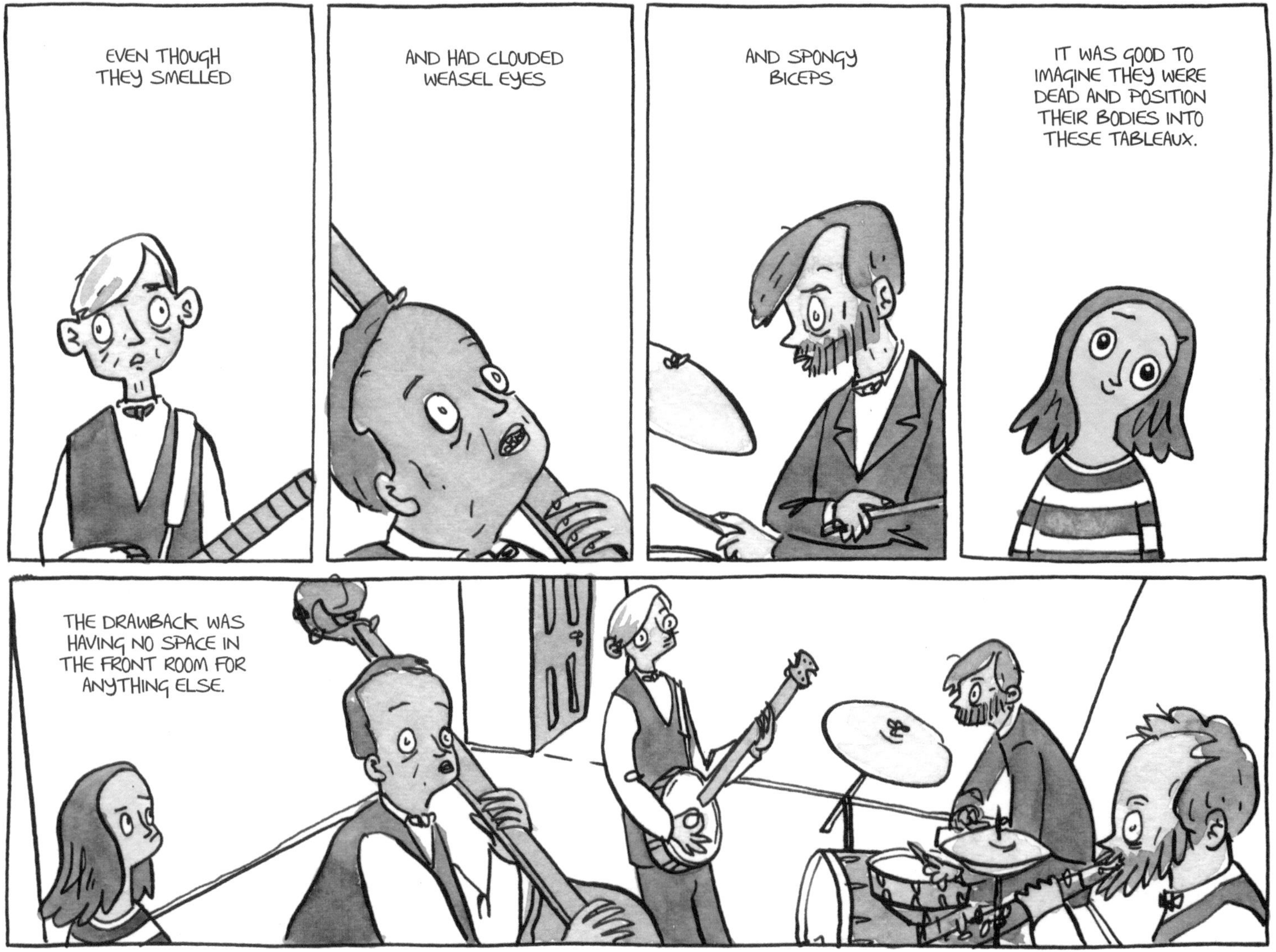
EVEN THOUGH THEY SMELLED
AND HAD CLOUDED WEASEL EYES
AND SPONGY BICEPS
IT WAS GOOD TO IMAGINE THEY WERE DEAD AND POSITION THEIR BODIES INTO THESE TABLEAUX.
THE DRAWBACK WAS HAVING NO SPACE IN THE FRONT ROOM FOR ANYTHING ELSE.

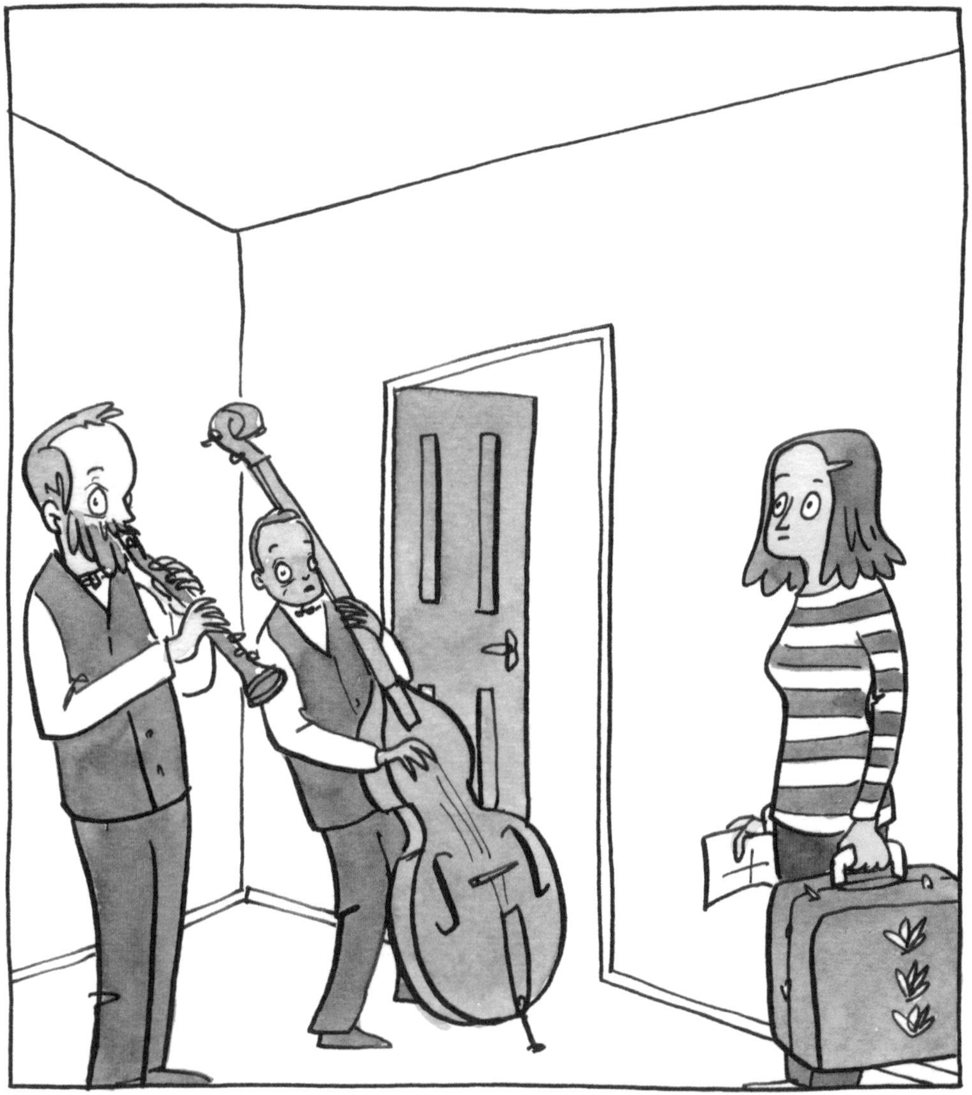

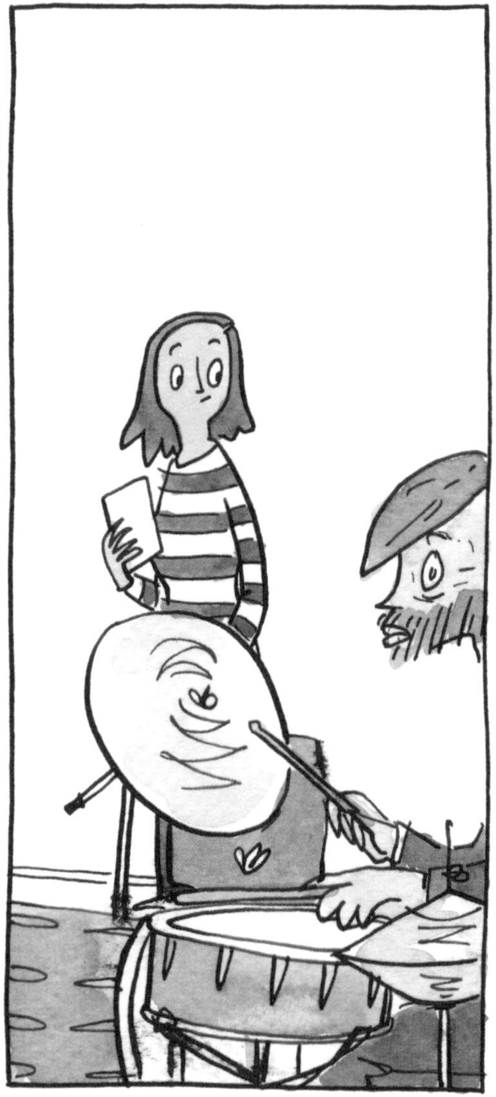

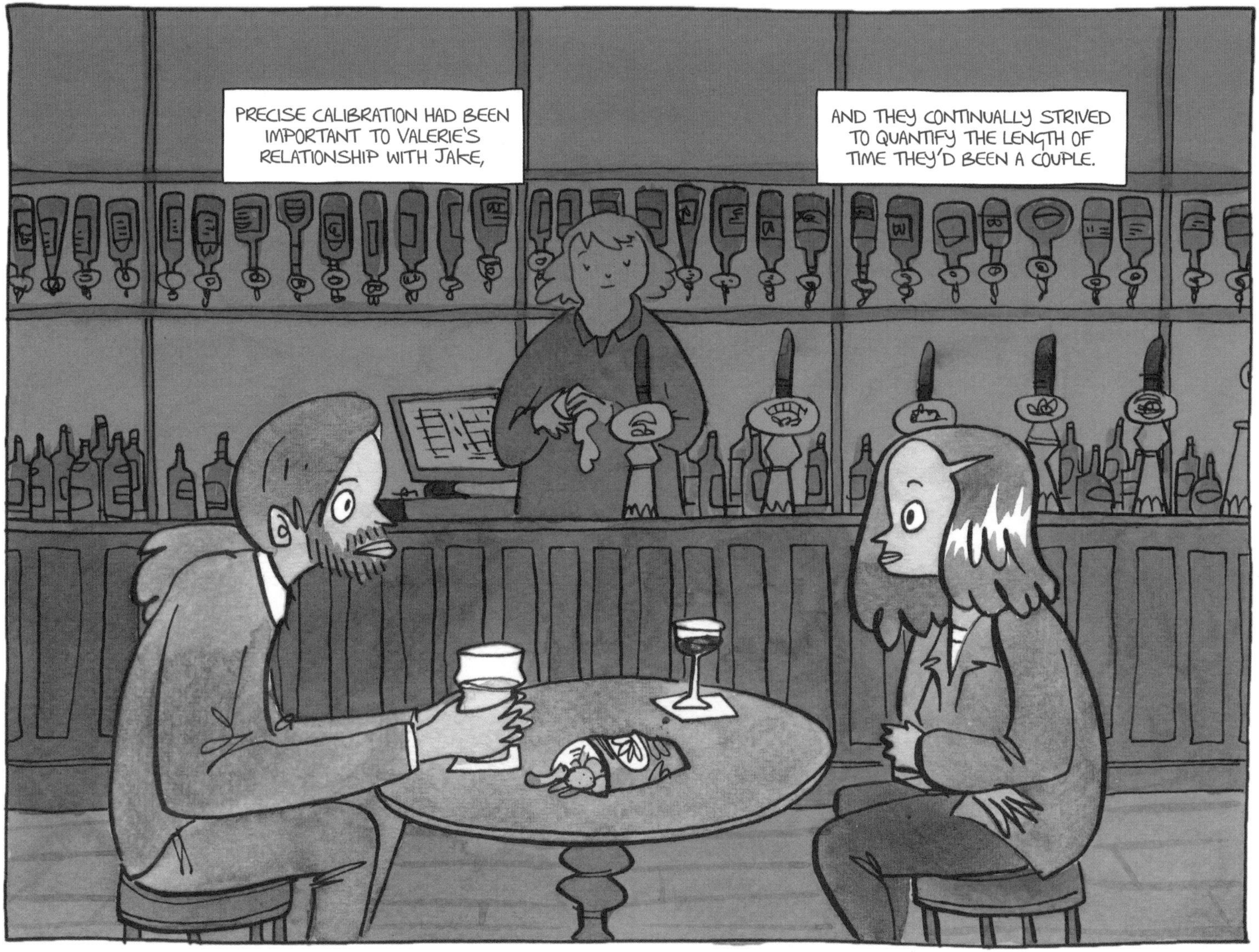
PRECISE CALIBRATION HAD BEEN IMPORTANT TO VALERIE'S RELATIONSHIP WITH JAKE,
AND THEY CONTINUALLY STRIVED TO QUANTIFY THE LENGTH OF TIME THEY'D BEEN A COUPLE.

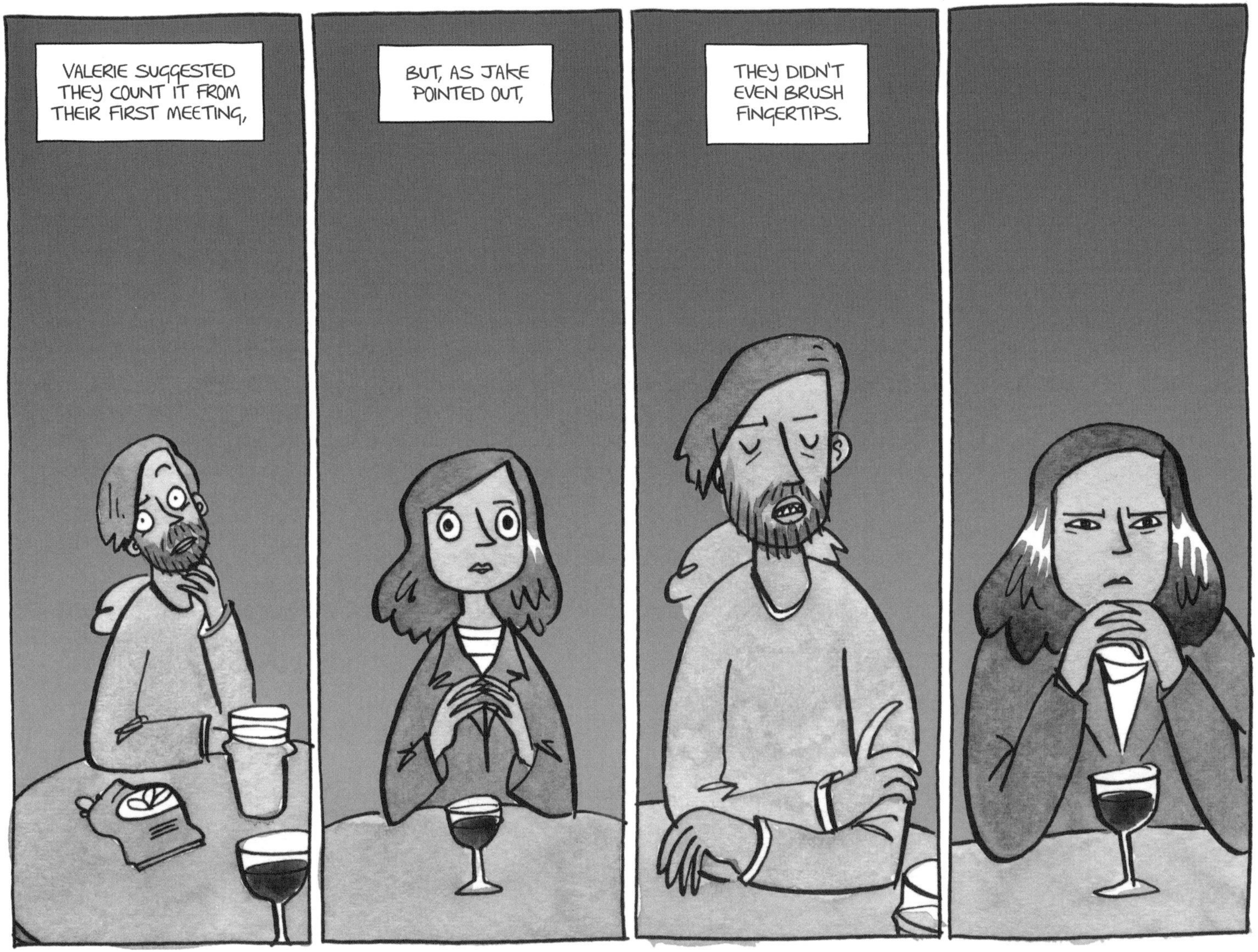
VALERIE SUGGESTED THEY COUNT IT FROM THEIR FIRST MEETING,
BUT, AS JAKE POINTED OUT,
THEY DIDN'T EVEN BRUSH FINGERTIPS.

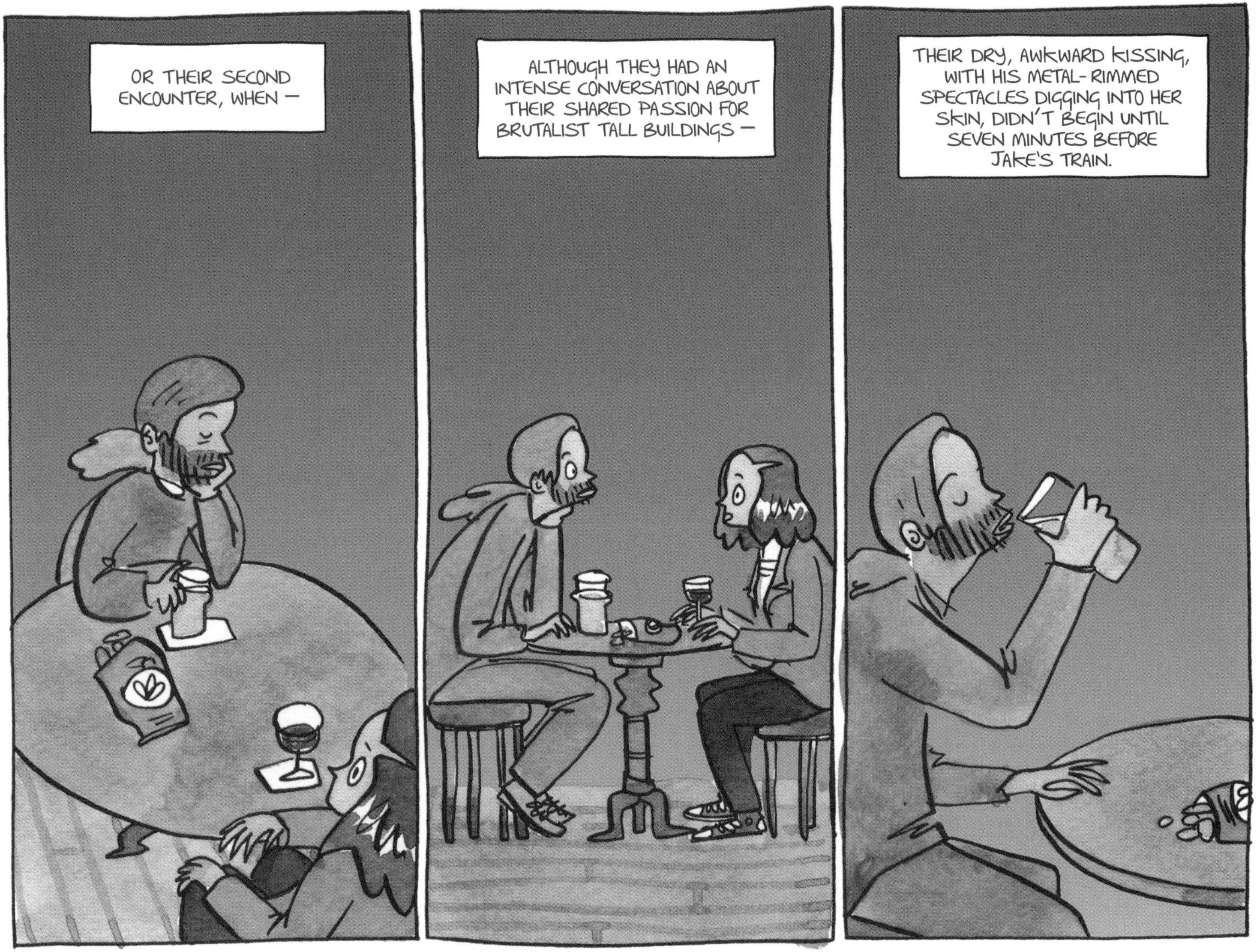
OR THEIR SECOND ENCOUNTER, WHEN —
ALTHOUGH THEY HAD AN INTENSE CONVERSATION ABOUT THEIR SHARED PASSION FOR BRUTALIST TALL BUILDINGS —
THEIR DRY, AWKWARD KISSING, WITH HIS METAL-RIMMED SPECTACLES DIGGING INTO HER SKIN, DIDN'T BEGIN UNTIL SEVEN MINUTES BEFORE JAKE'S TRAIN.

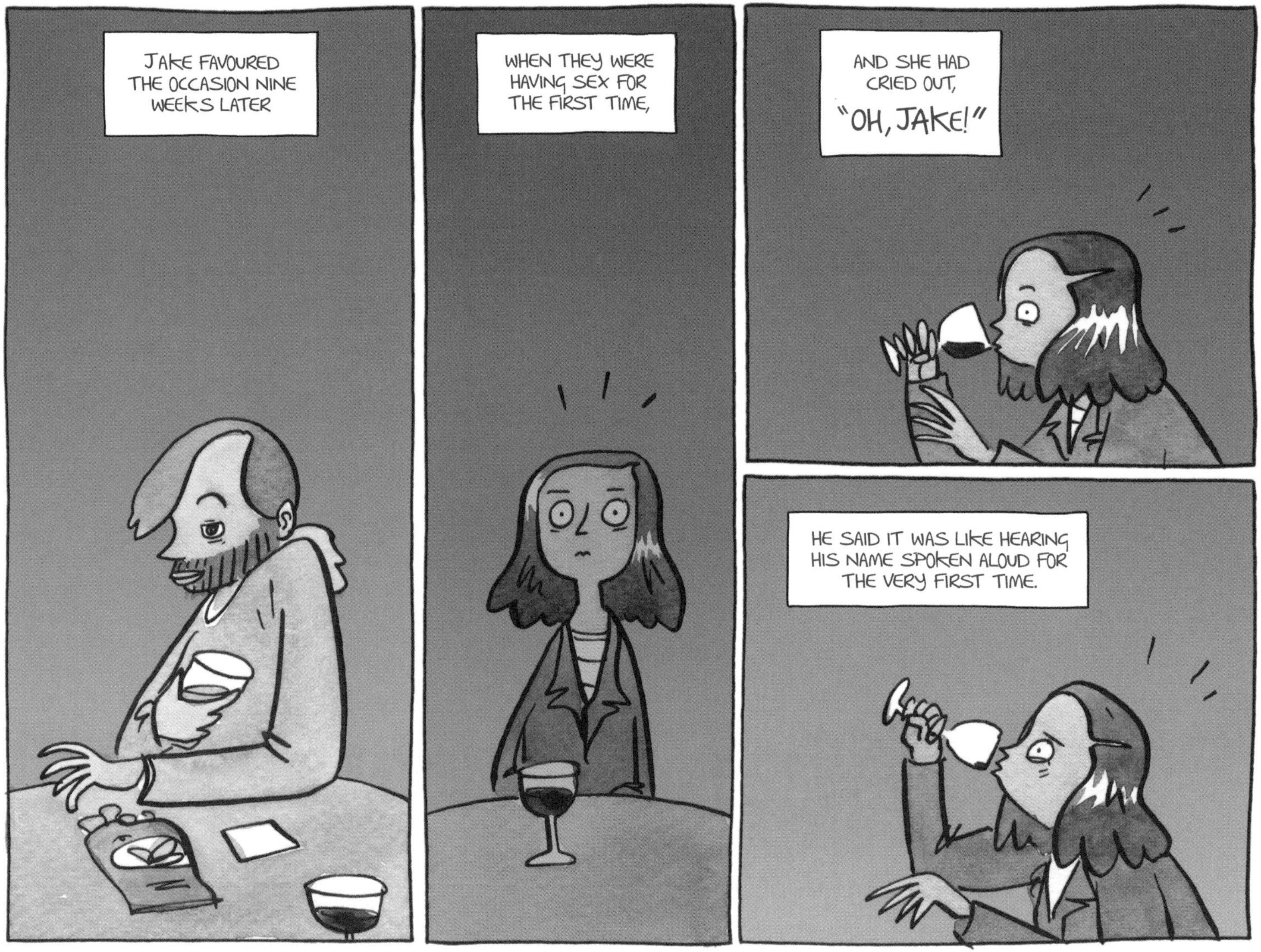
JAKE FAVOURED THE OCCASION NINE WEEKS LATER
WHEN THEY WERE HAVING SEX FOR THE FIRST TIME,
AND SHE HAD CRIED OUT, "OH, JAKE!"
HE SAID IT WAS LIKE HEARING HIS NAME SPOKEN ALOUD FOR THE VERY FIRST TIME.

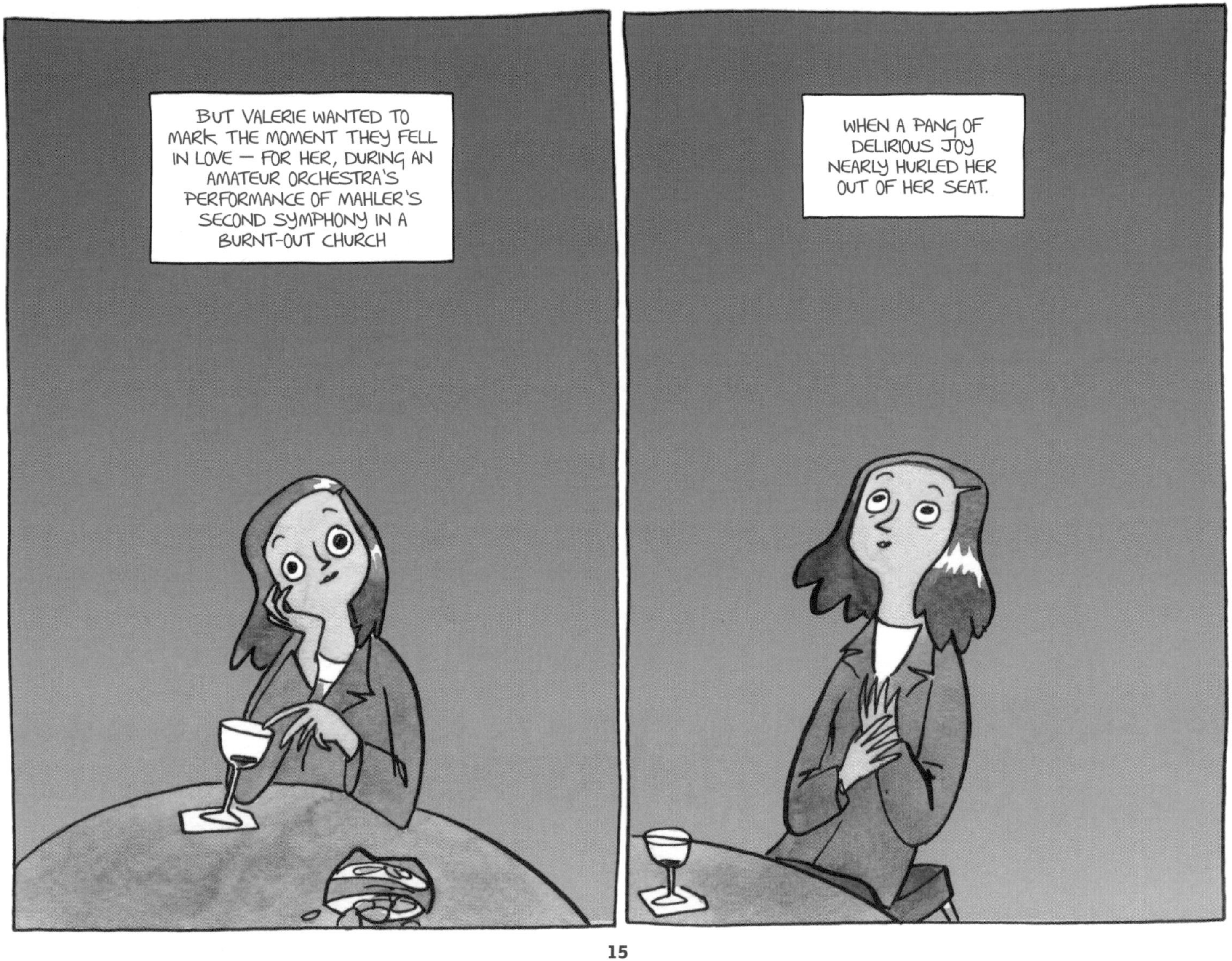
BUT VALERIE WANTED TO MARK THE MOMENT THEY FELL IN LOVE — FOR HER, DURING AN AMATEUR ORCHESTRA'S PERFORMANCE OF MAHLER'S SECOND SYMPHONY IN A BURNT-OUT CHURCH
WHEN A PANG OF DELIRIOUS JOY NEARLY HURLED HER OUT OF HER SEAT.

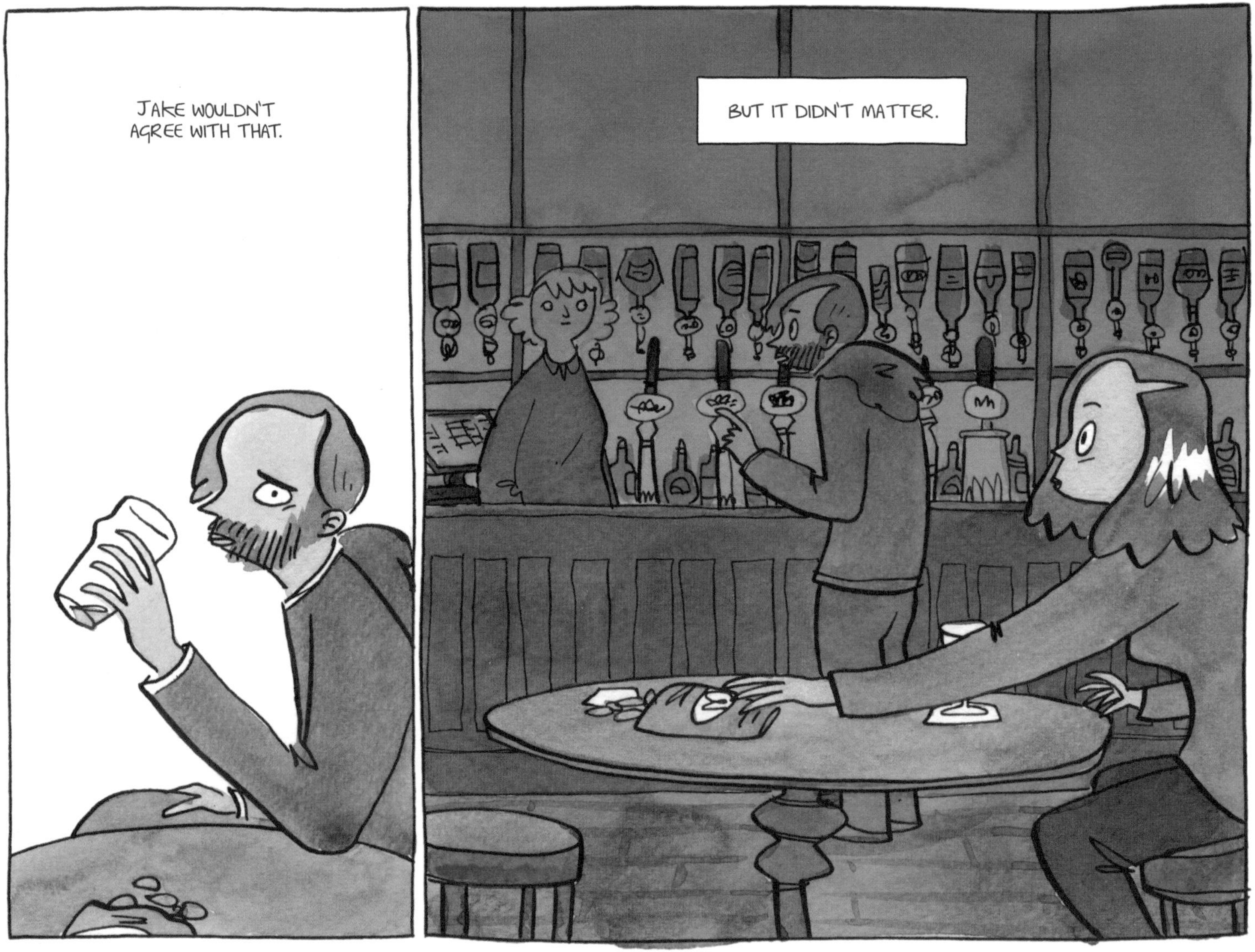
JAKE WOULDN'T AGREE WITH THAT.
BUT IT DIDN'T MATTER.

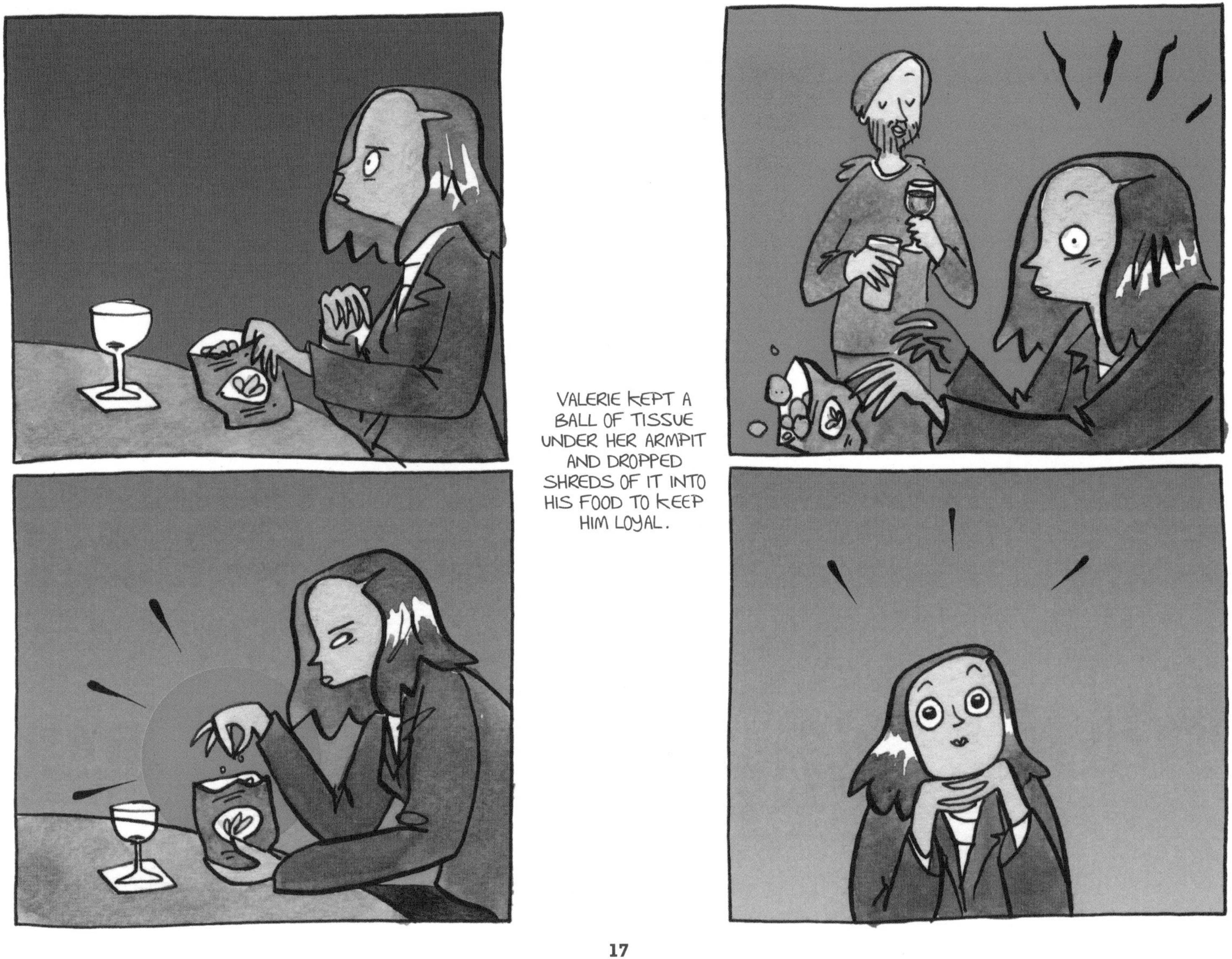
VALERIE KEPT A BALL OF TISSUE UNDER HER ARMPIT AND DROPPED SHREDS OF IT INTO HIS FOOD TO KEEP HIM LOYAL.

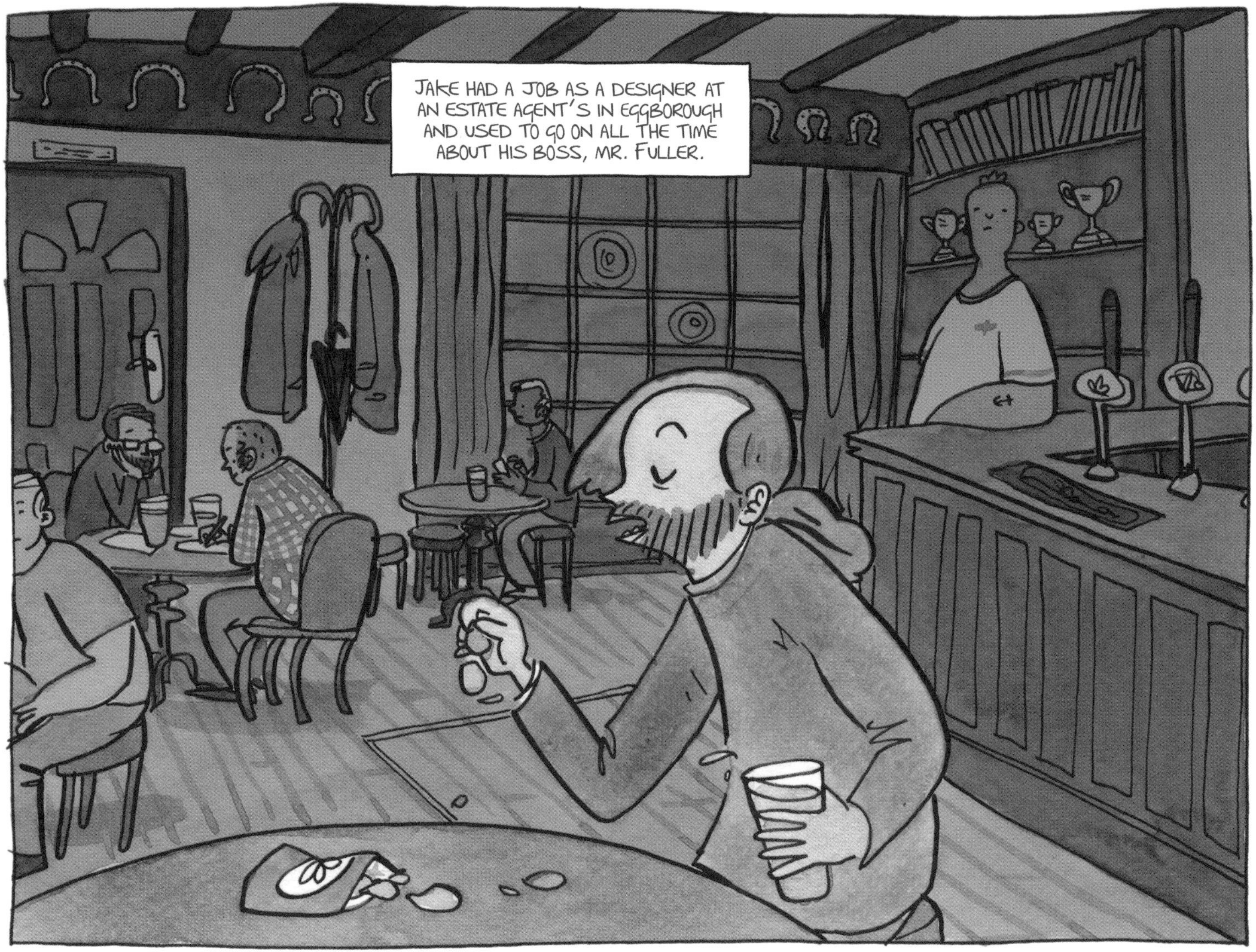
JAKE HAD A JOB AS A DESIGNER AT AN ESTATE AGENT'S IN EGGBOROUGH AND USED TO GO ON ALL THE TIME ABOUT HIS BOSS, MR. FULLER.

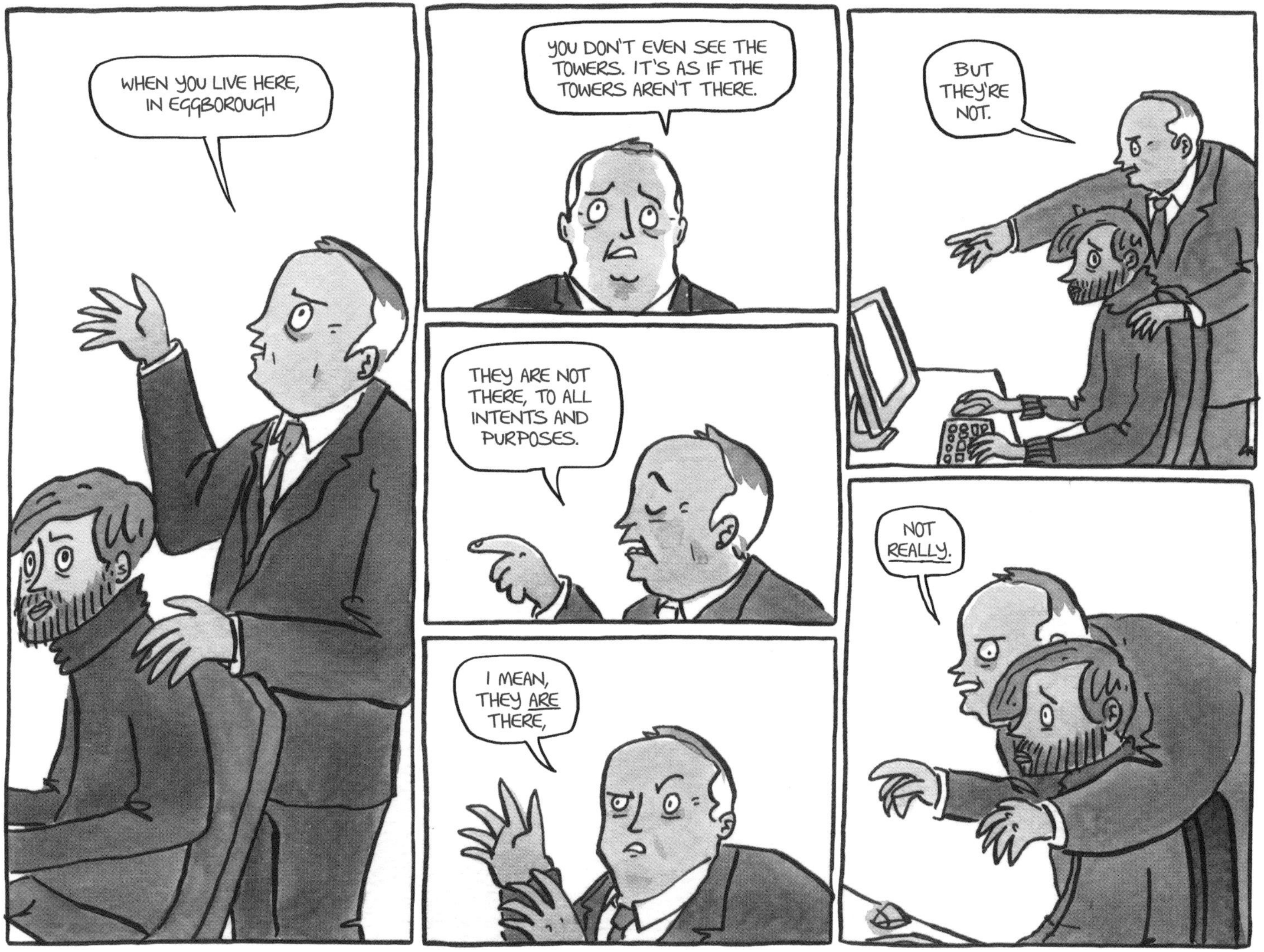

WHEN YOU LIVE HERE, IN EGGBOROUGH
YOU DON'T EVEN SEE THE TOWERS. IT'S AS IF THE TOWERS AREN'T THERE.
THEY ARE NOT THERE, TO ALL INTENTS AND PURPOSES.
I MEAN, THEY ARE THERE,
BUT THEY'RE NOT.
NOT REALLY.

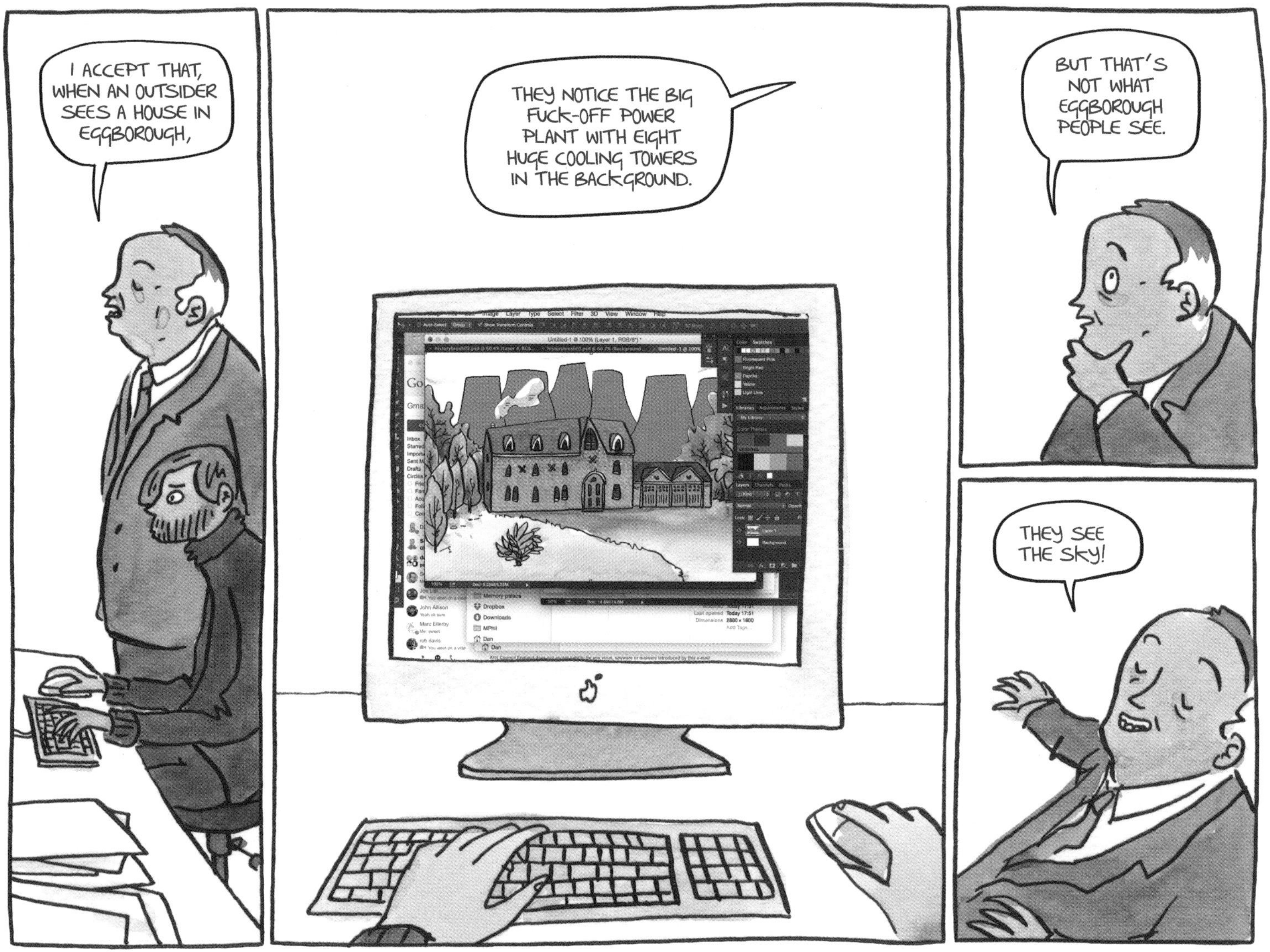
I ACCEPT THAT, WHEN AN OUTSIDER SEES A HOUSE IN EGGBOROUGH,
THEY NOTICE THE BIG FUCK-OFF POWER PLANT WITH EIGHT HUGE COOLING TOWERS IN THE BACKGROUND.
BUT THAT'S NOT WHAT EGGBOROUGH PEOPLE SEE.
THEY SEE THE SKY!

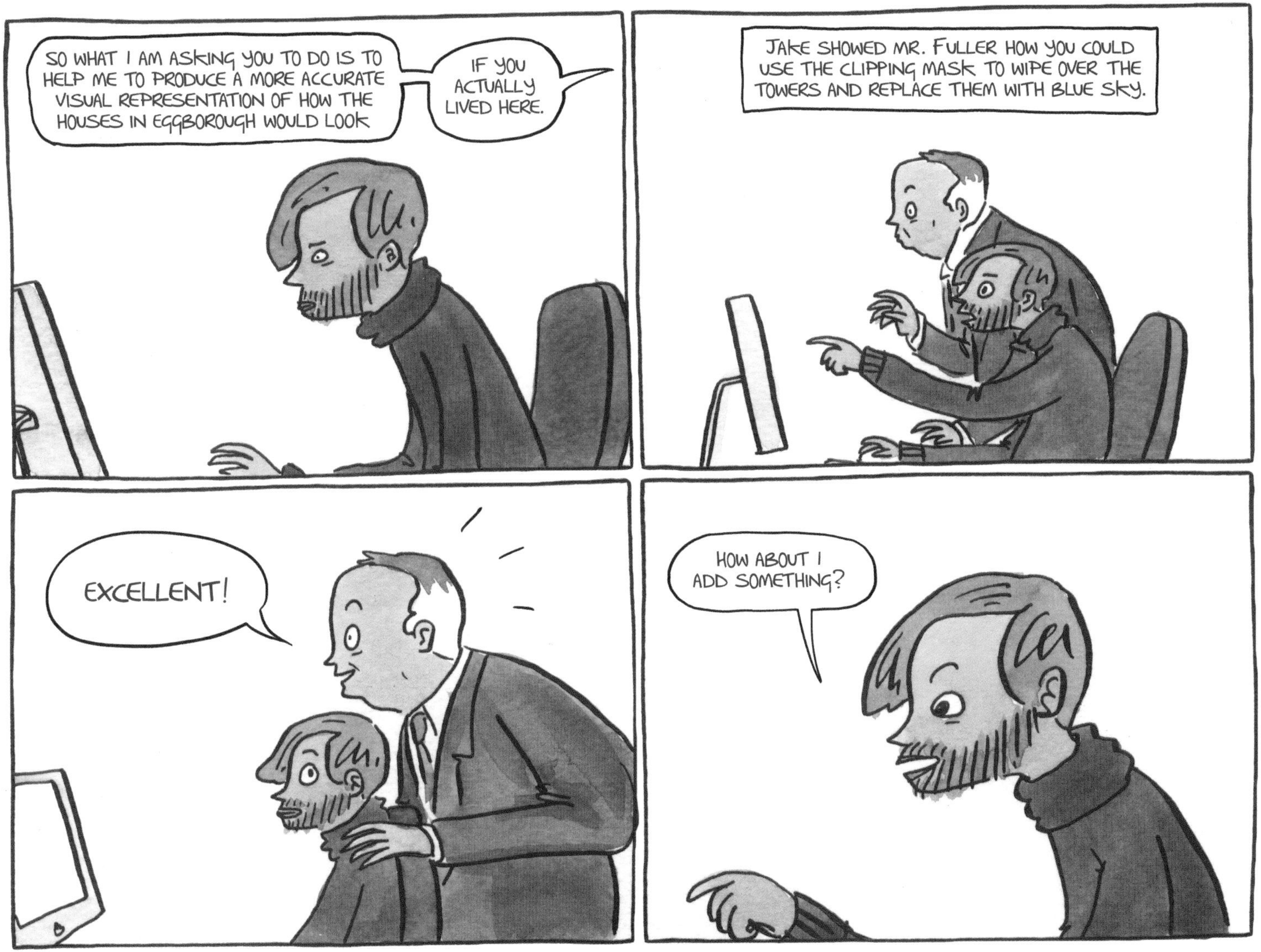
SO WHAT I AM ASKING YOU TO DO IS TO HELP ME TO PRODUCE A MORE ACCURATE VISUAL REPRESENTATION OF HOW THE HOUSES IN EGGBOROUGH WOULD LOOK
IF YOU ACTUALLY LIVED HERE.
JAKE SHOWED MR. FULLER HOW YOU COULD USE THE CLIPPING MASK TO WIPE OVER THE TOWERS AND REPLACE THEM WITH BLUE SKY.
EXCELLENT!
HOW ABOUT I ADD SOMETHING?

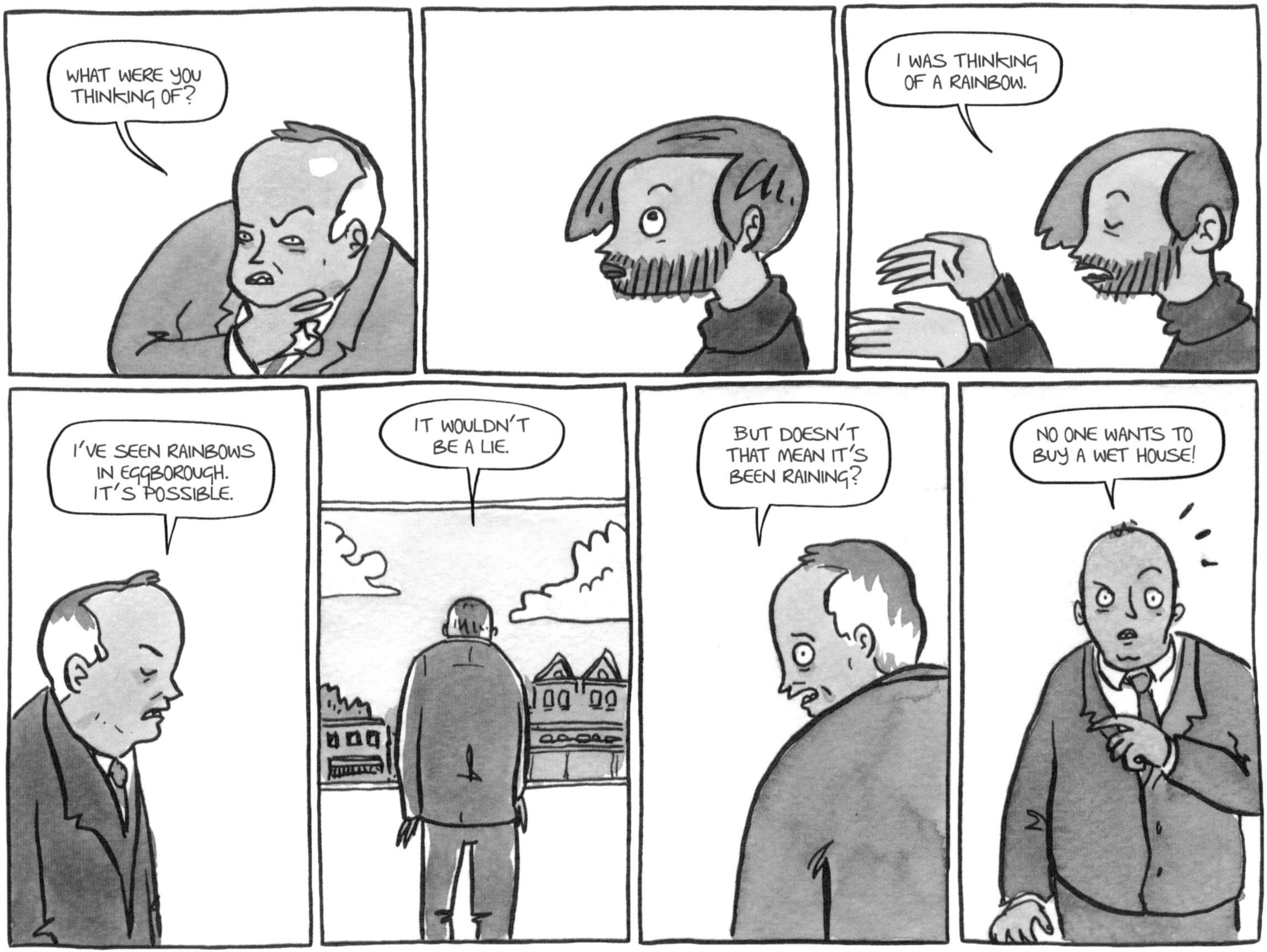
WHAT WERE YOU THINKING OF?
I WAS THINKING OF A RAINBOW.
I'VE SEEN RAINBOWS IN EGGBOROUGH. IT'S POSSIBLE.
IT WOULDN'T BE A LIE.
BUT DOESN'T THAT MEAN IT'S BEEN RAINING?
NO ONE WANTS TO BUY A WET HOUSE!

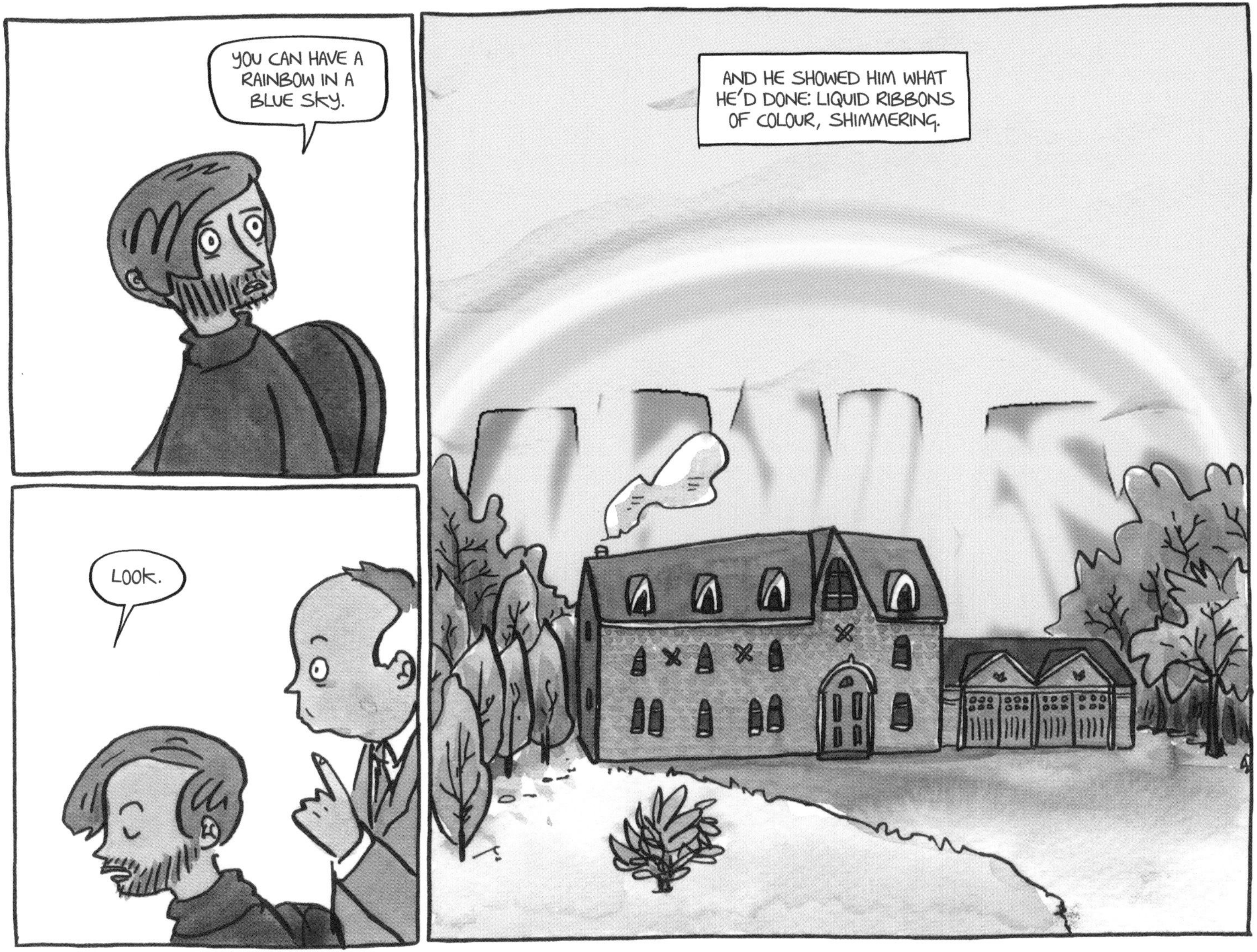
YOU CAN HAVE A RAINBOW IN A BLUE SKY.
LOOK.
AND HE SHOWED HIM WHAT HE'D DONE: LIQUID RIBBONS OF COLOUR, SHIMMERING.

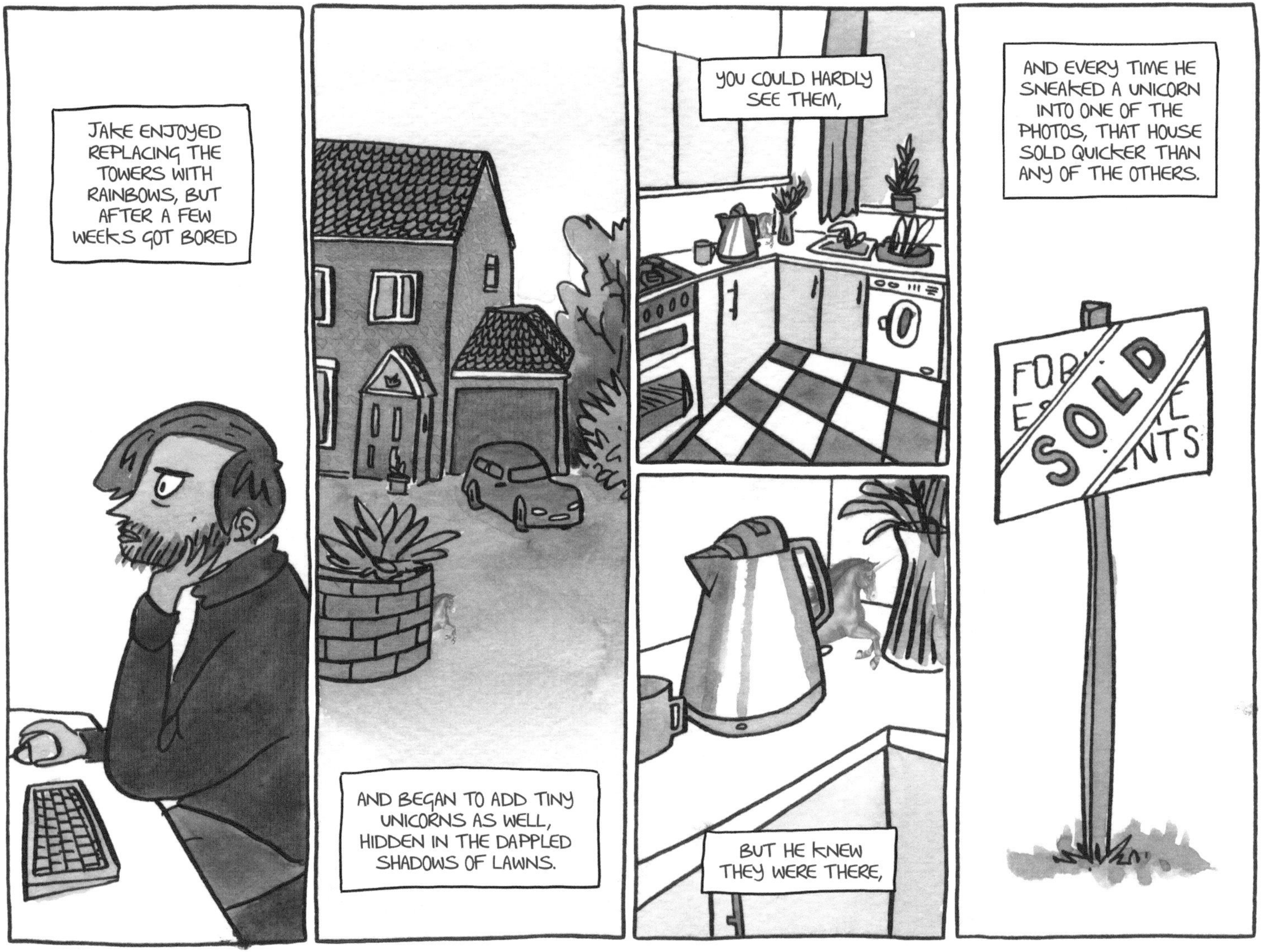
JAKE ENJOYED REPLACING THE TOWERS WITH RAINBOWS, BUT AFTER A FEW WEEKS GOT BORED
AND BEGAN TO ADD TINY UNICORNS AS WELL, HIDDEN IN THE DAPPLED SHADOWS OF LAWNS.
YOU COULD HARDLY SEE THEM,
BUT HE KNEW THEY WERE THERE,
AND EVERY TIME HE SNEAKED A UNICORN INTO ONE OF THE PHOTOS, THAT HOUSE SOLD QUICKER THAN ANY OF THE OTHERS.
SOLD

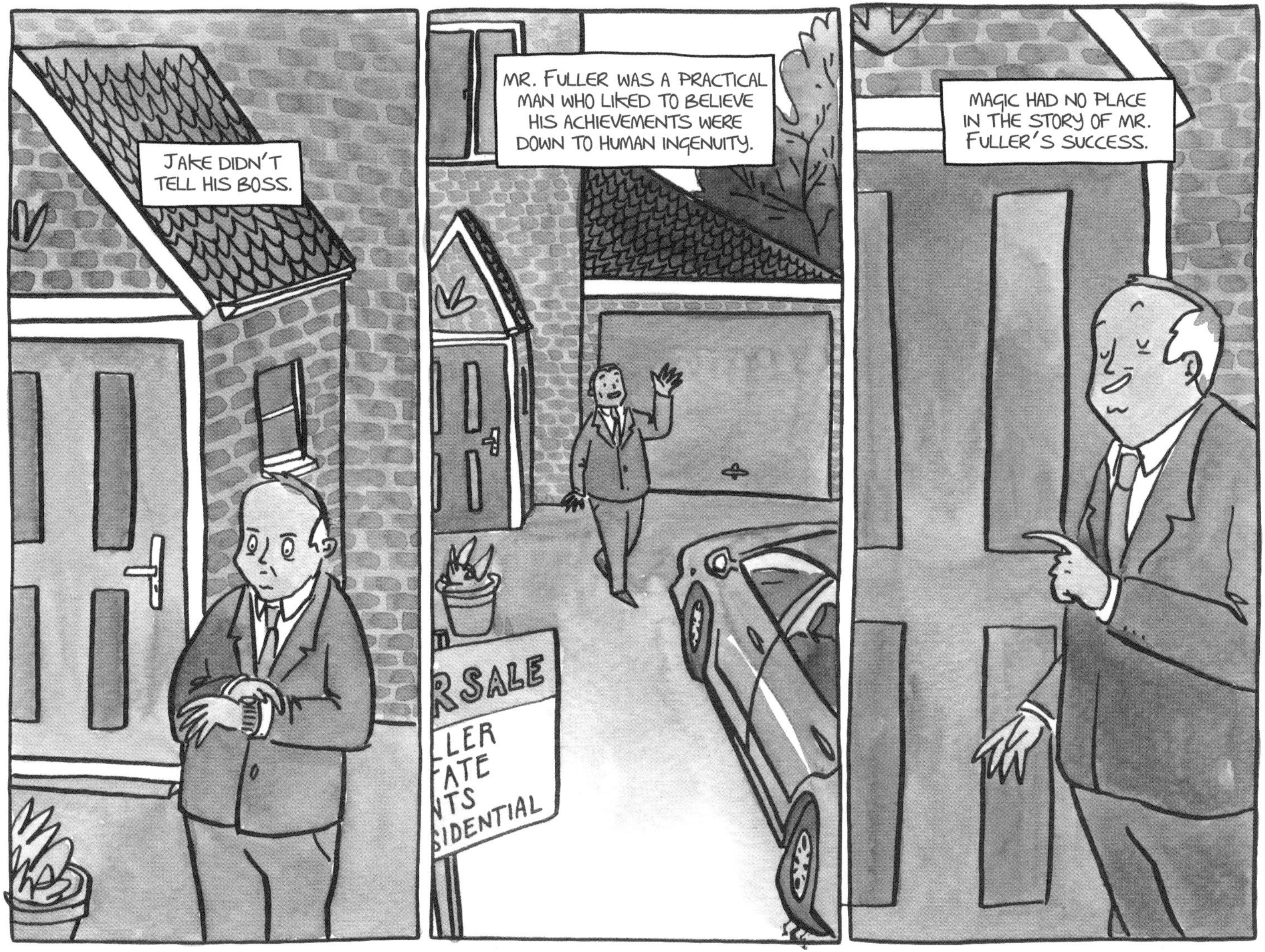
JAKE DIDN'T TELL HIS BOSS.
MR. FULLER WAS A PRACTICAL MAN WHO LIKED TO BELIEVE HIS ACHIEVEMENTS WERE DOWN TO HUMAN INGENUITY.
RSALE
LLER
TATE
NTS
SIDENTIAL
MAGIC HAD NO PLACE IN THE STORY OF MR. FULLER'S SUCCESS.

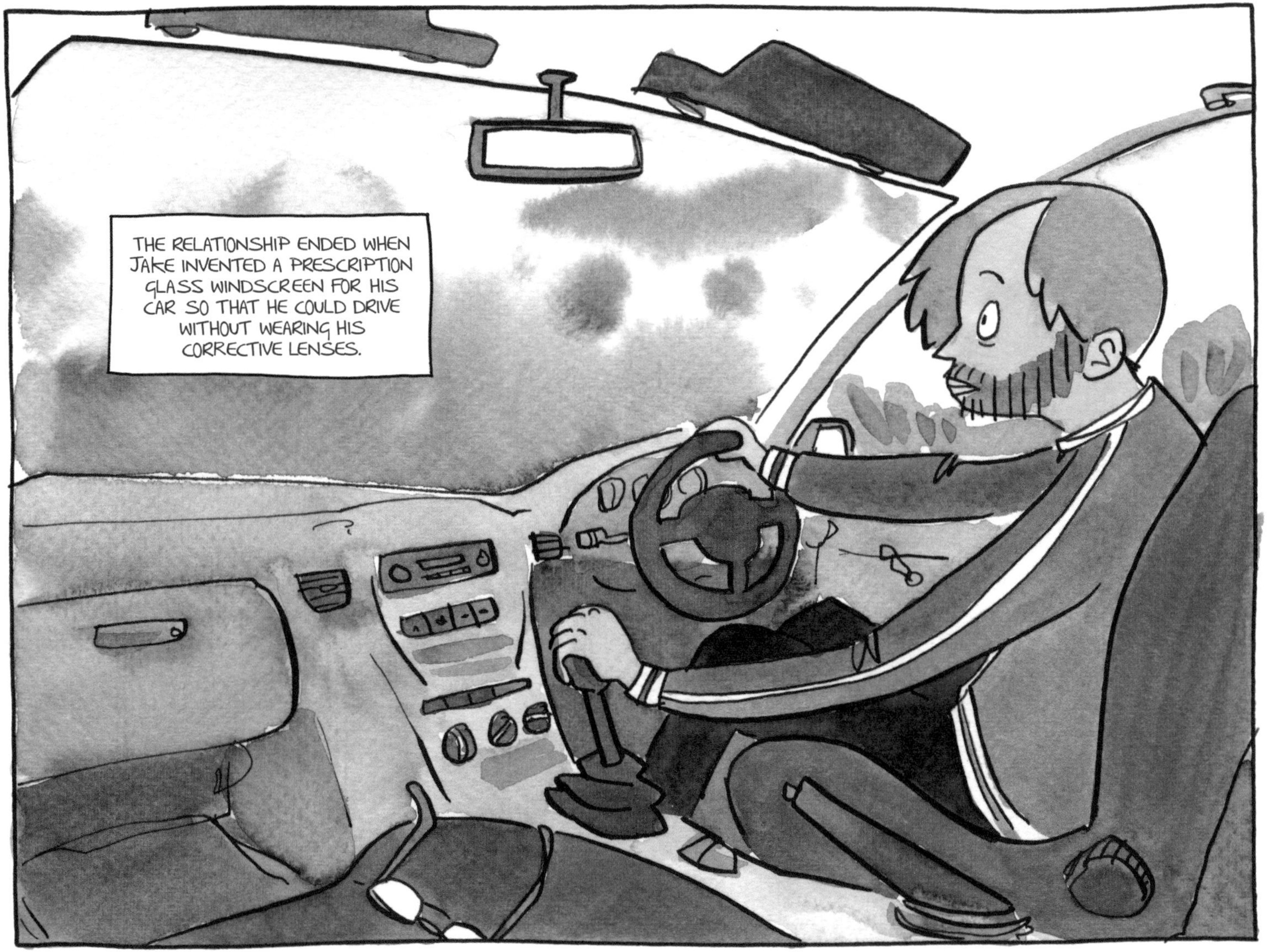
THE RELATIONSHIP ENDED WHEN JAKE INVENTED A PRESCRIPTION GLASS WINDSCREEN FOR HIS CAR SO THAT HE COULD DRIVE WITHOUT WEARING HIS CORRECTIVE LENSES.

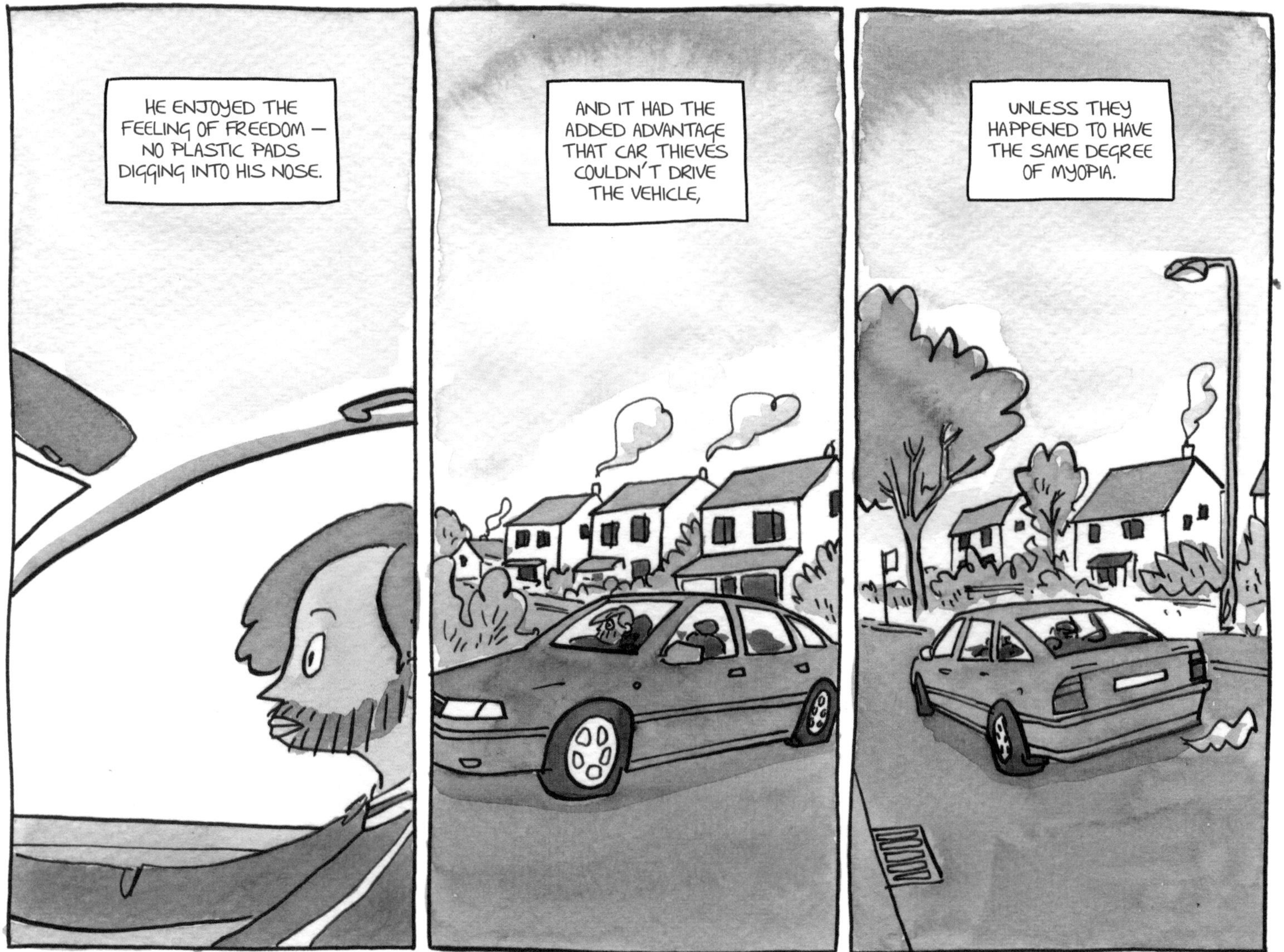
HE ENJOYED THE FEELING OF FREEDOM — NO PLASTIC PADS DIGGING INTO HIS NOSE.
AND IT HAD THE ADDED ADVANTAGE THAT CAR THIEVES COULDN'T DRIVE THE VEHICLE,
UNLESS THEY HAPPENED TO HAVE THE SAME DEGREE OF MYOPIA.

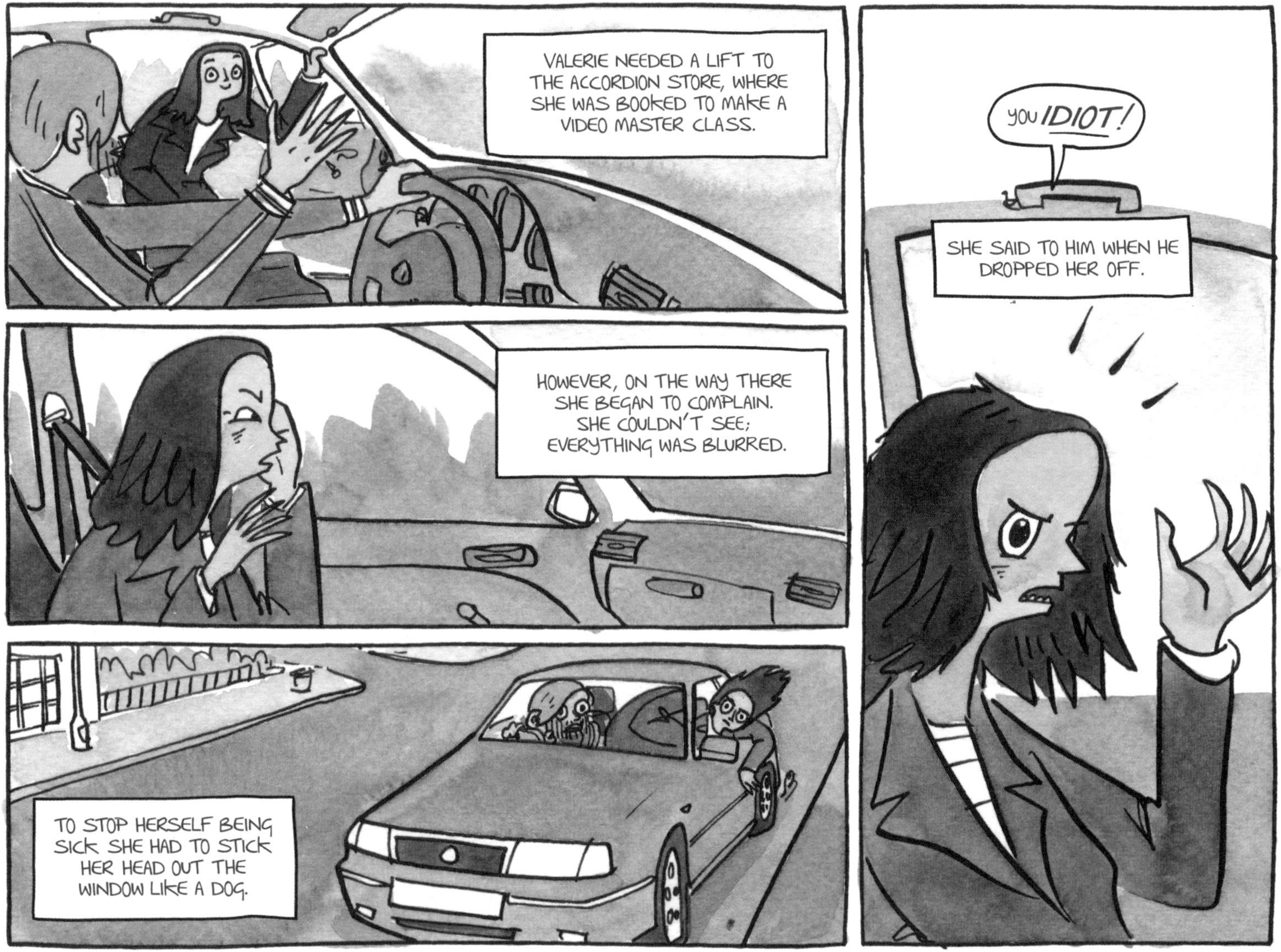
VALERIE NEEDED A LIFT TO THE ACCORDION STORE, WHERE SHE WAS BOOKED TO MAKE A VIDEO MASTER CLASS.
HOWEVER, ON THE WAY THERE SHE BEGAN TO COMPLAIN. SHE COULDN'T SEE; EVERYTHING WAS BLURRED.
TO STOP HERSELF BEING SICK SHE HAD TO STICK HER HEAD OUT THE WINDOW LIKE A DOG.
YOU IDIOT!
SHE SAID TO HIM WHEN HE DROPPED HER OFF.

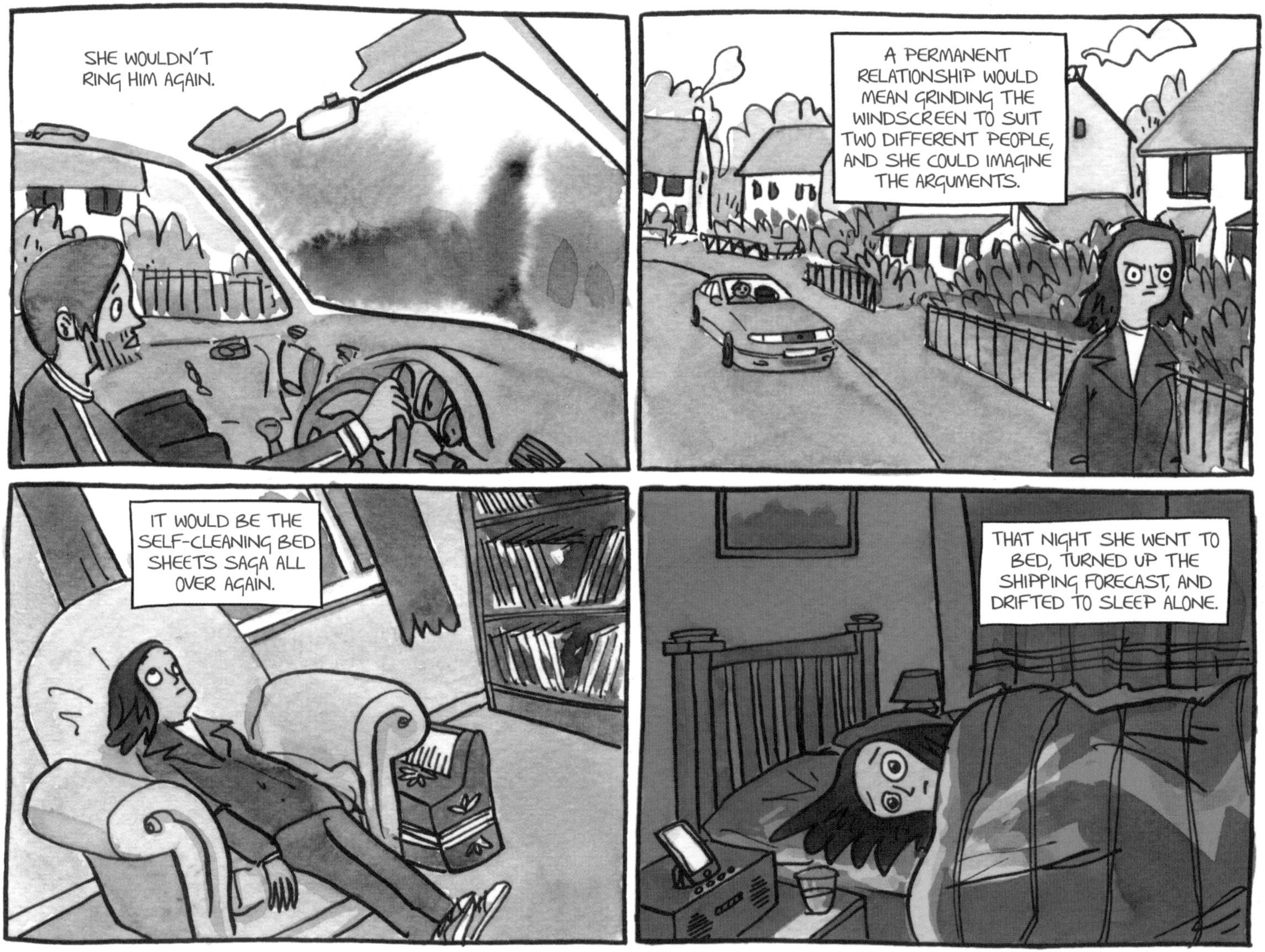
SHE WOULDN'T RING HIM AGAIN.
A PERMANENT RELATIONSHIP WOULD MEAN GRINDING THE WINDSCREEN TO SUIT TWO DIFFERENT PEOPLE, AND SHE COULD IMAGINE THE ARGUMENTS.
IT WOULD BE THE SELF-CLEANING BED SHEETS SAGA ALL OVER AGAIN.
THAT NIGHT SHE WENT TO BED, TURNED UP THE SHIPPING FORECAST, AND DRIFTED TO SLEEP ALONE.

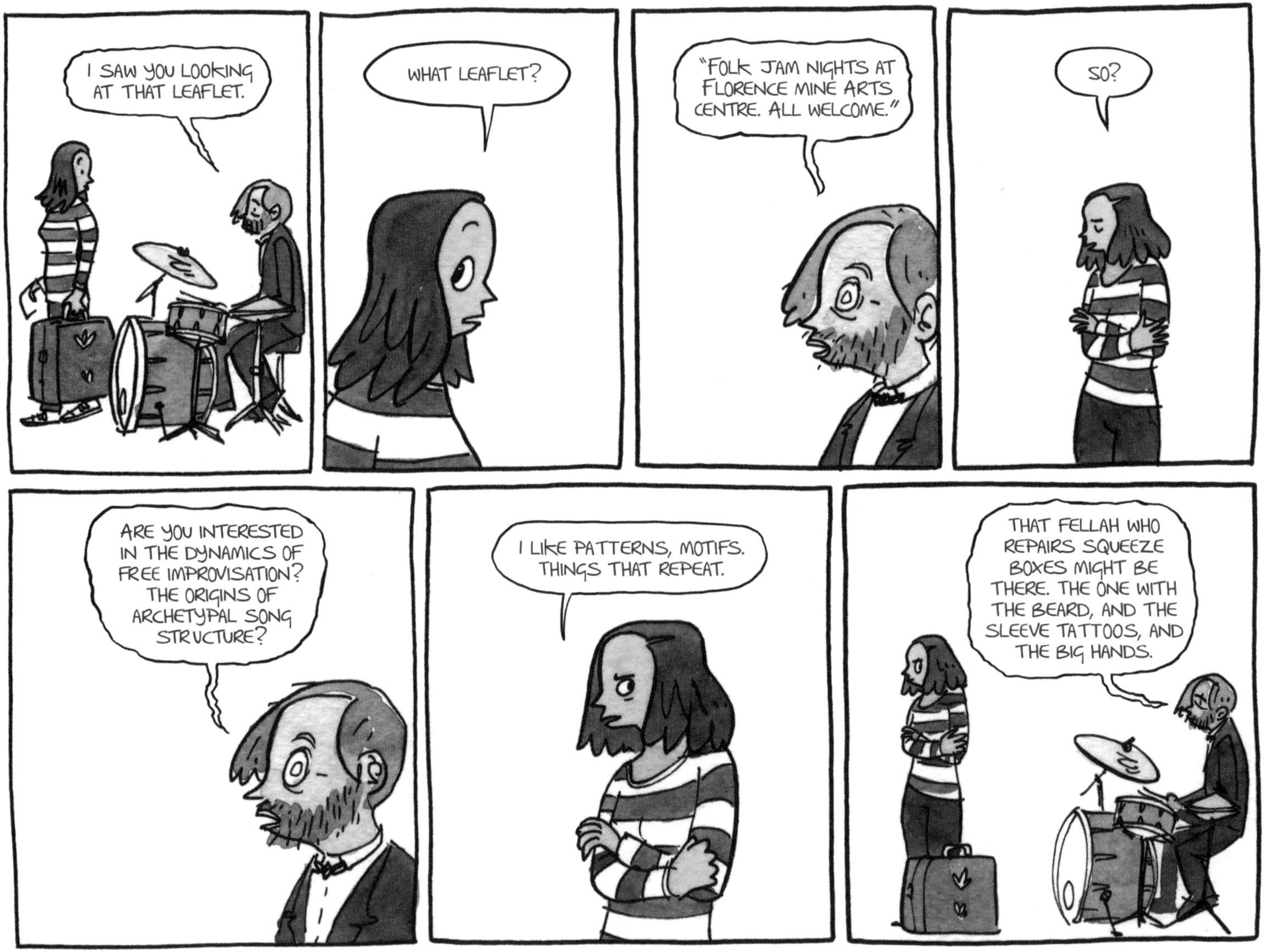
I SAW YOU LOOKING AT THAT LEAFLET.
WHAT LEAFLET?
"FOLK JAM NIGHTS AT FLORENCE MINE ARTS CENTRE. ALL WELCOME."
SO?
ARE YOU INTERESTED IN THE DYNAMICS OF FREE IMPROVISATION? THE ORIGINS OF ARCHETYPAL SONG STRUCTURE?
I LIKE PATTERNS, MOTIFS. THINGS THAT REPEAT.
THAT FELLAH WHO REPAIRS SQUEEZE BOXES MIGHT BE THERE. THE ONE WITH THE BEARD, AND THE SLEEVE TATTOOS, AND THE BIG HANDS.

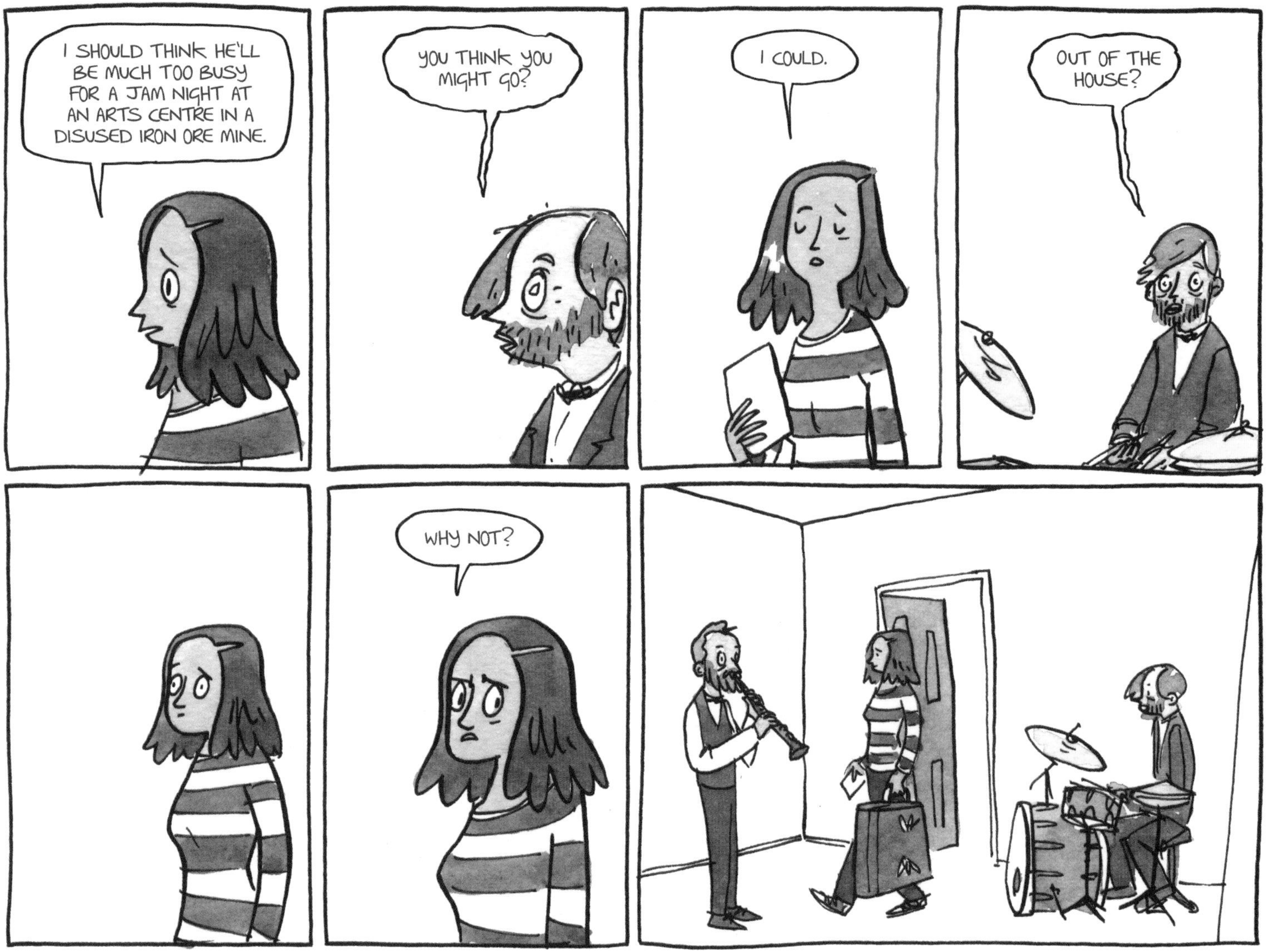
I SHOULD THINK HE'LL BE MUCH TOO BUSY FOR A JAM NIGHT AT AN ARTS CENTRE IN A DISUSED IRON ORE MINE.
YOU THINK YOU MIGHT GO?
I COULD.
OUT OF THE HOUSE?
WHY NOT?

ON THEIR SECOND
DATE, VALERIE AND
BRETT BROKE INTO
THE DERELICT PUMP
HOUSE AT THE OLD
MINE, AND BRETT
THREW HIMSELF ON
ALL FOURS AND
TOUCHED THE GROUND
WITH HIS TONGUE.

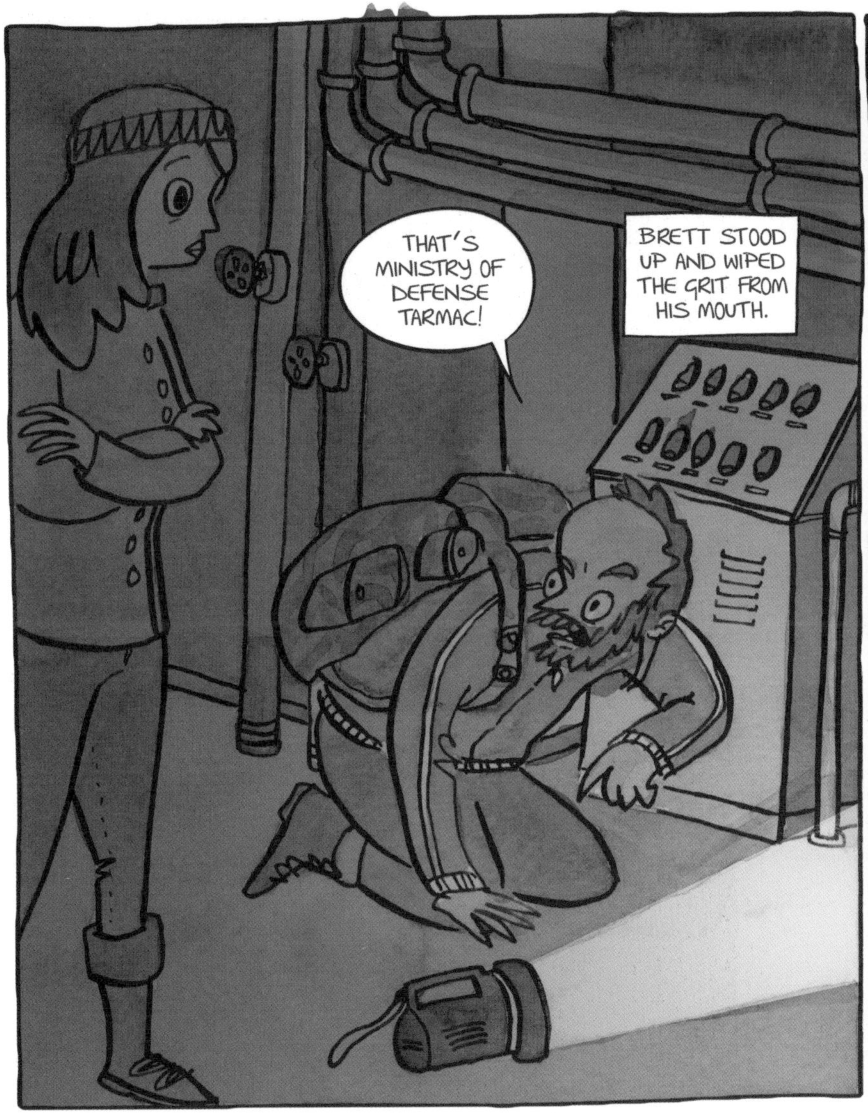
THAT'S MINISTRY OF DEFENSE TARMAC!
BRETT STOOD UP AND WIPED THE GRIT FROM HIS MOUTH.

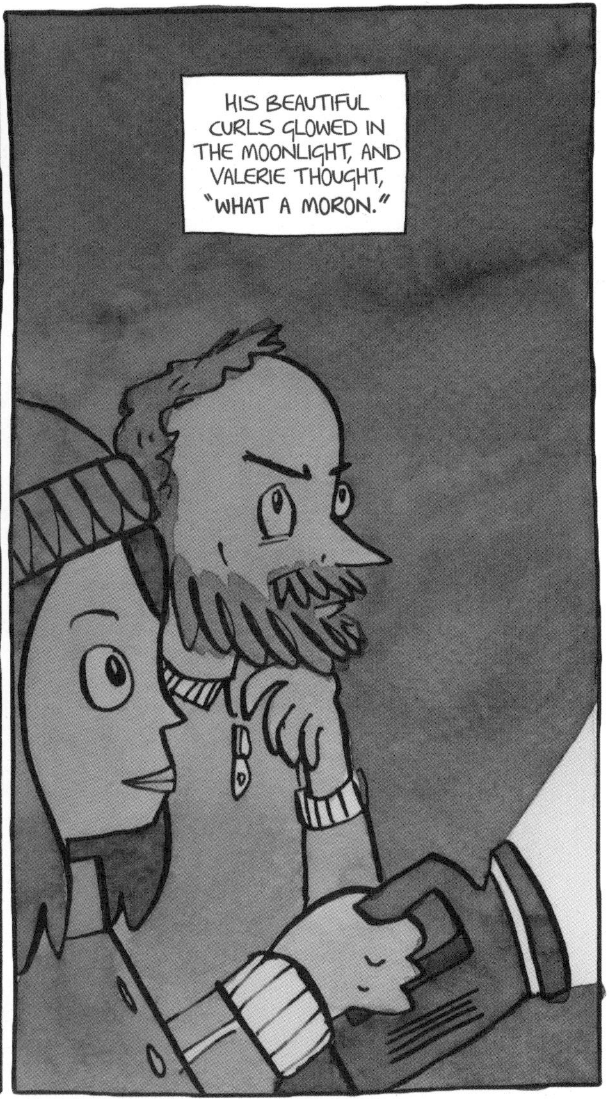
HIS BEAUTIFUL CURLS GLOWED IN THE MOONLIGHT, AND VALERIE THOUGHT, "WHAT A MORON."

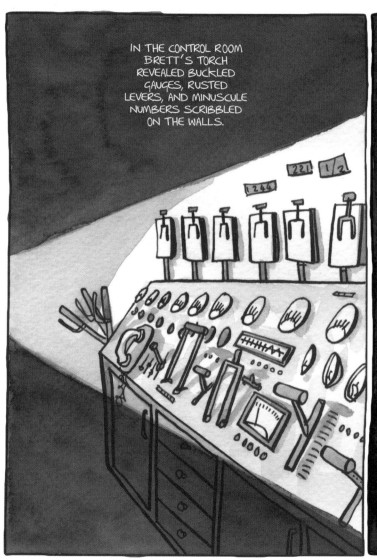

IN THE CONTROL ROOM BRETT'S TORCH REVEALED BUCKLED GAUGES, RUSTED LEVERS, AND MINUSCULE NUMBERS SCRIBBLED ON THE WALLS.

HE SWITCHED OFF THE LIGHT, THEN KISSED AND FUMBLED AT HER.

THE AIR SEEMED TO THICKEN, AND SHE PUSHED HIM AWAY.

THAT DOESN'T MAKE SENSE, BRETT; THE TARMAC BEING MINISTRY OF DEFENSE? THIS WAS A COAL MINE.

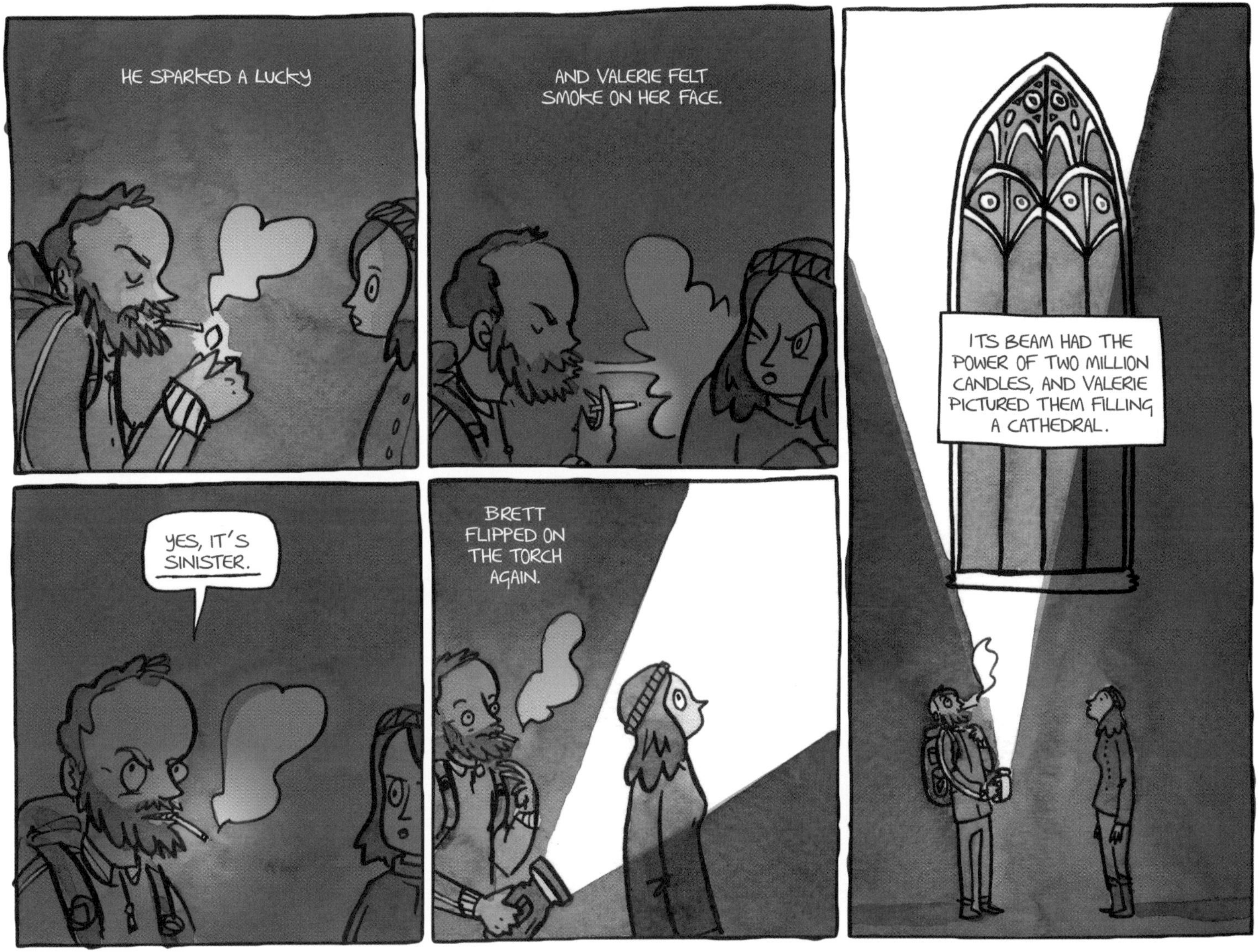
HE SPARKED A LUCKY
AND VALERIE FELT SMOKE ON HER FACE.
YES, IT'S SINISTER.
BRETT FLIPPED ON THE TORCH AGAIN.
ITS BEAM HAD THE POWER OF TWO MILLION CANDLES, AND VALERIE PICTURED THEM FILLING A CATHEDRAL.

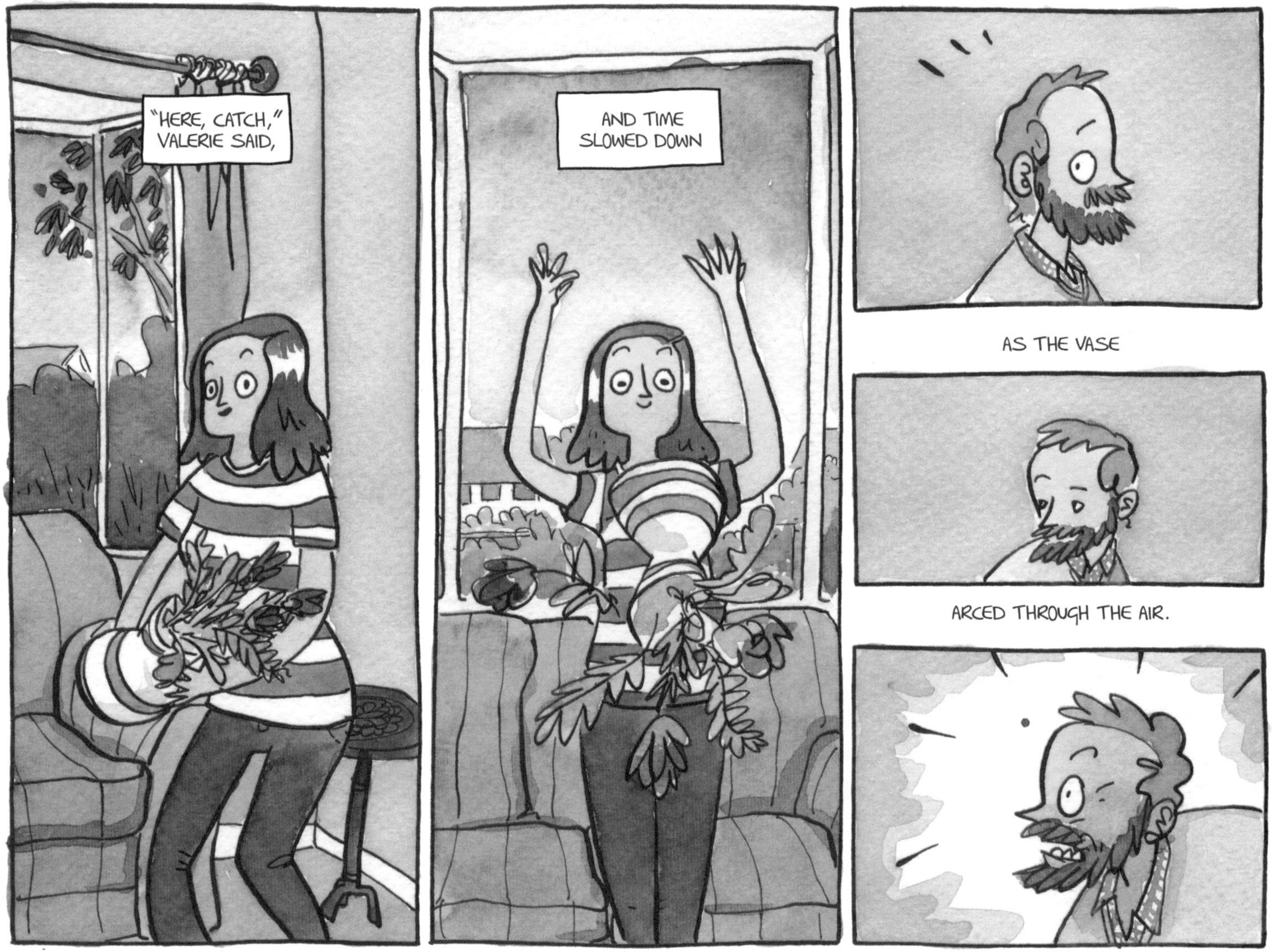
"HERE, CATCH," VALERIE SAID,
AND TIME SLOWED DOWN
AS THE VASE
ARCED THROUGH THE AIR.

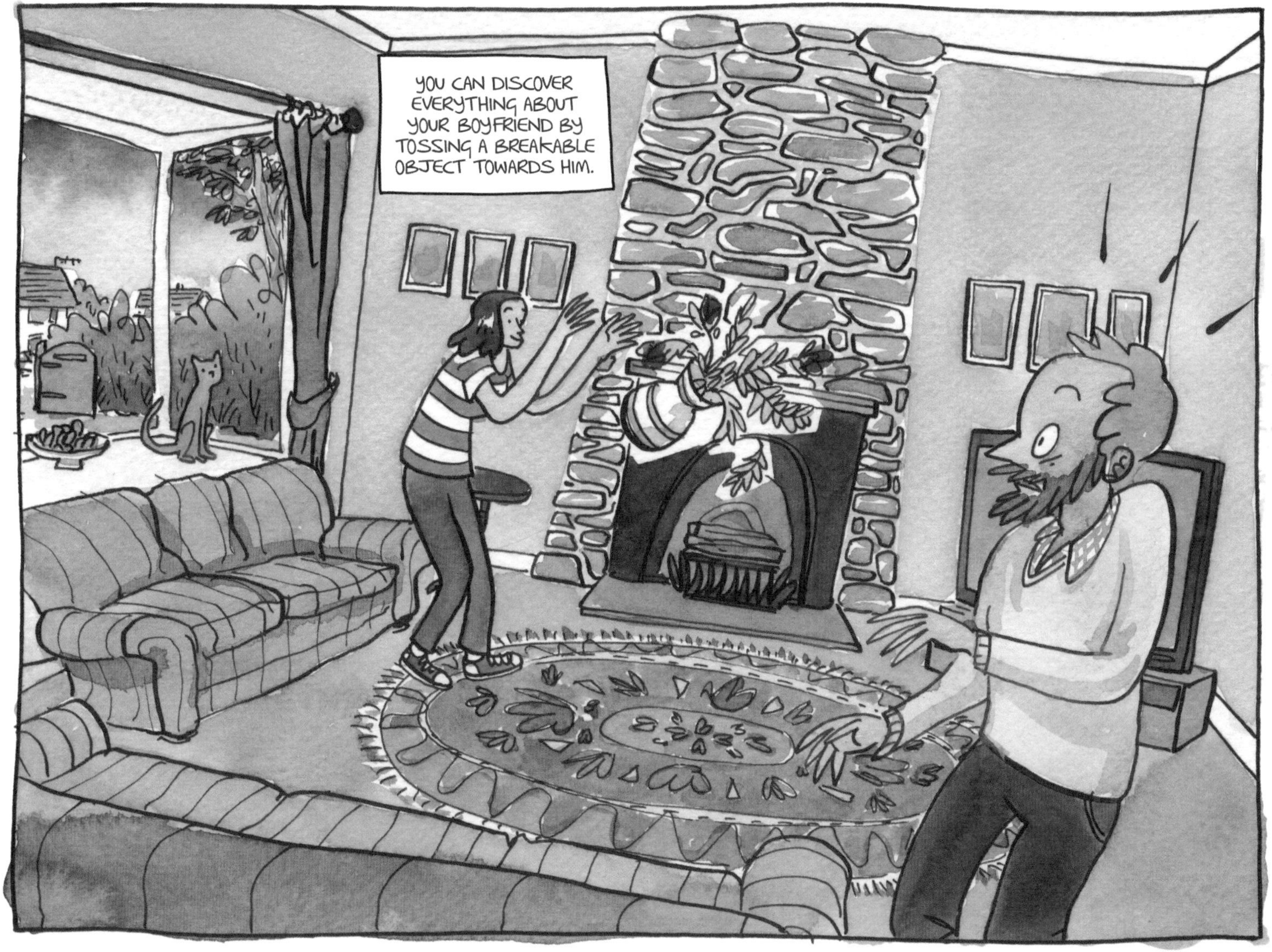
YOU CAN DISCOVER EVERYTHING ABOUT YOUR BOYFRIEND BY TOSSING A BREAKABLE OBJECT TOWARDS HIM.

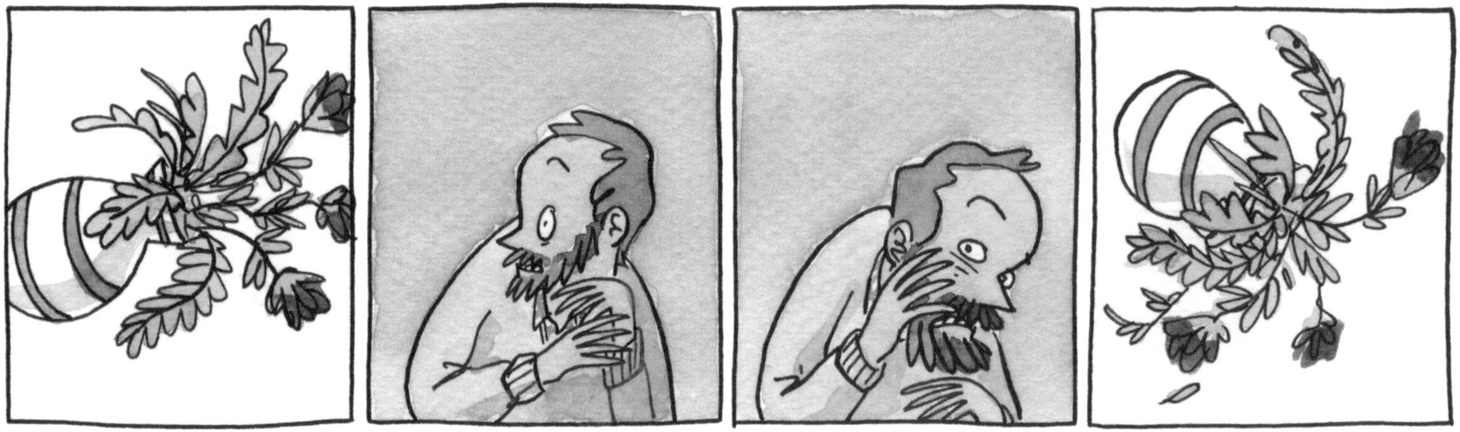

IS HE POISED?

CONFIDENT IN HIS JUDGEMENTS?

DOES HE SEEM WILLING TO TAKE RESPONSIBILITY FOR SOMEONE ELSE'S ACTIONS?

IS HE COMFORTABLE WITH SPONTANEITY?

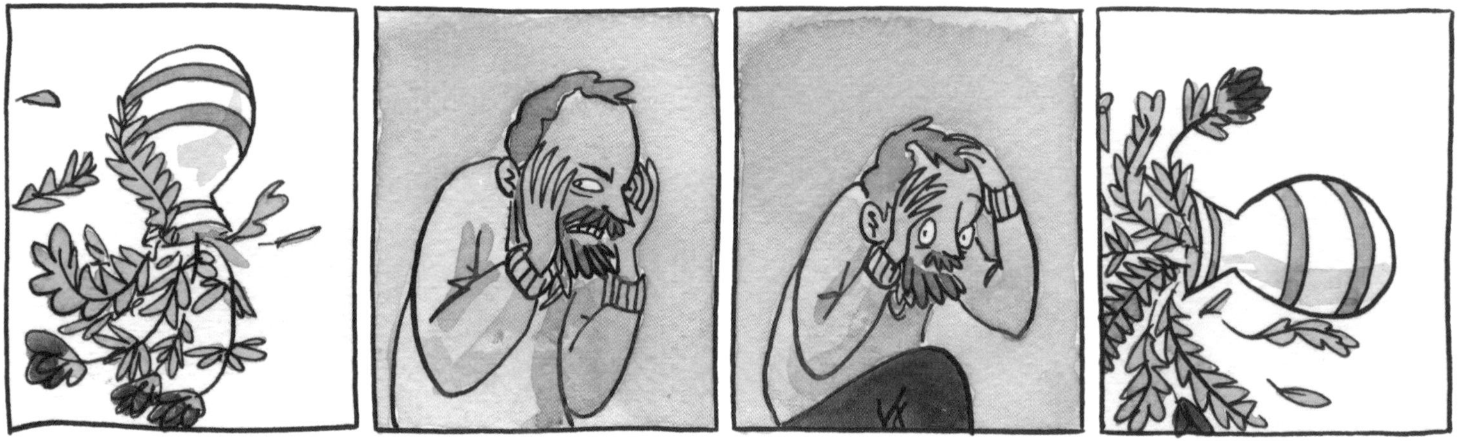

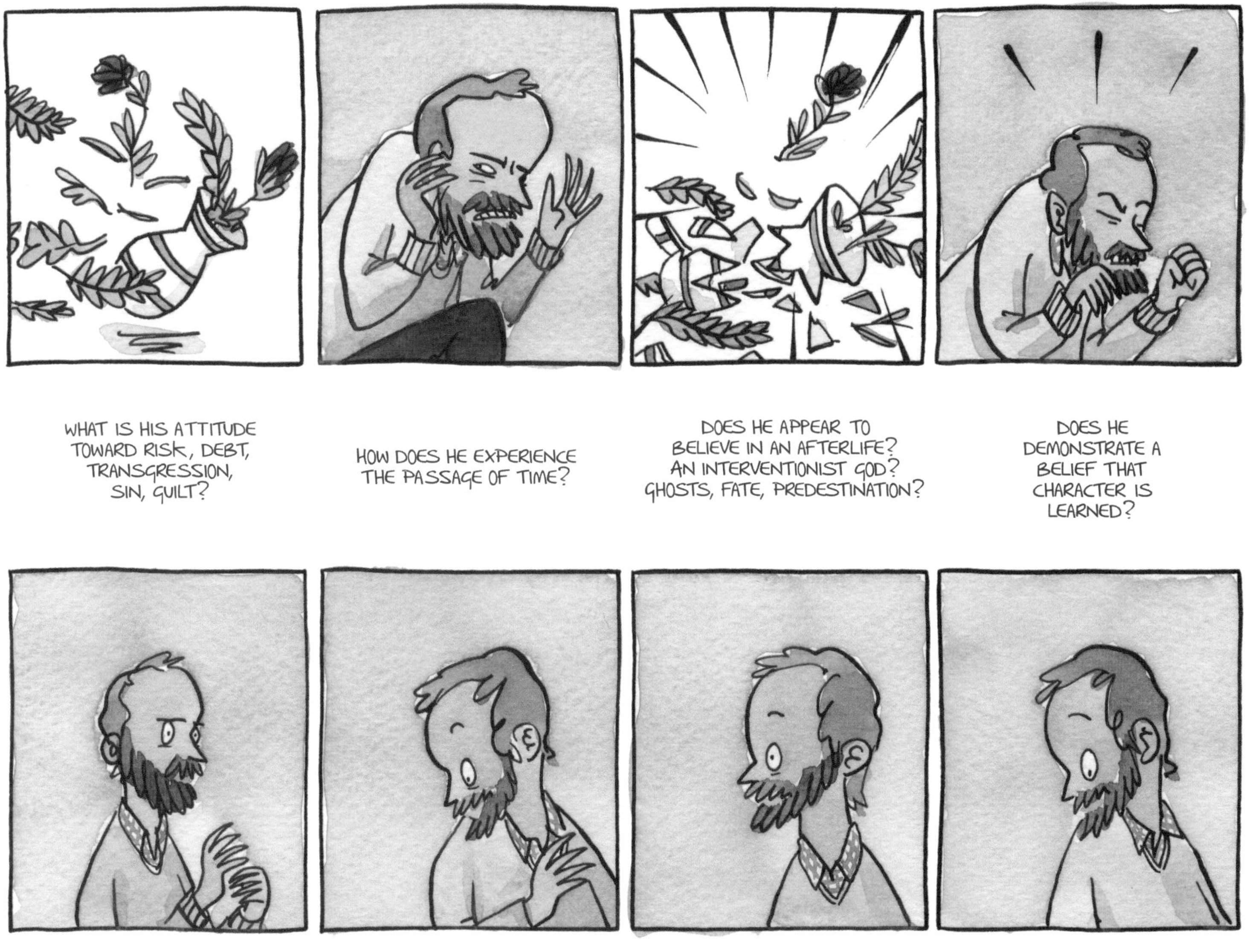
WHAT IS HIS ATTITUDE TOWARD RISK, DEBT, TRANSGRESSION, SIN, GUILT?
HOW DOES HE EXPERIENCE THE PASSAGE OF TIME?
DOES HE APPEAR TO BELIEVE IN AN AFTERLIFE? AN INTERVENTIONIST GOD? GHOSTS, FATE, PREDESTINATION?
DOES HE DEMONSTRATE A BELIEF THAT CHARACTER IS LEARNED?

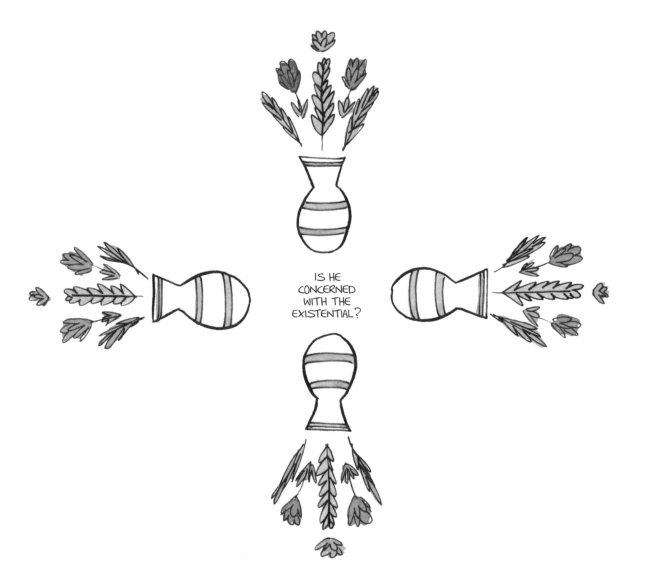

IS HE
CONCERNED
WITH THE
EXISTENTIAL?

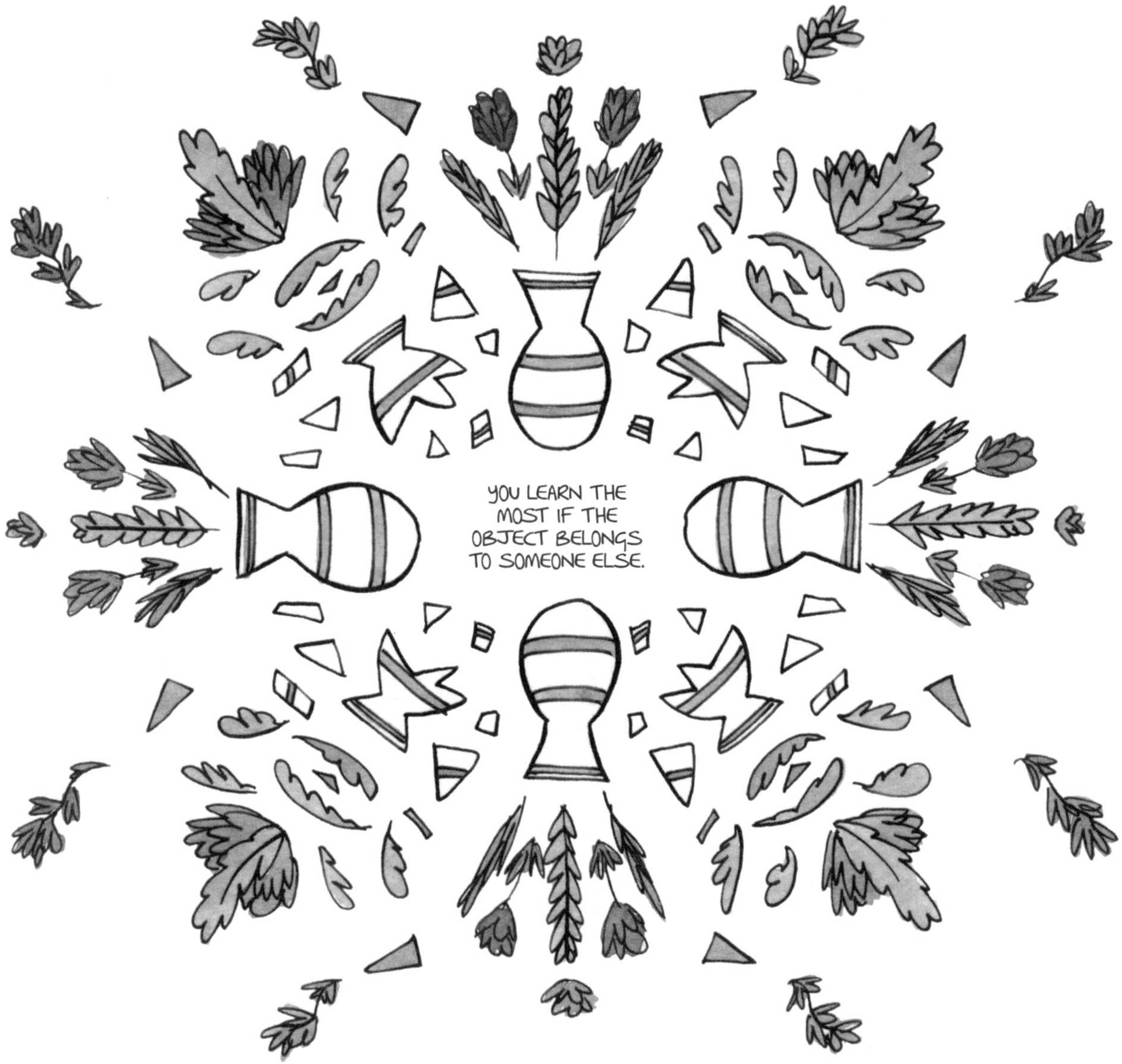
YOU LEARN THE MOST IF THE OBJECT BELONGS TO SOMEONE ELSE.

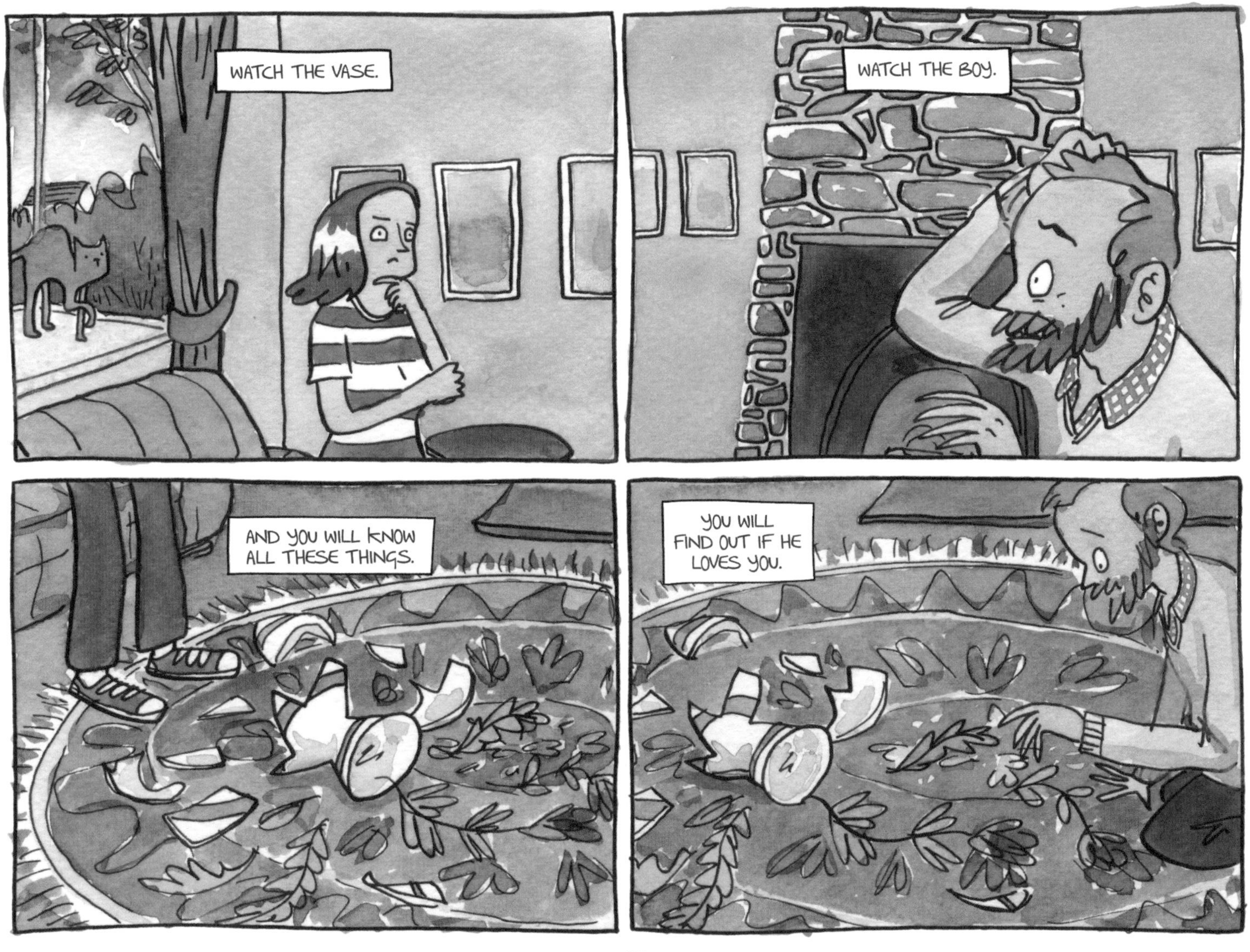
WATCH THE VASE.
WATCH THE BOY.
AND YOU WILL KNOW ALL THESE THINGS.
YOU WILL FIND OUT IF HE LOVES YOU.

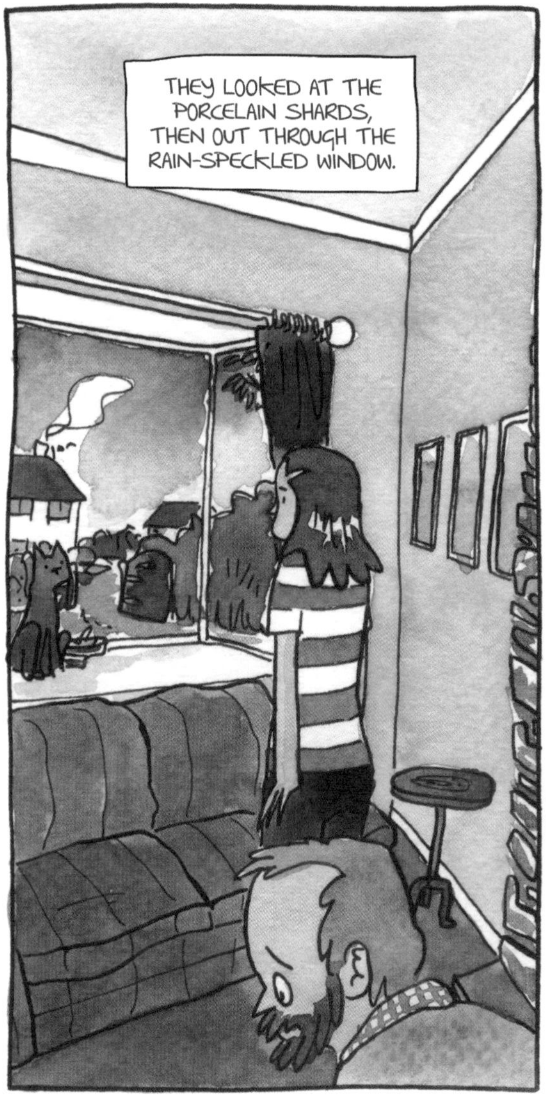
THEY LOOKED AT THE PORCELAIN SHARDS, THEN OUT THROUGH THE RAIN-SPECKLED WINDOW.

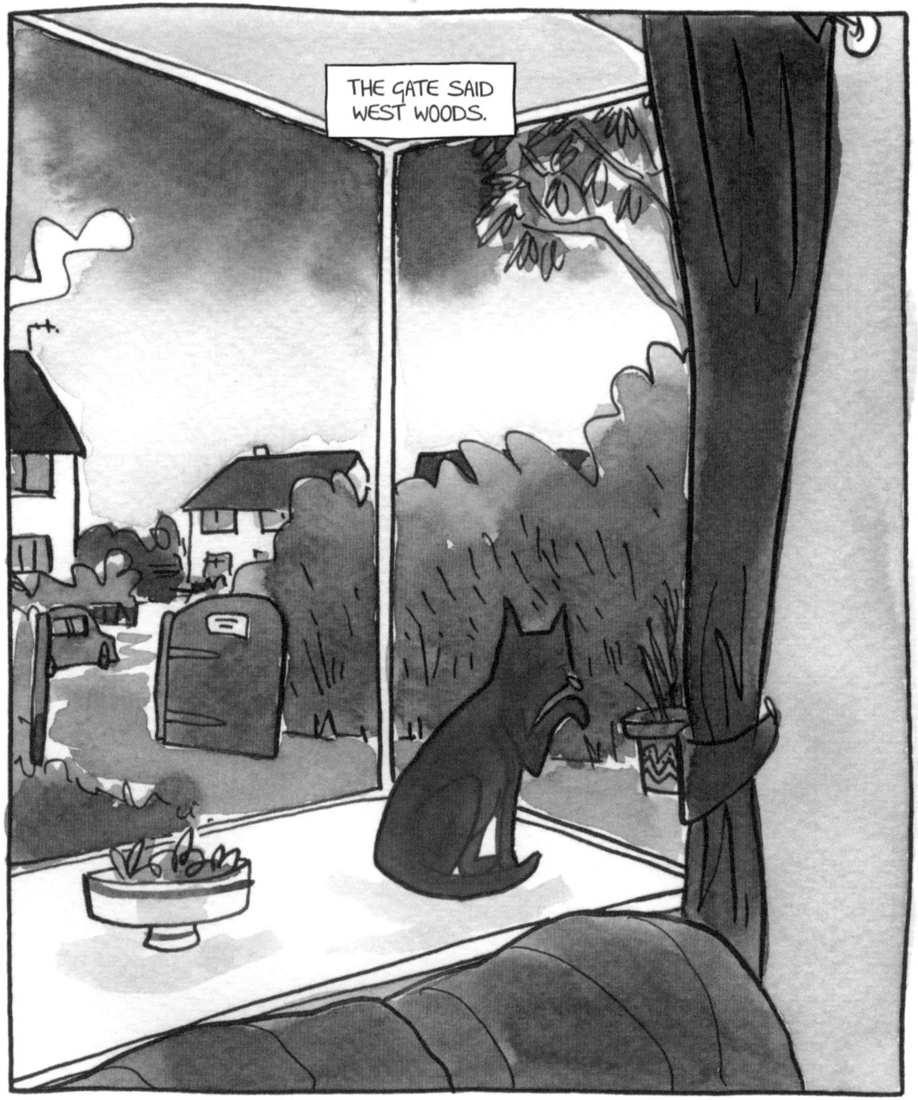
THE GATE SAID WEST WOODS.

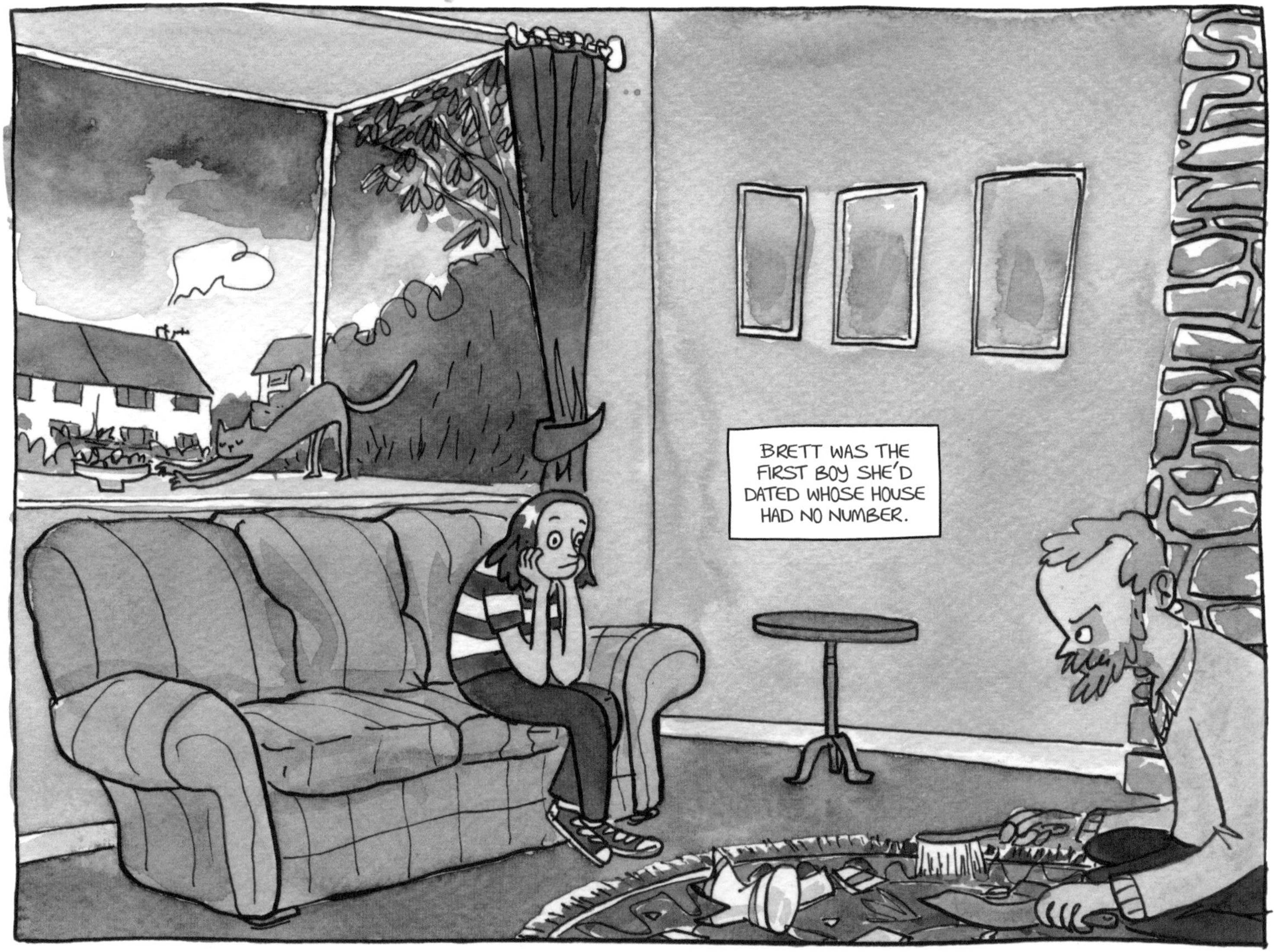
BRETT WAS THE FIRST BOY SHE'D DATED WHOSE HOUSE HAD NO NUMBER.

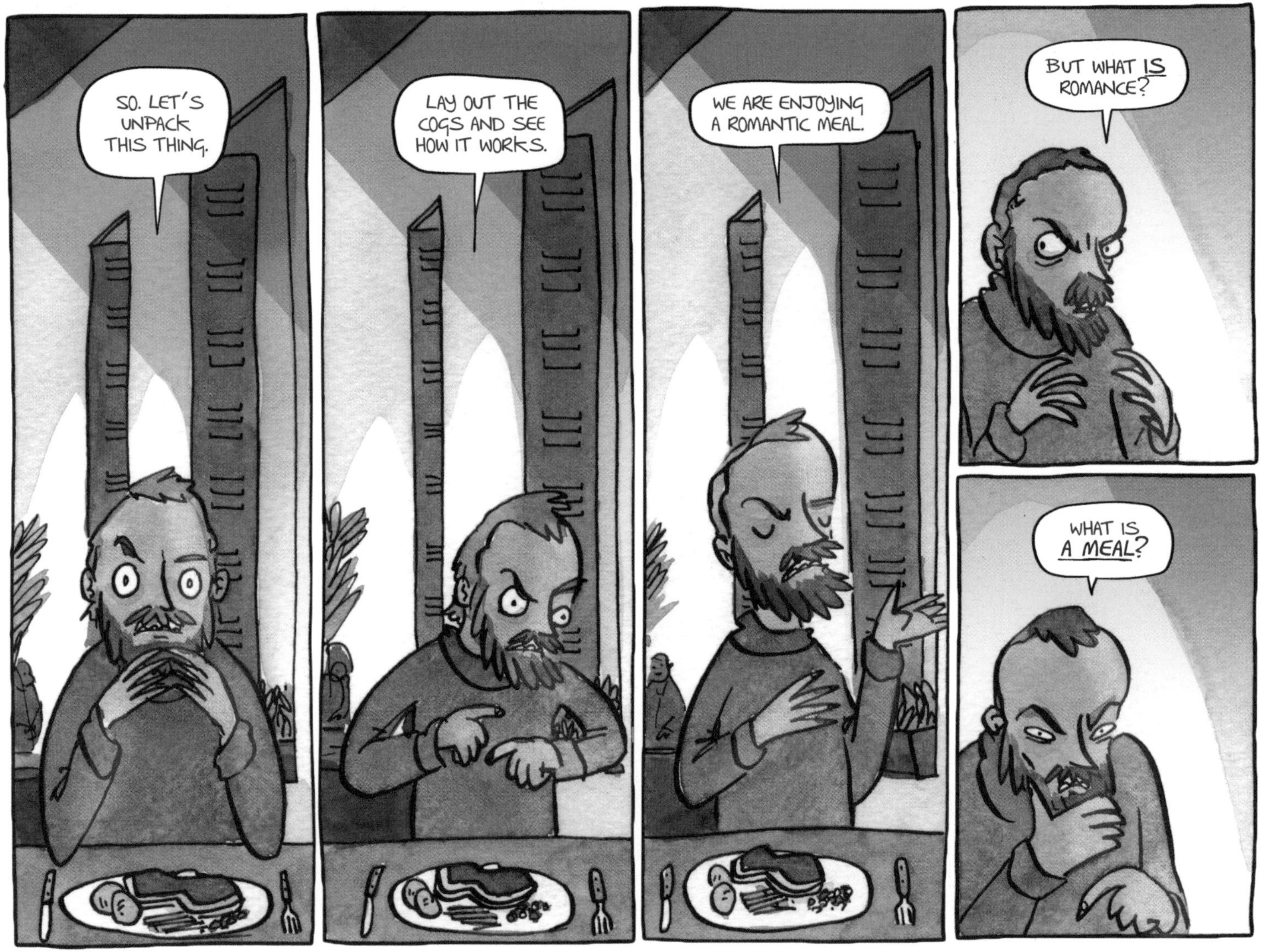
SO. LET'S UNPACK THIS THING.
LAY OUT THE COGS AND SEE HOW IT WORKS.
WE ARE ENJOYING A ROMANTIC MEAL.
BUT WHAT IS ROMANCE?
WHAT IS A MEAL?

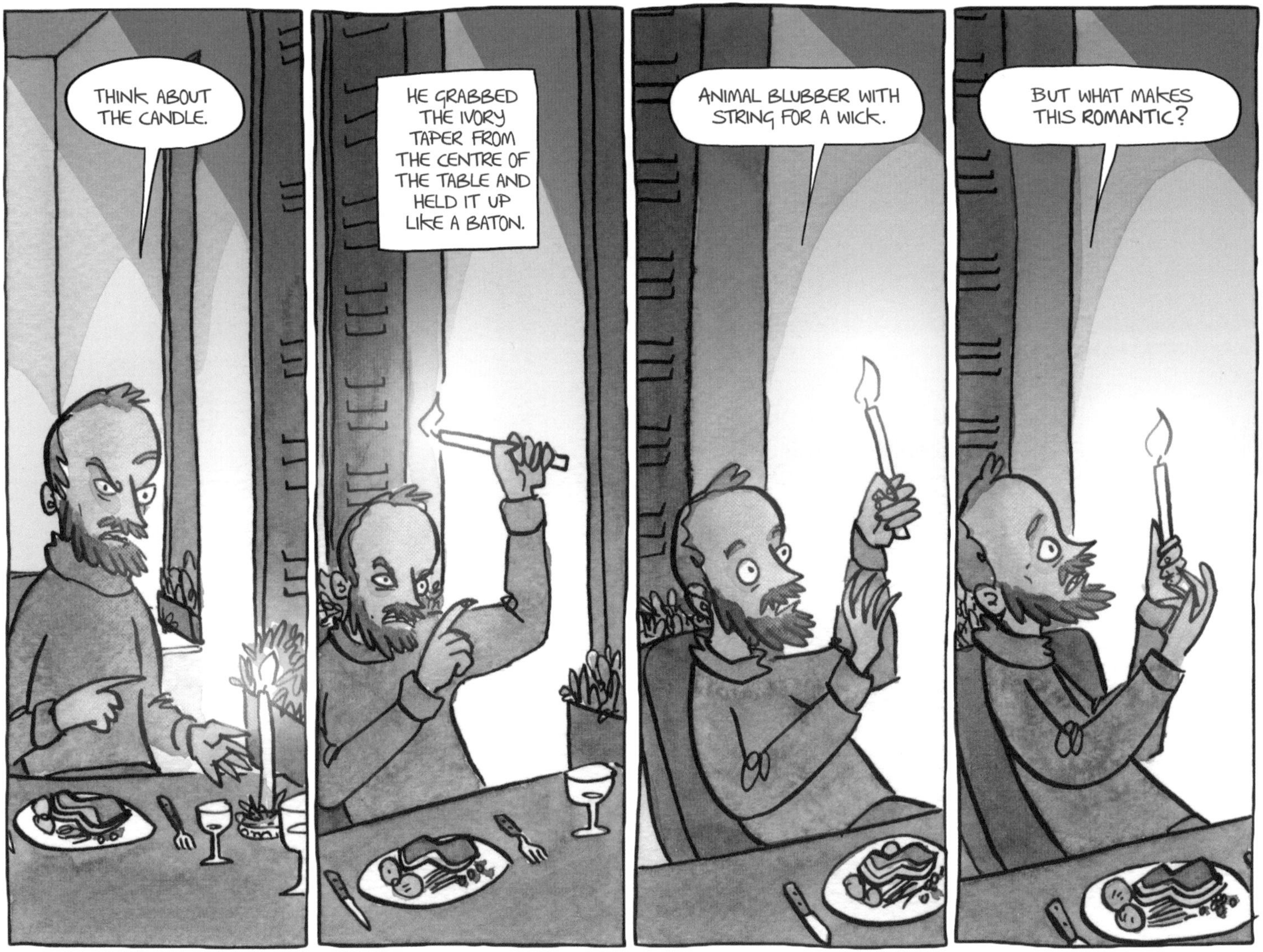
THINK ABOUT THE CANDLE.
HE GRABBED THE IVORY TAPER FROM THE CENTRE OF THE TABLE AND HELD IT UP LIKE A BATON.
ANIMAL BLUBBER WITH STRING FOR A WICK.
BUT WHAT MAKES THIS ROMANTIC?

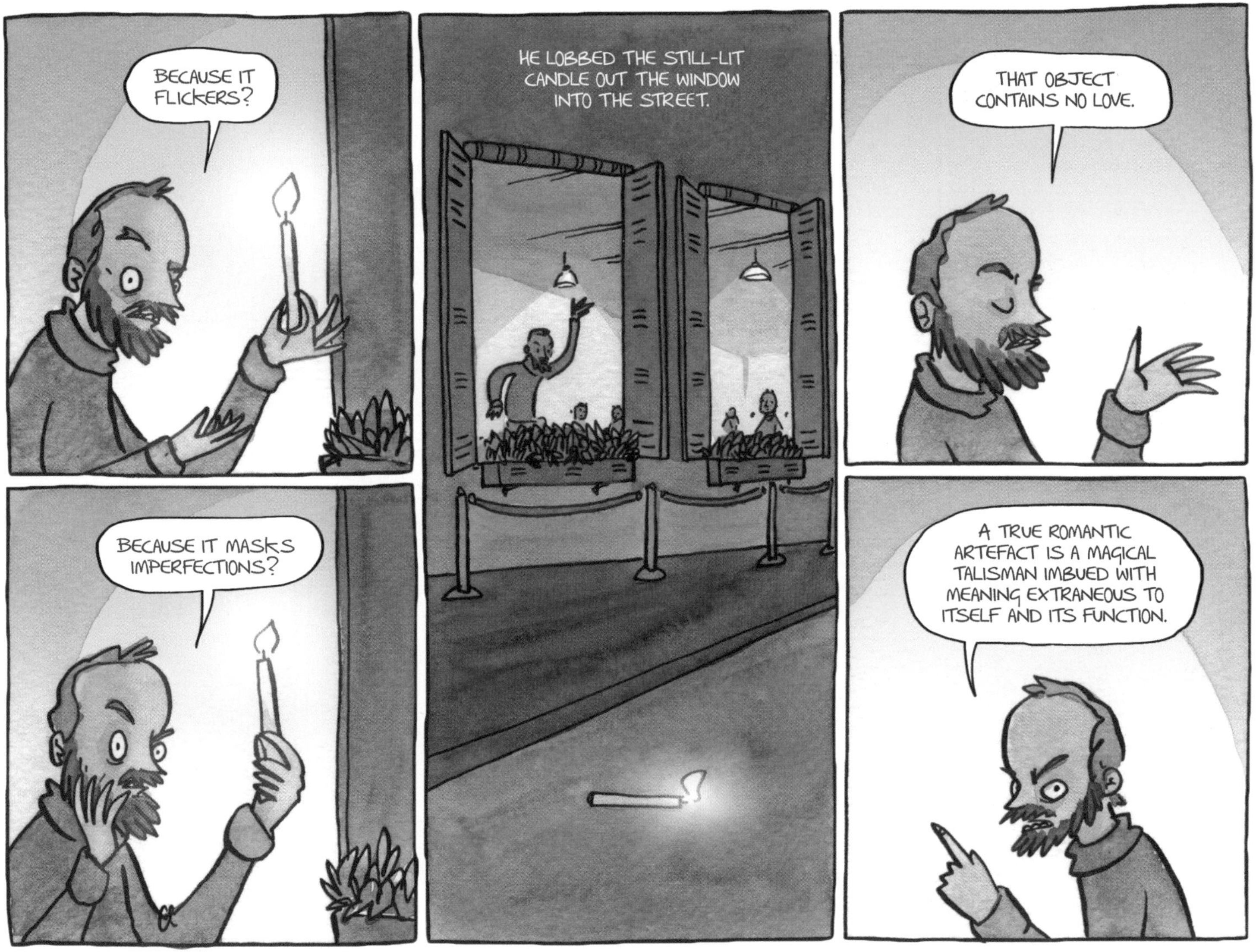
BECAUSE IT FLICKERS?
BECAUSE IT MASKS IMPERFECTIONS?
HE LOBBED THE STILL-LIT CANDLE OUT THE WINDOW INTO THE STREET.
THAT OBJECT CONTAINS NO LOVE.
A TRUE ROMANTIC ARTEFACT IS A MAGICAL TALISMAN IMBUED WITH MEANING EXTRANEOUS TO ITSELF AND ITS FUNCTION.

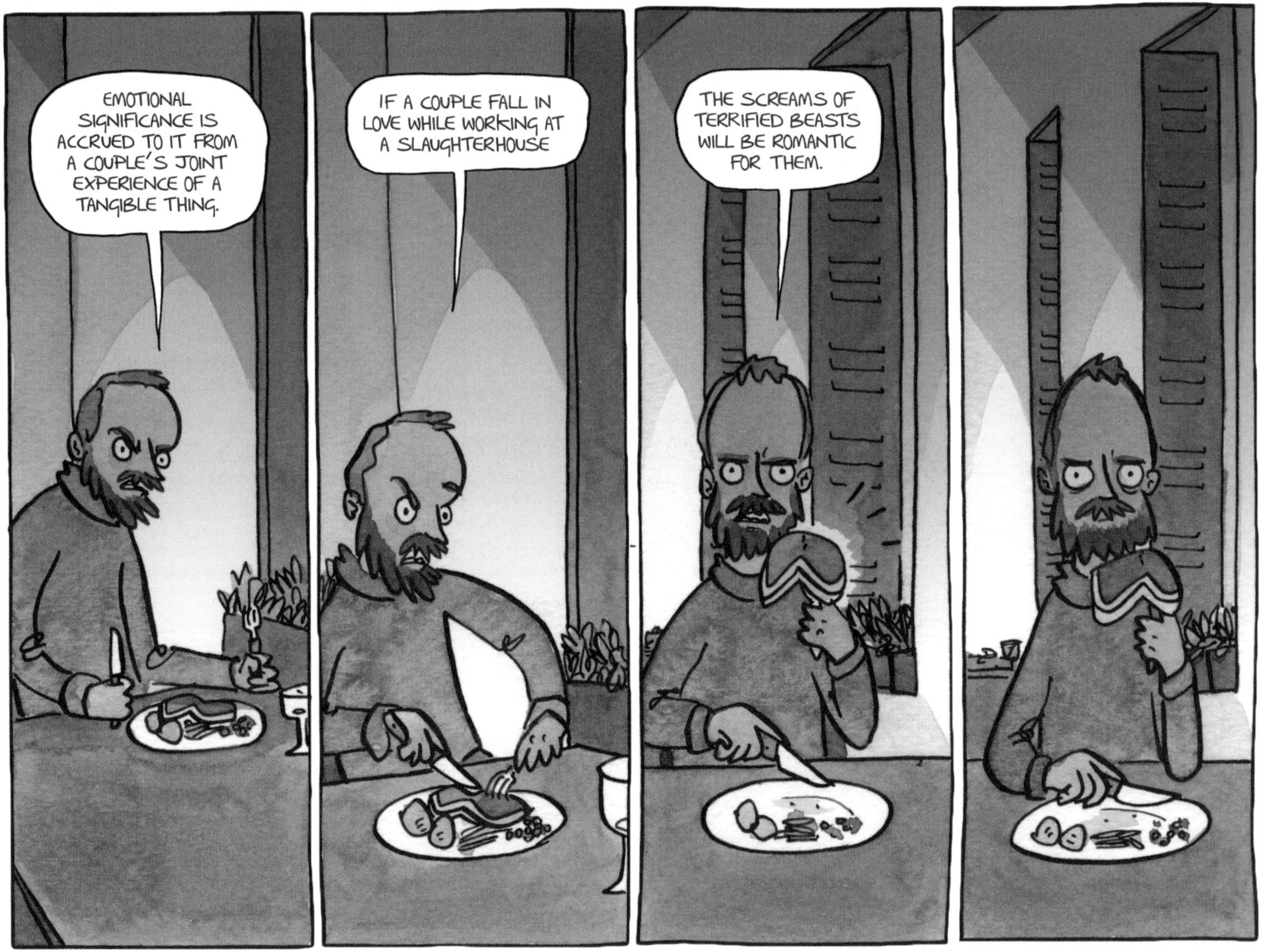
EMOTIONAL SIGNIFICANCE IS ACCRUED TO IT FROM A COUPLE'S JOINT EXPERIENCE OF A TANGIBLE THING.
IF A COUPLE FALL IN LOVE WHILE WORKING AT A SLAUGHTERHOUSE
THE SCREAMS OF TERRIFIED BEASTS WILL BE ROMANTIC FOR THEM.

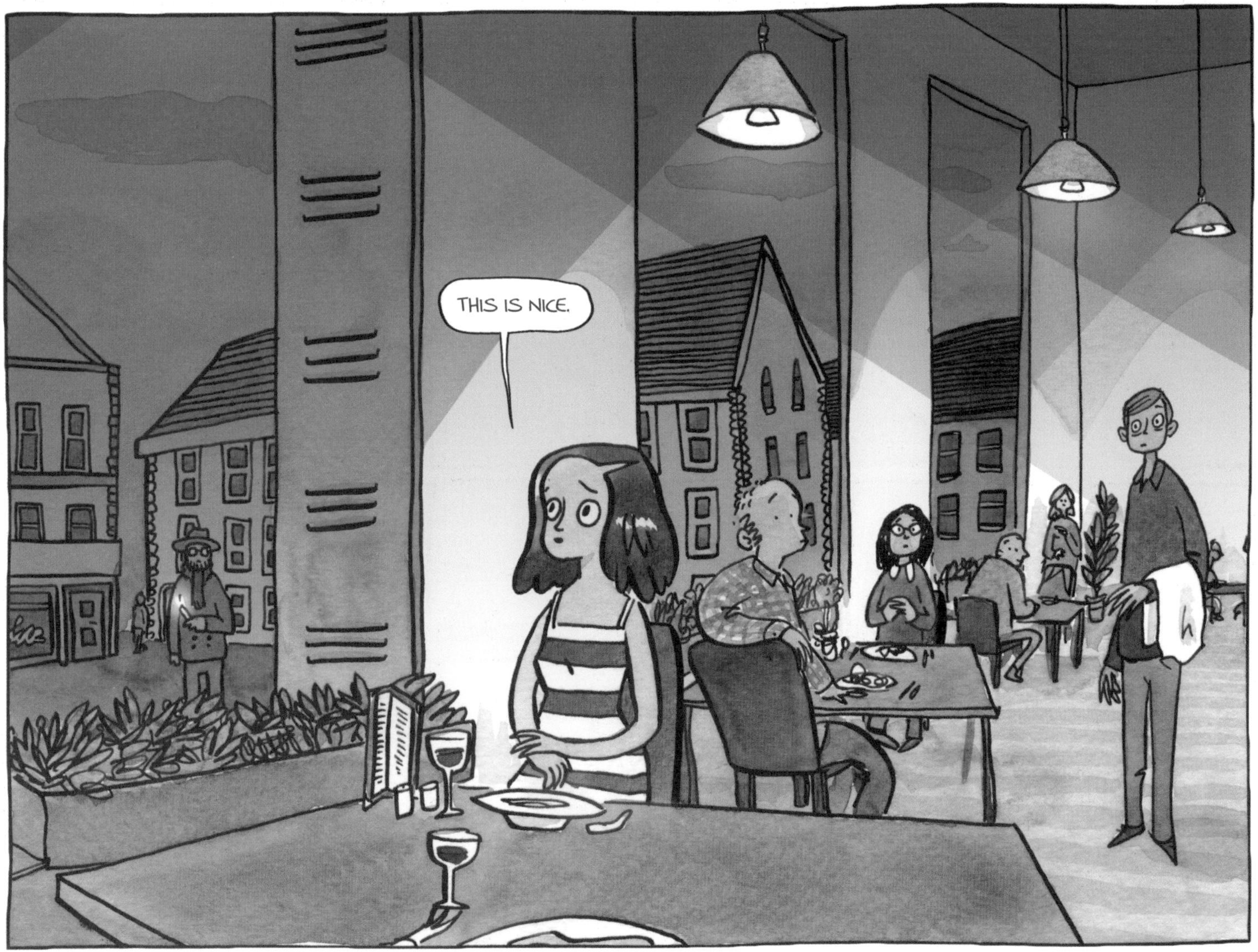
THIS IS NICE.

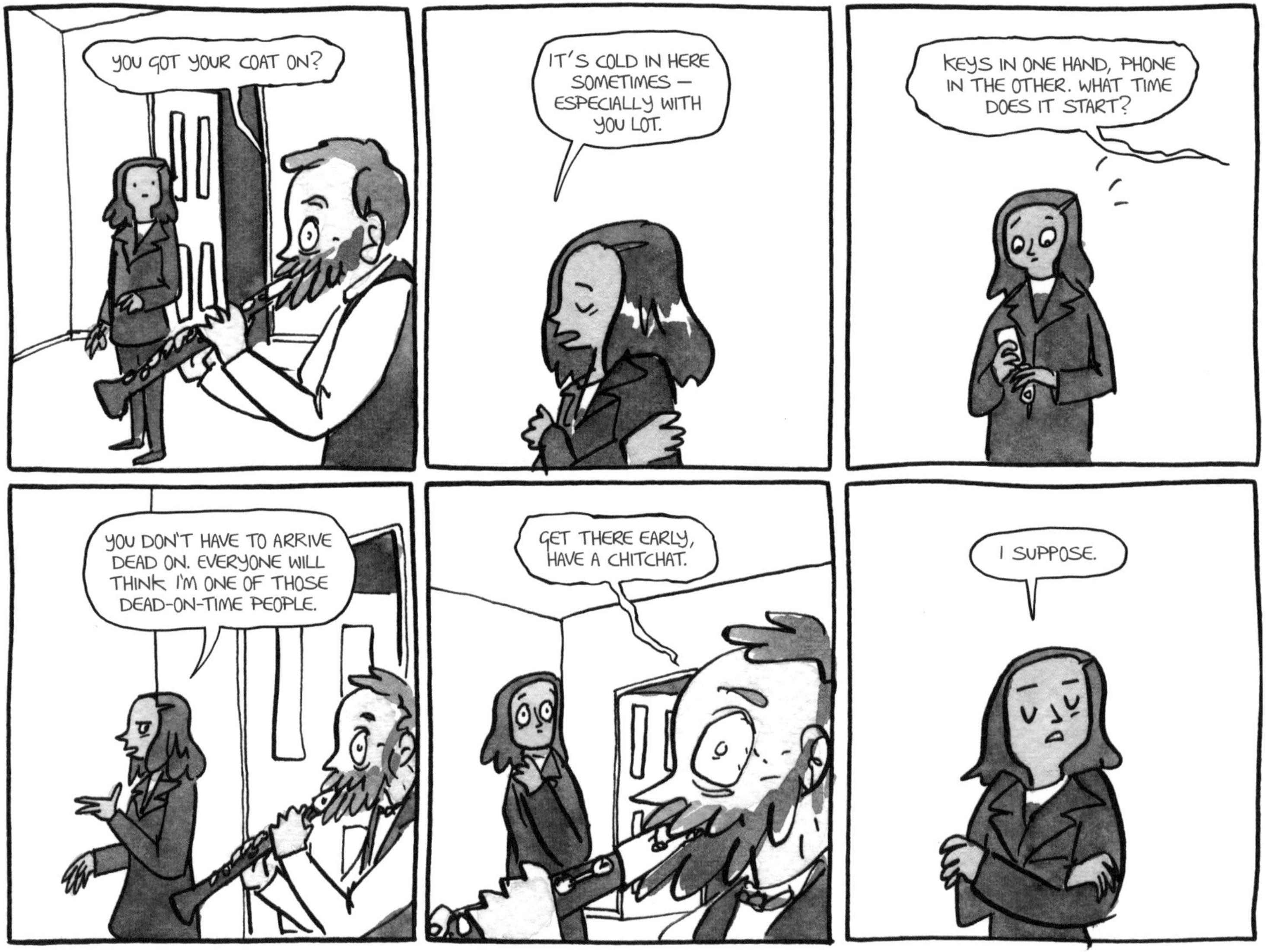
YOU GOT YOUR COAT ON?
IT'S COLD IN HERE SOMETIMES — ESPECIALLY WITH YOU LOT.
KEYS IN ONE HAND, PHONE IN THE OTHER. WHAT TIME DOES IT START?
YOU DON'T HAVE TO ARRIVE DEAD ON. EVERYONE WILL THINK I'M ONE OF THOSE DEAD-ON-TIME PEOPLE.
GET THERE EARLY, HAVE A CHITCHAT.
I SUPPOSE.

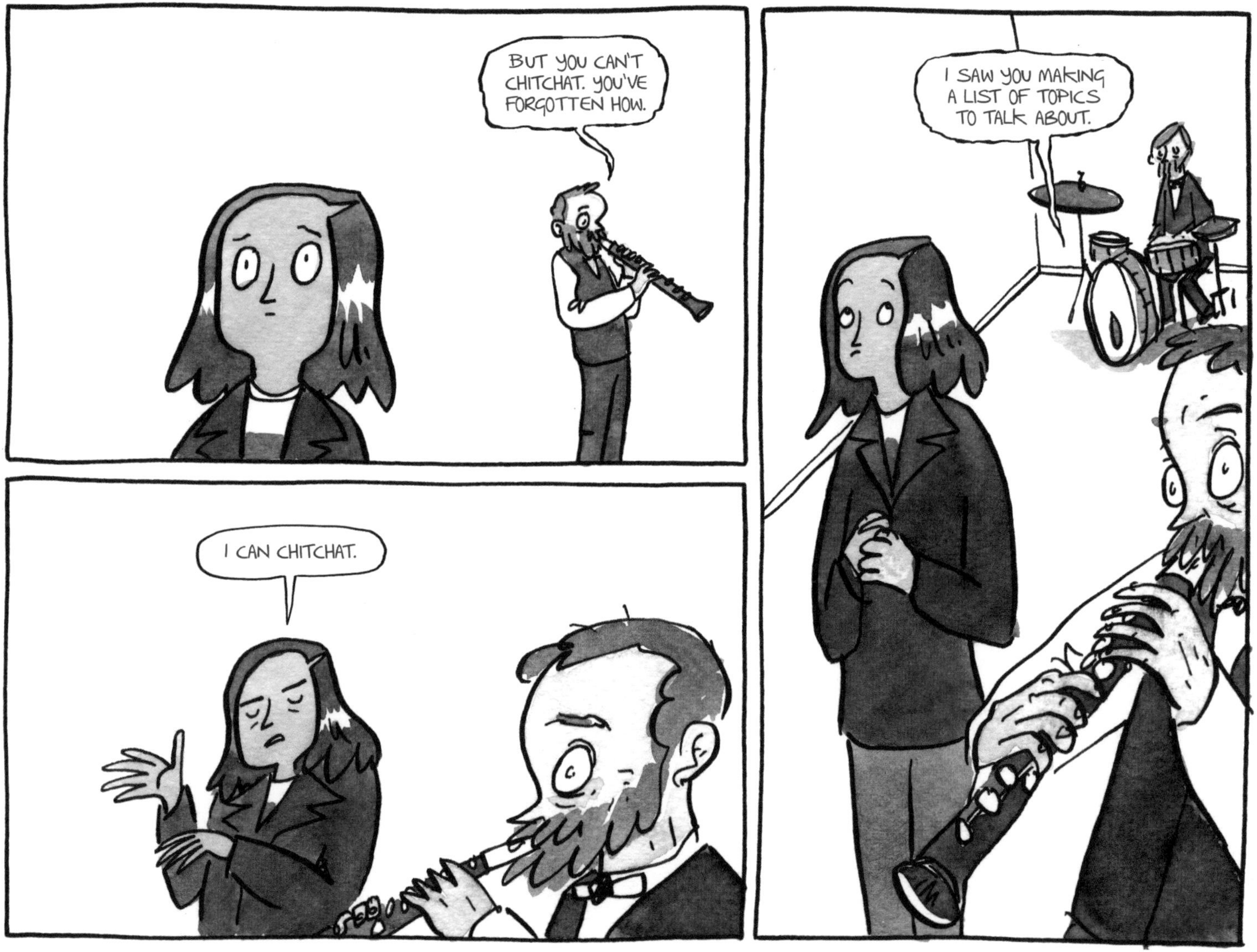
BUT YOU CAN'T CHITCHAT. YOU'VE FORGOTTEN HOW.
I CAN CHITCHAT.
I SAW YOU MAKING A LIST OF TOPICS TO TALK ABOUT.

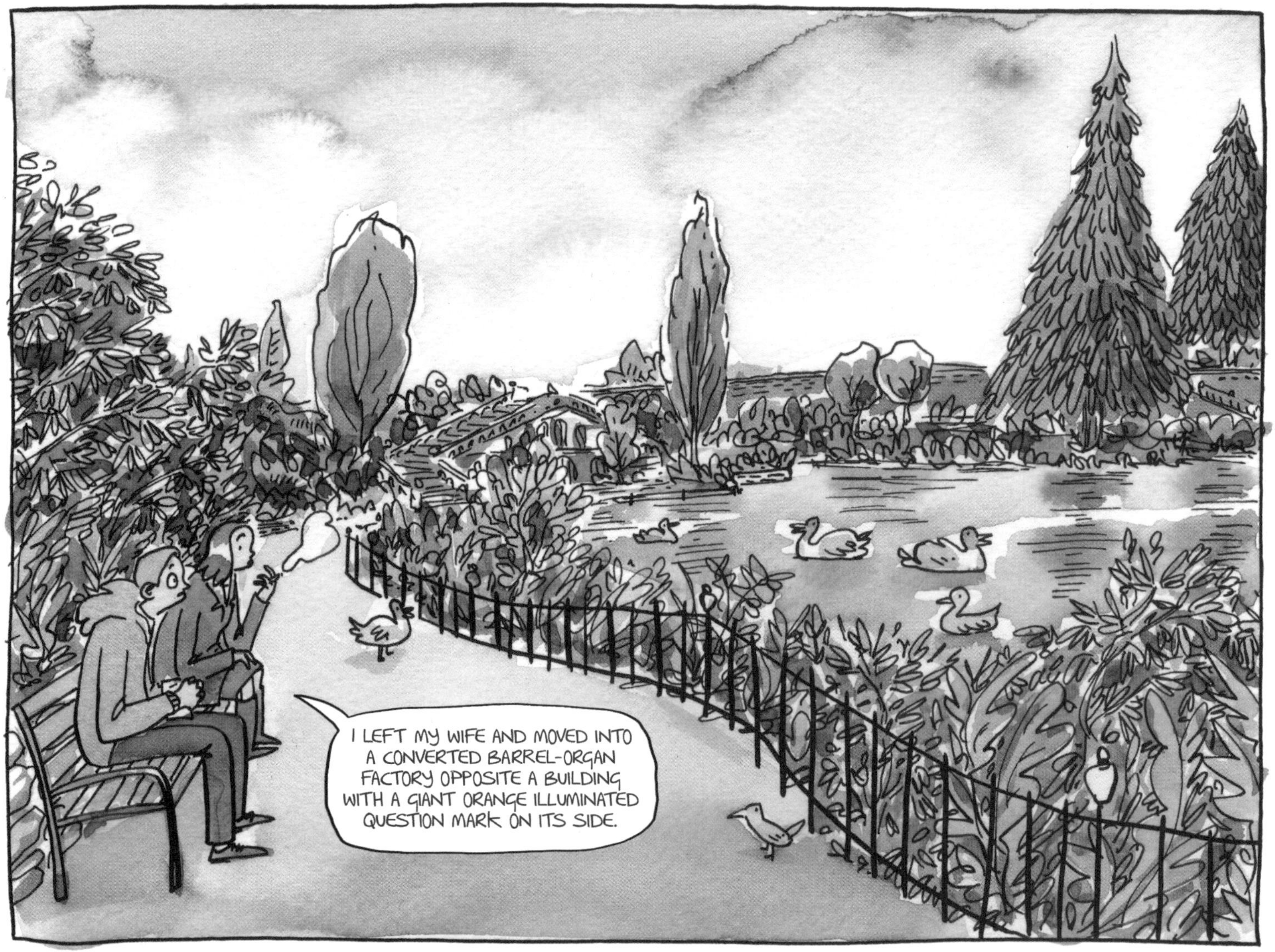
I LEFT MY WIFE AND MOVED INTO A CONVERTED BARREL-ORGAN FACTORY OPPOSITE A BUILDING WITH A GIANT ORANGE ILLUMINATED QUESTION MARK ON ITS SIDE.

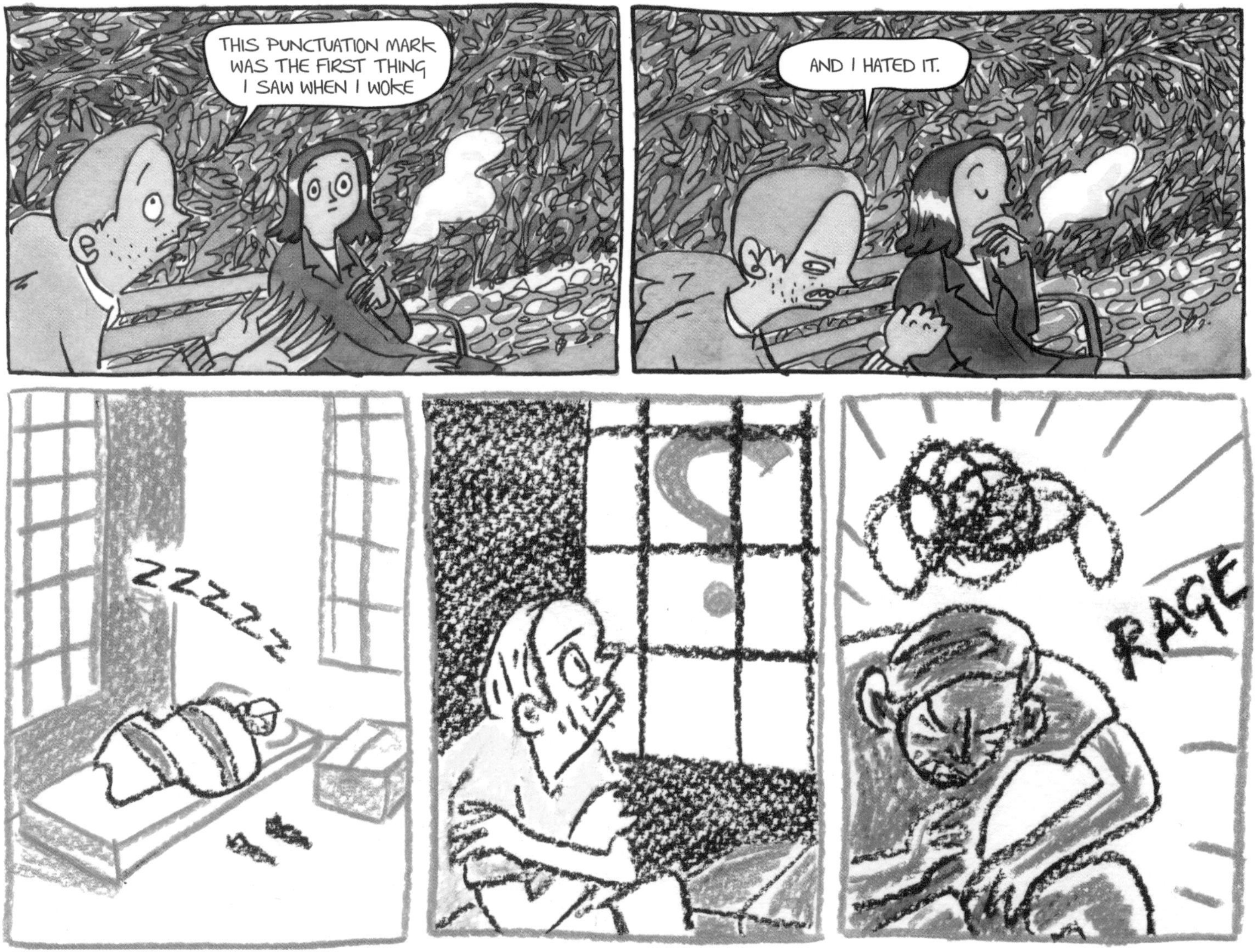
THIS PUNCTUATION MARK WAS THE FIRST THING I SAW WHEN I WOKE
AND I HATED IT.
ZZZZZZ
RAGE

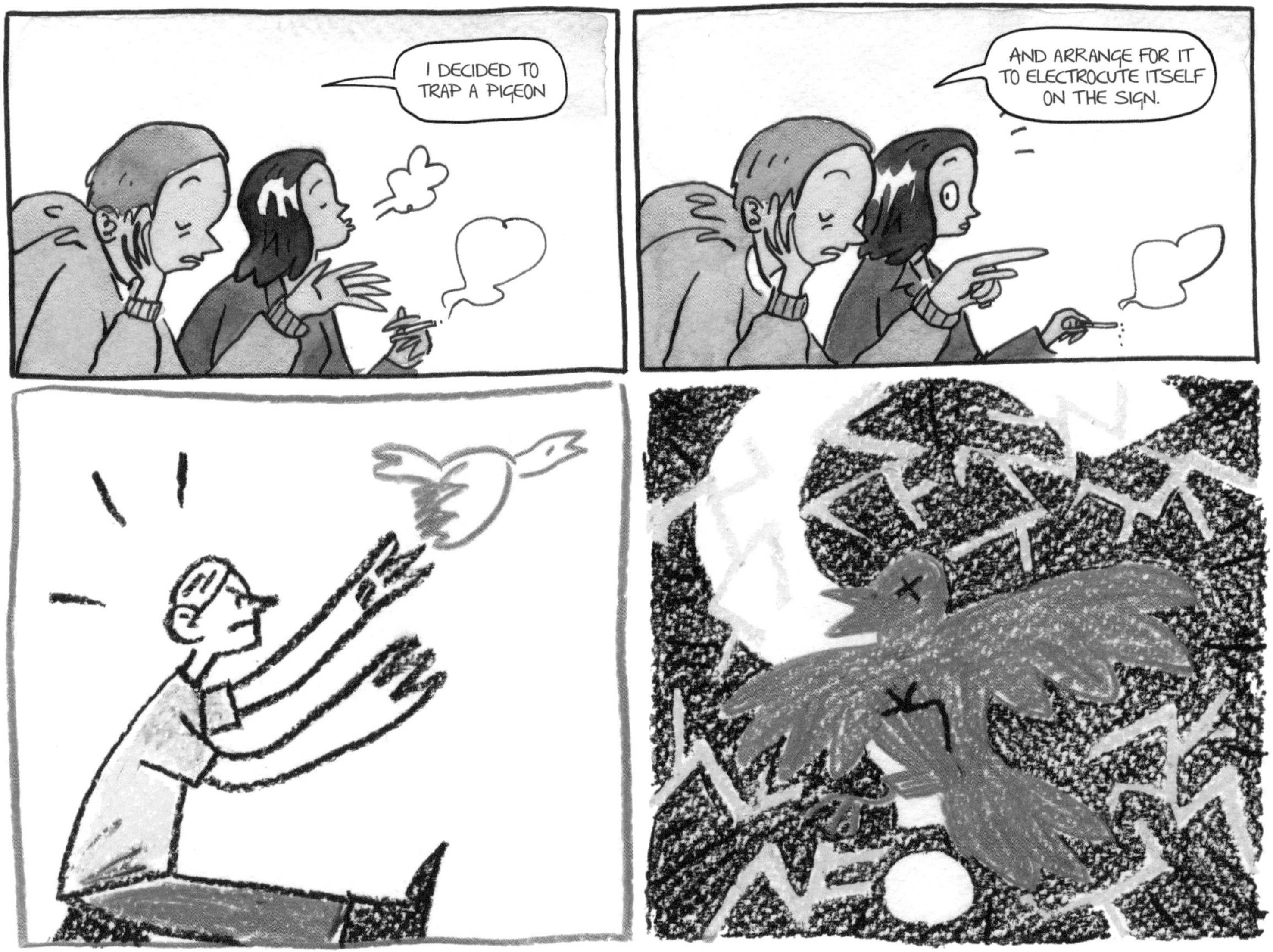
I DECIDED TO TRAP A PIGEON
AND ARRANGE FOR IT TO ELECTROCUTE ITSELF ON THE SIGN.

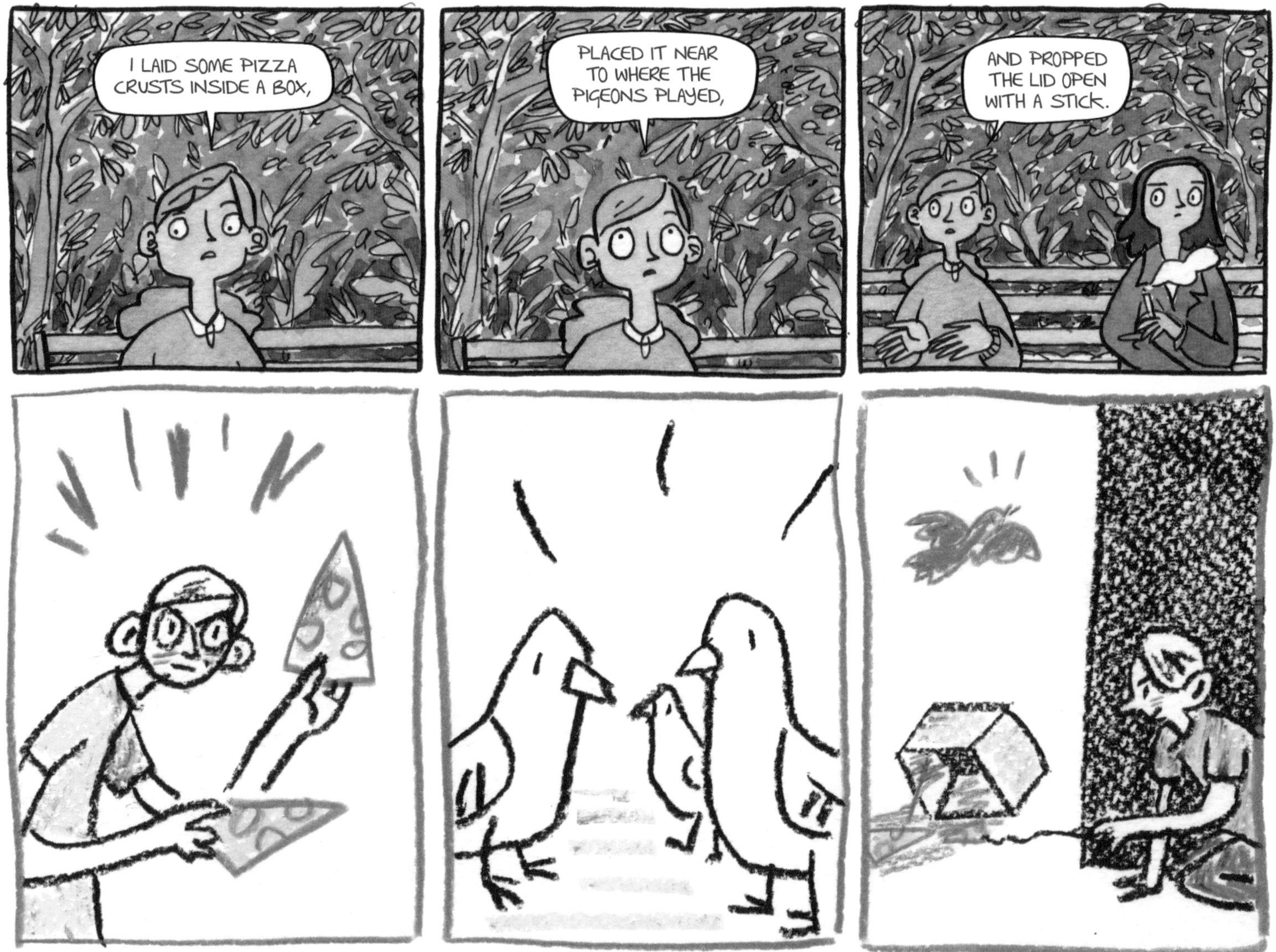
I LAID SOME PIZZA CRUSTS INSIDE A BOX,
PLACED IT NEAR TO WHERE THE PIGEONS PLAYED,
AND PROPPED THE LID OPEN WITH A STICK.

BUT THE BIRDS
IGNORED IT.

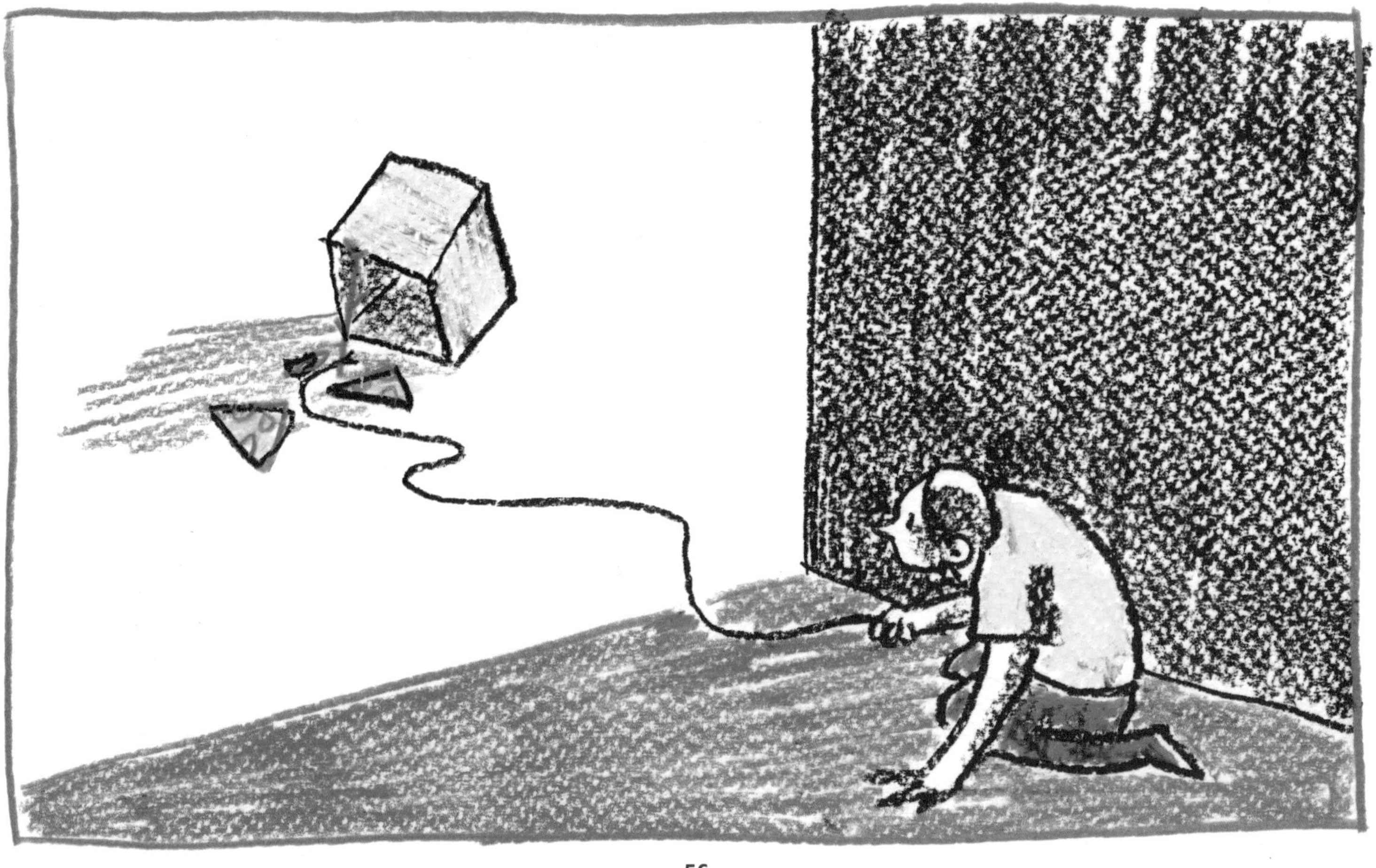

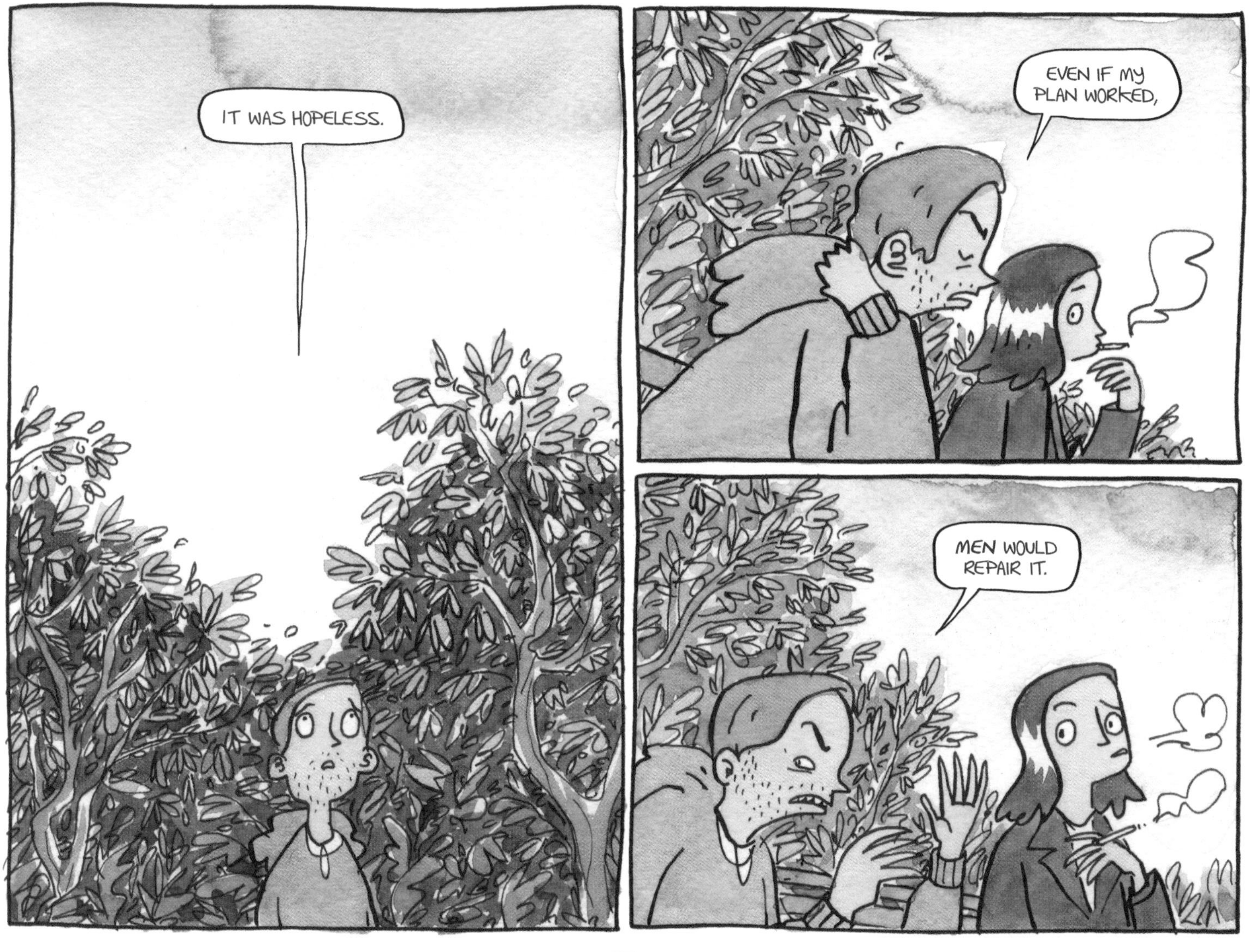
IT WAS HOPELESS.
EVEN IF MY PLAN WORKED,
MEN WOULD REPAIR IT.

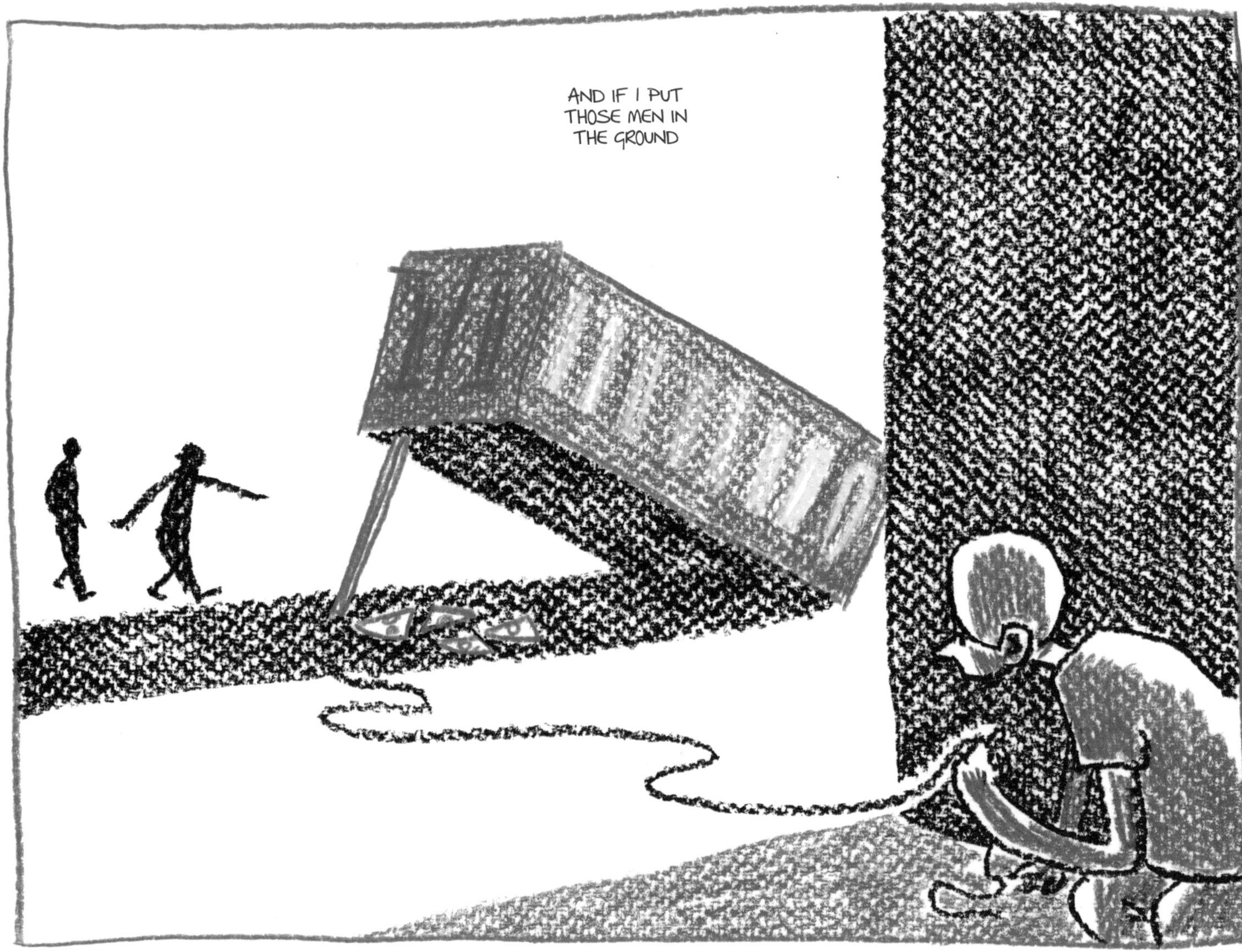
AND IF I PUT
THOSE MEN IN
THE GROUND

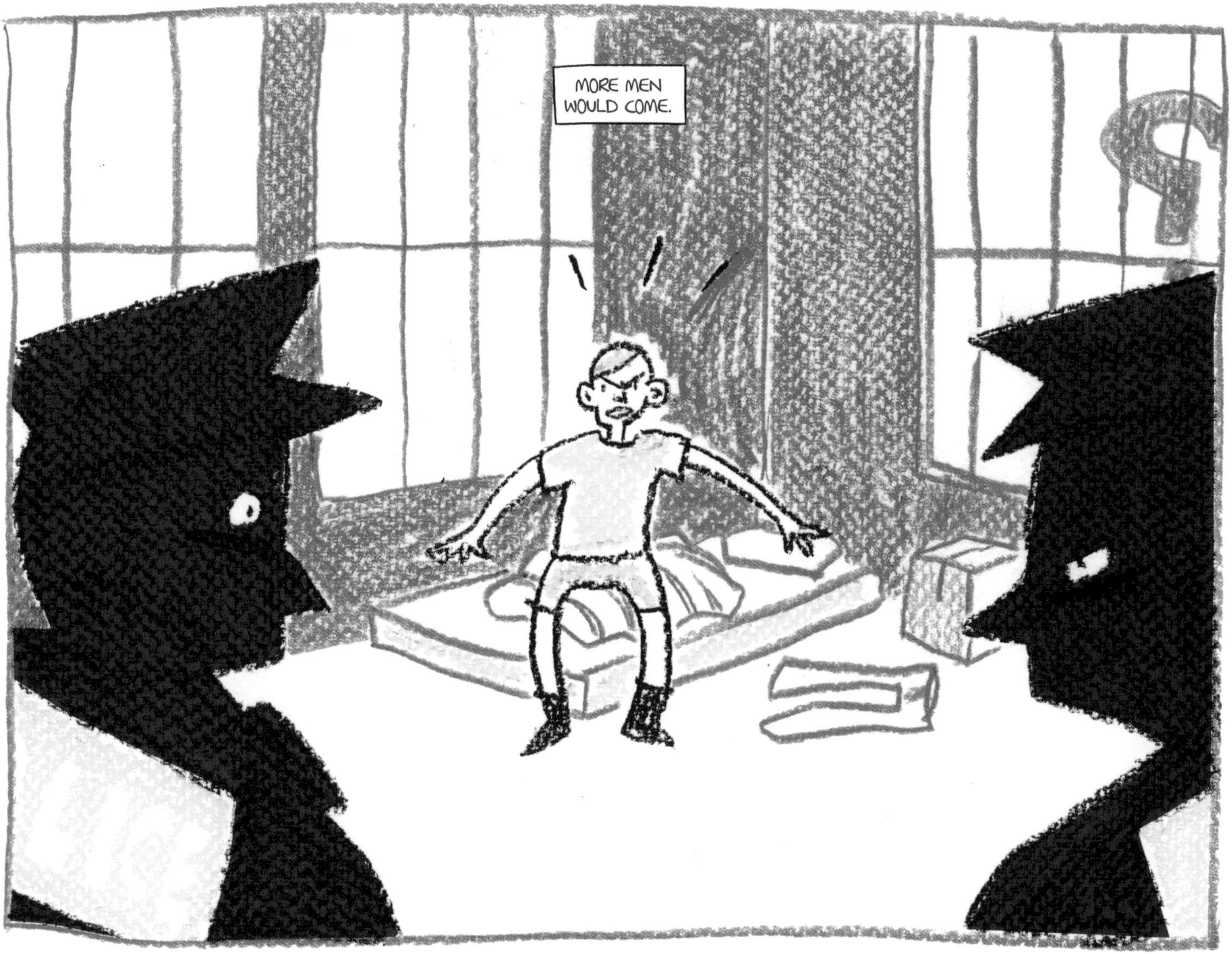
MORE MEN
WOULD COME.

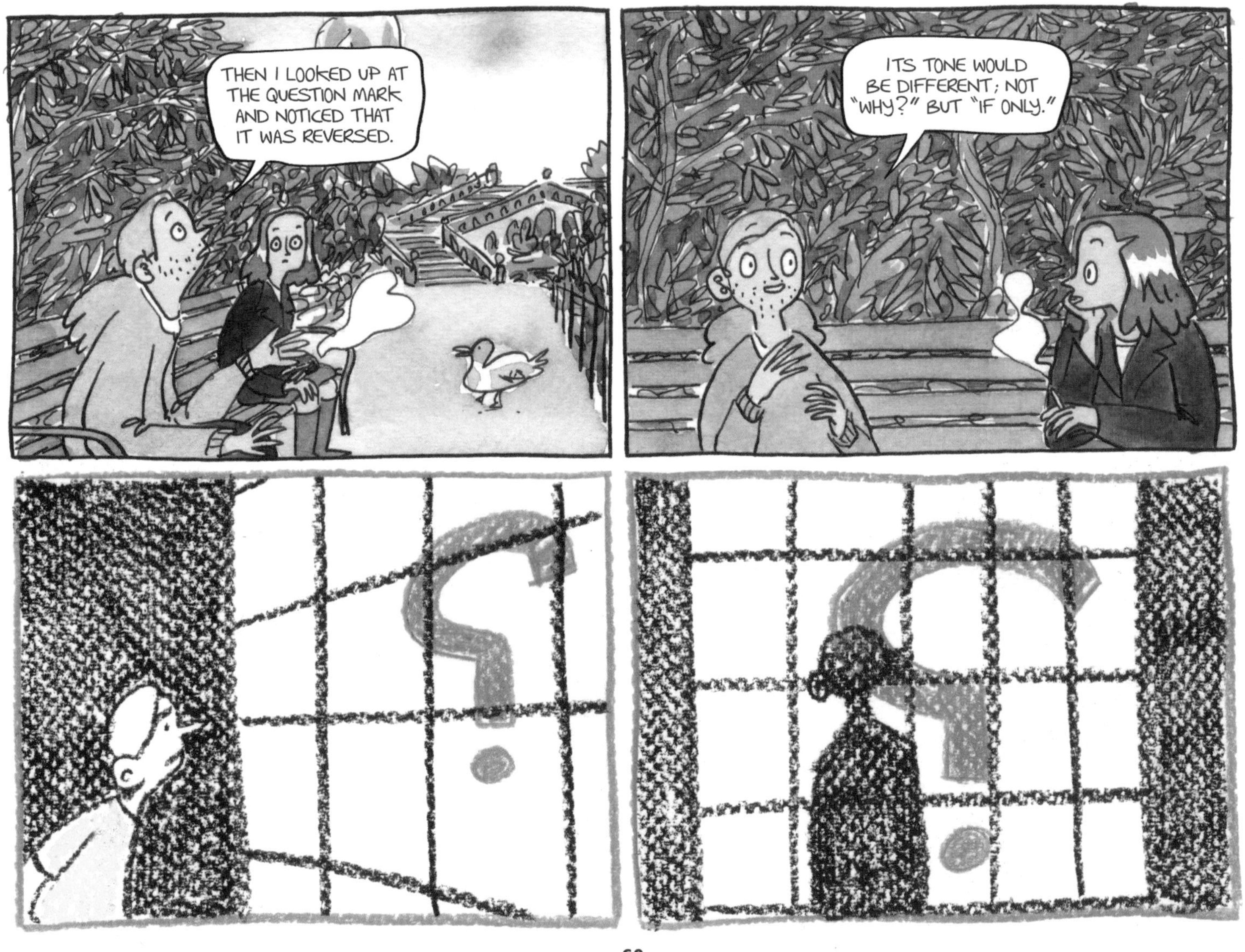
THEN I LOOKED UP AT THE QUESTION MARK AND NOTICED THAT IT WAS REVERSED.
ITS TONE WOULD BE DIFFERENT; NOT "WHY?" BUT "IF ONLY."

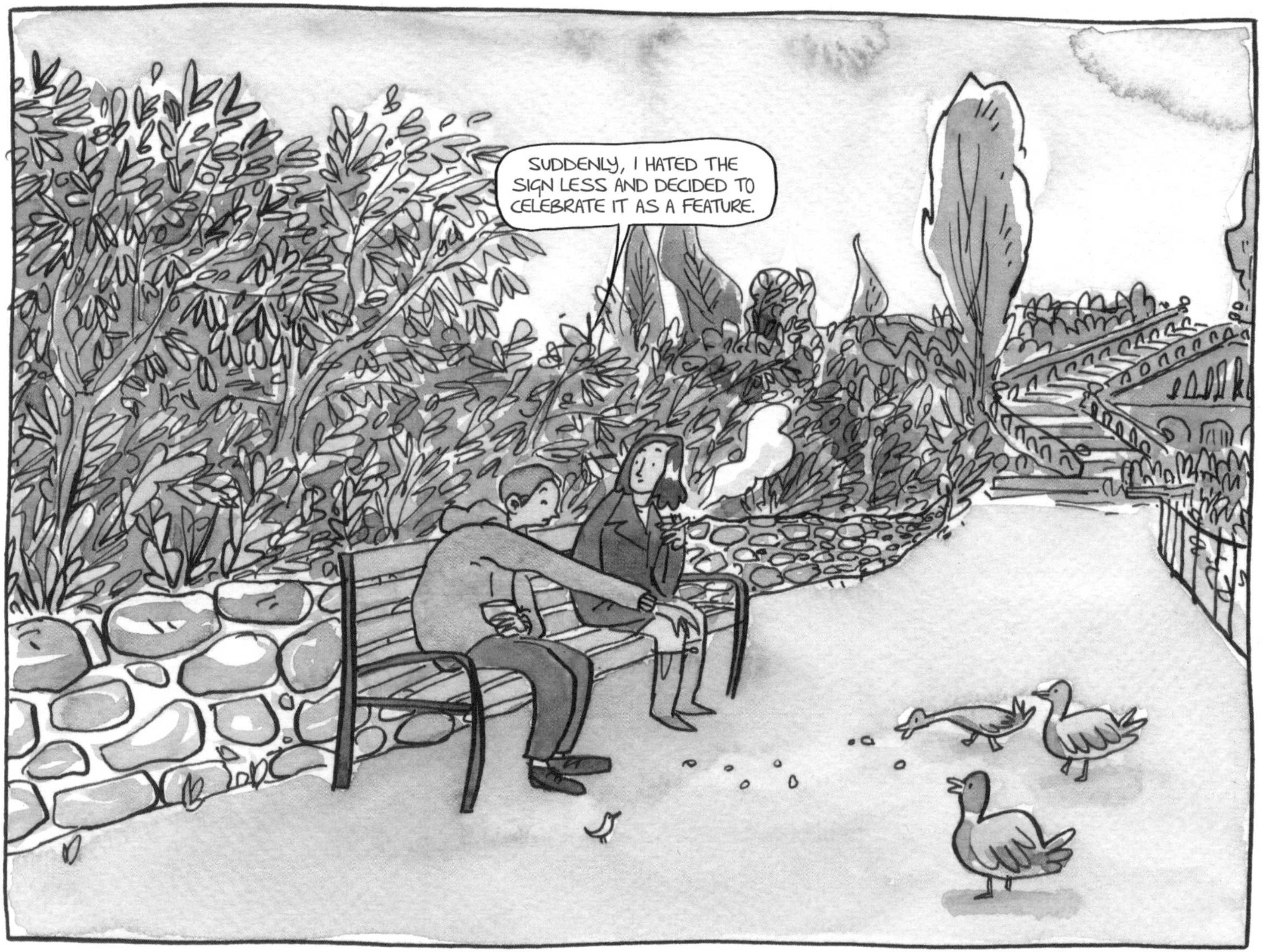
SUDDENLY, I HATED THE SIGN LESS AND DECIDED TO CELEBRATE IT AS A FEATURE.

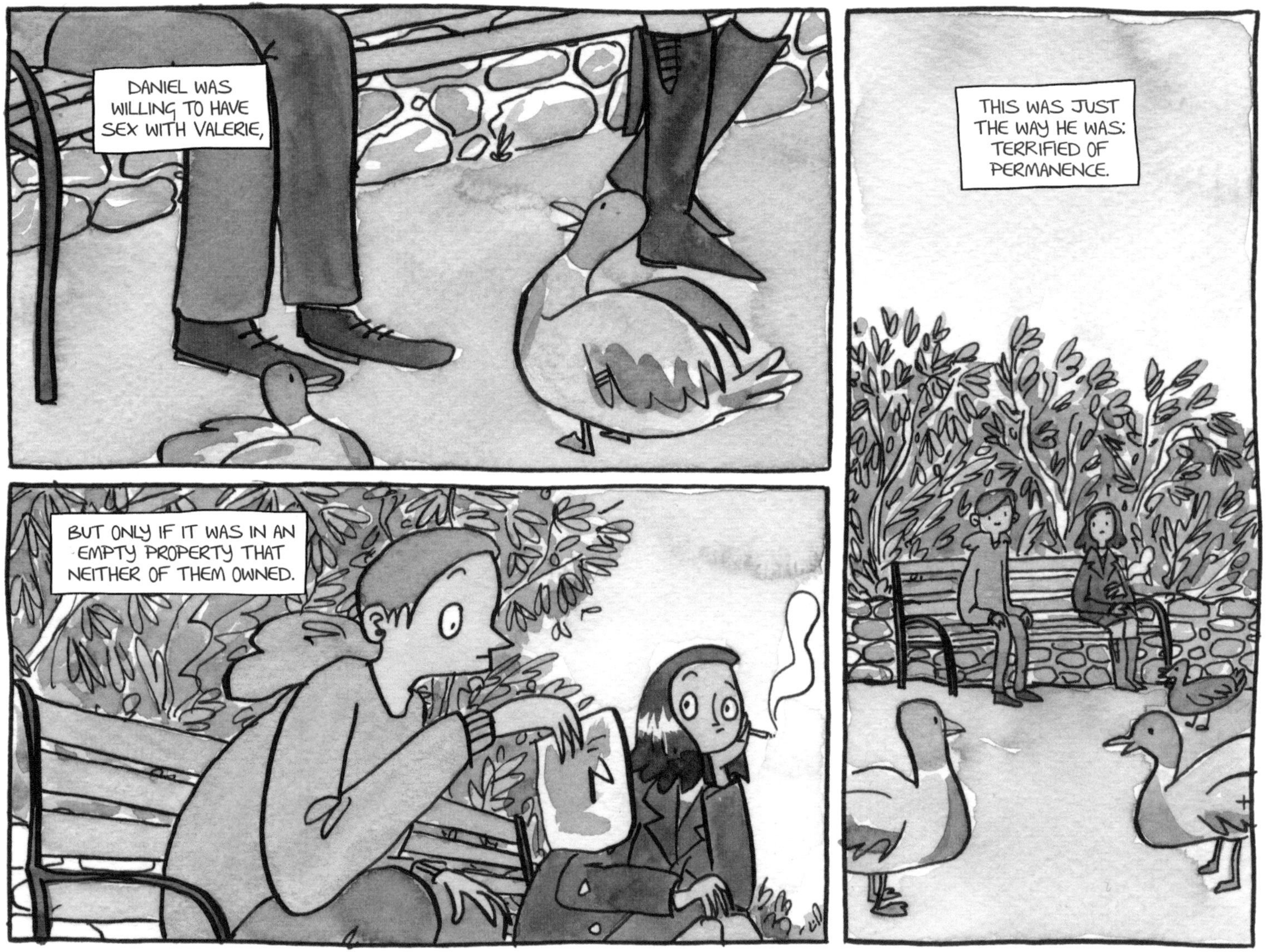
DANIEL WAS WILLING TO HAVE SEX WITH VALERIE,
BUT ONLY IF IT WAS IN AN EMPTY PROPERTY THAT NEITHER OF THEM OWNED.
THIS WAS JUST THE WAY HE WAS: TERRIFIED OF PERMANENCE.

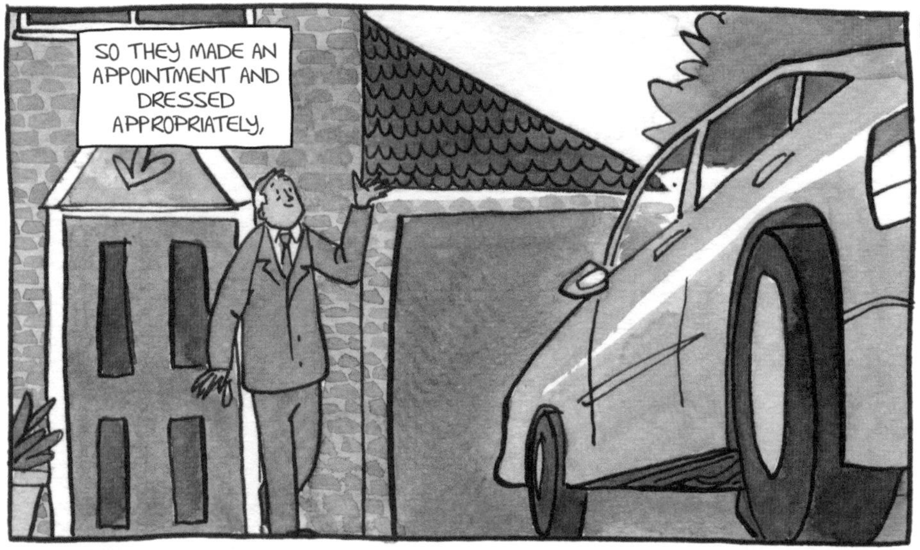
SO THEY MADE AN APPOINTMENT AND DRESSED APPROPRIATELY,

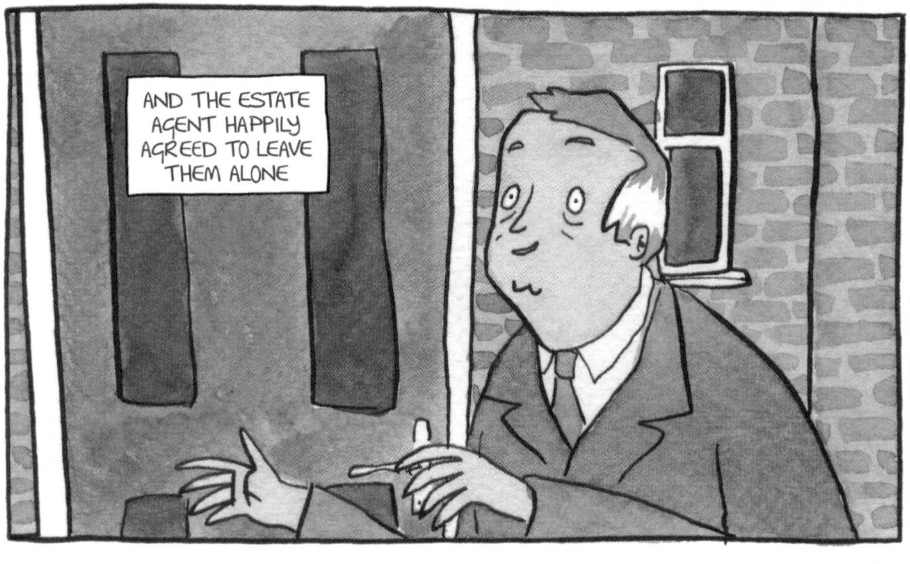
AND THE ESTATE AGENT HAPPILY AGREED TO LEAVE THEM ALONE

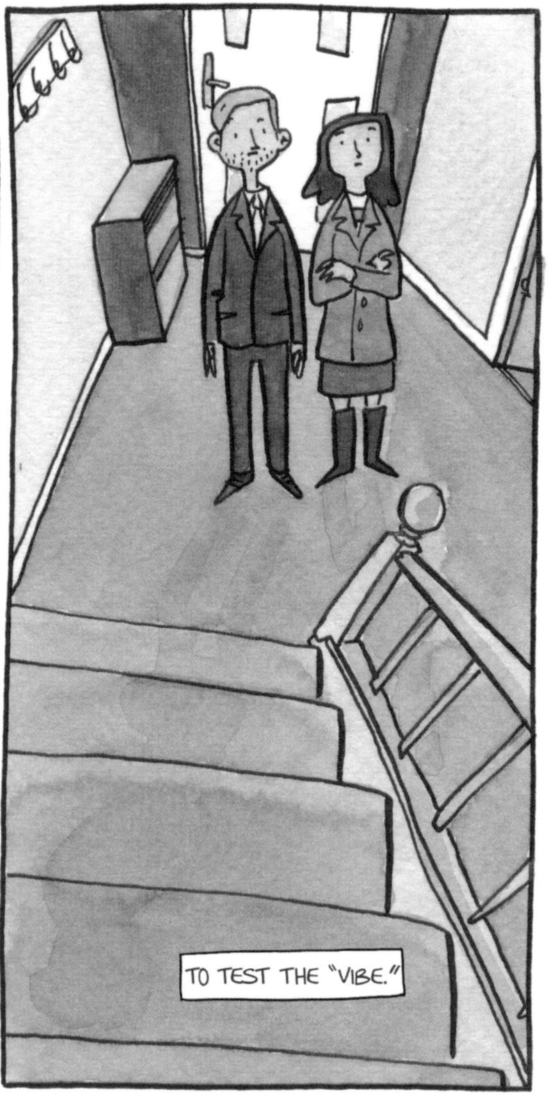
TO TEST THE "VIBE."

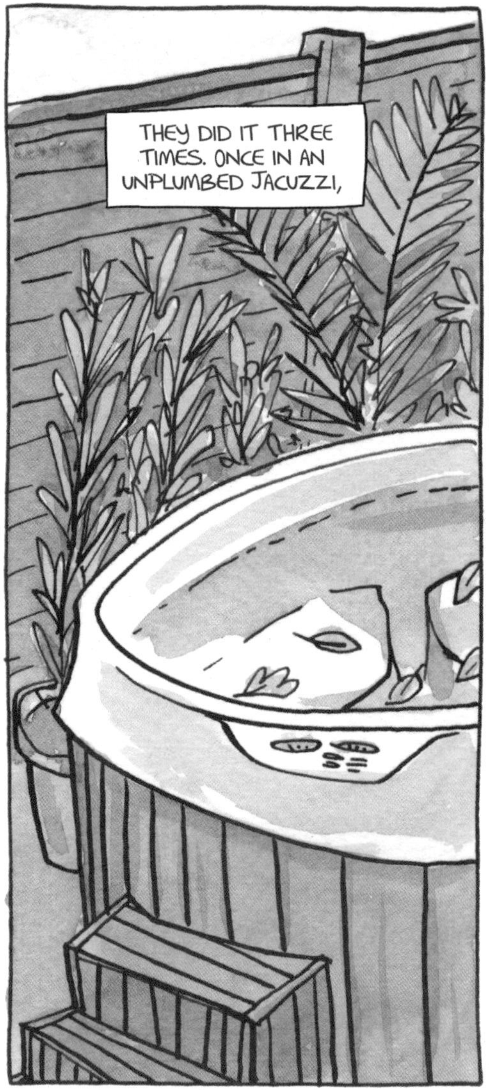
THEY DID IT THREE TIMES. ONCE IN AN UNPLUMBED JACUZZI,
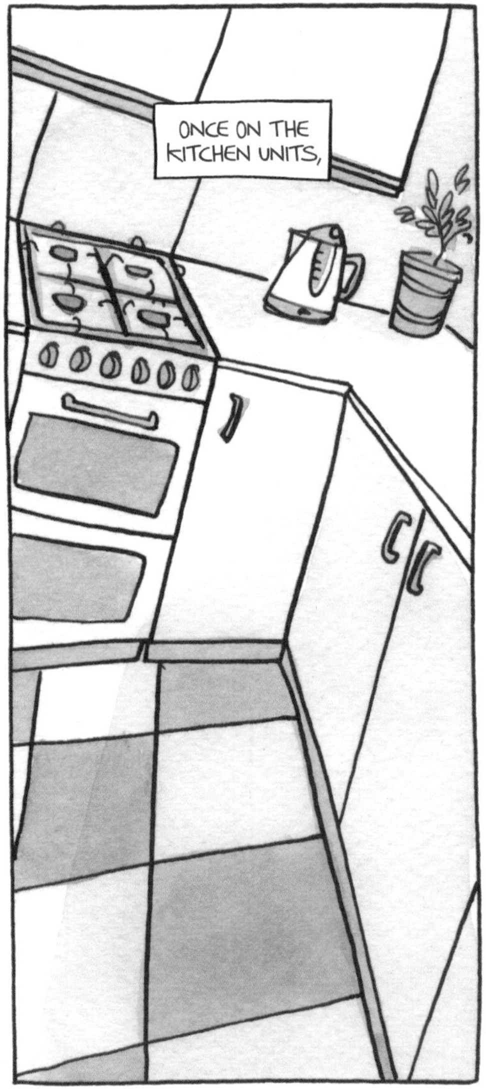
ONCE ON THE KITCHEN UNITS,
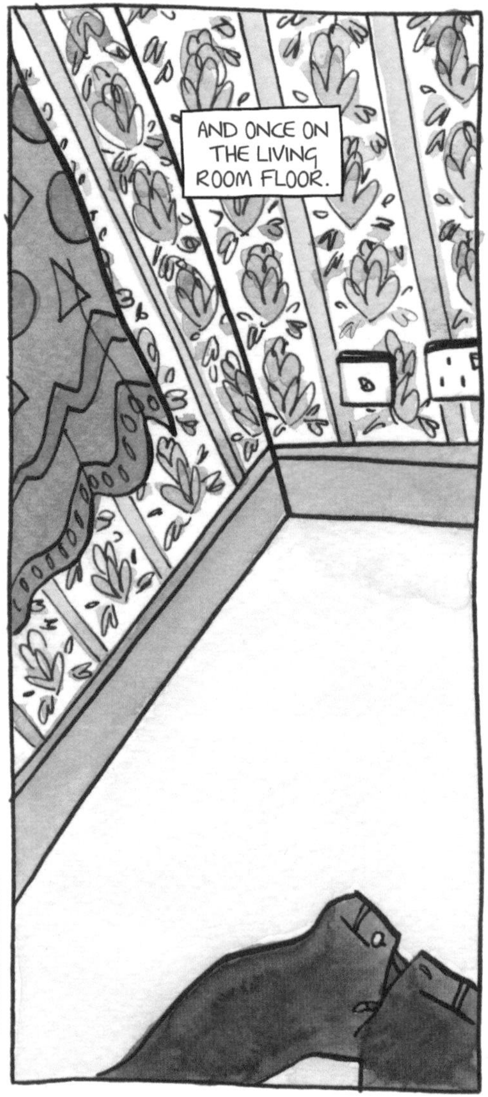
AND ONCE ON THE LIVING ROOM FLOOR.

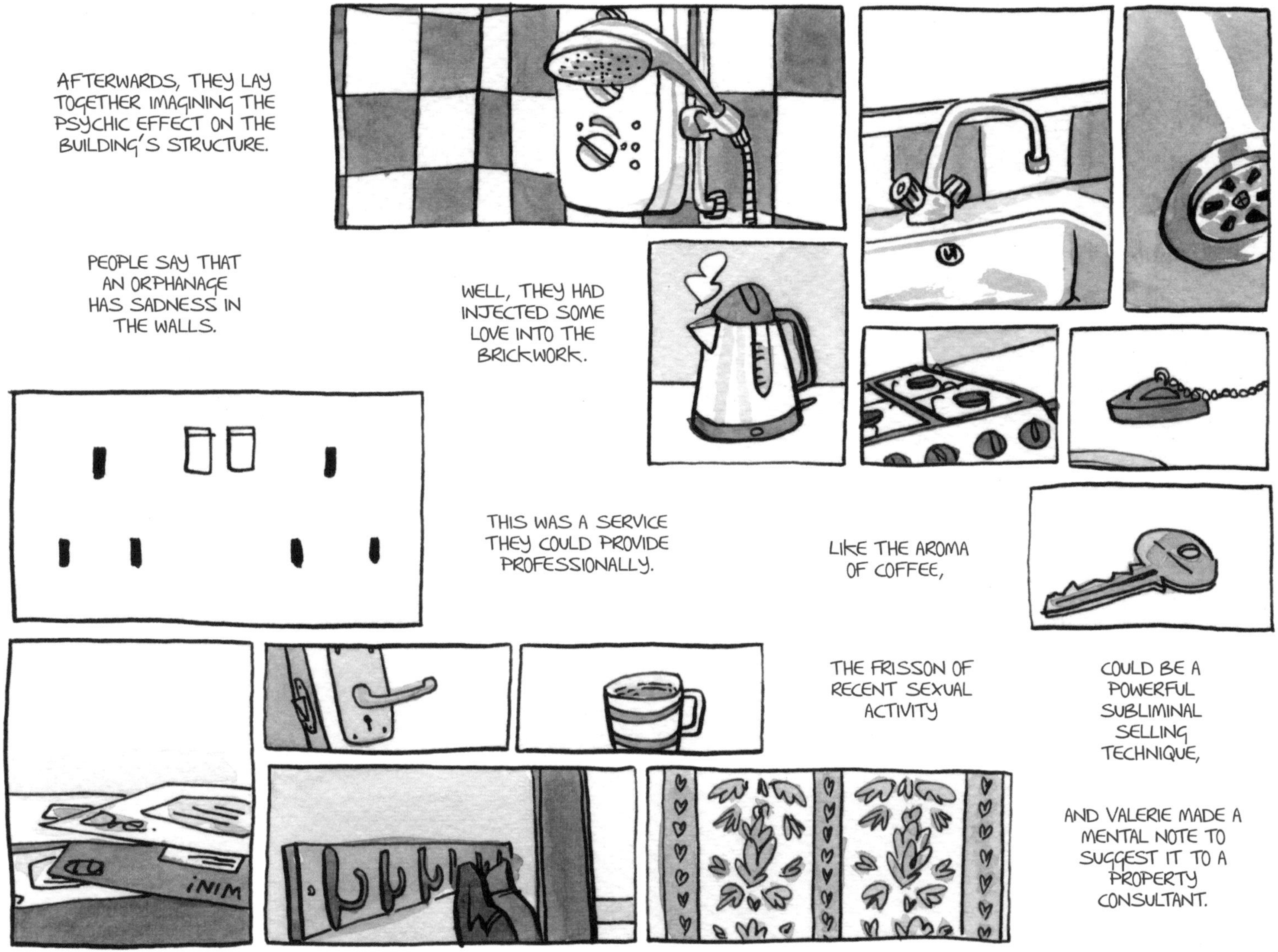
AFTERWARDS, THEY LAY TOGETHER IMAGINING THE PSYCHIC EFFECT ON THE BUILDING'S STRUCTURE.
PEOPLE SAY THAT AN ORPHANAGE HAS SADNESS IN THE WALLS.
WELL, THEY HAD INJECTED SOME LOVE INTO THE BRICKWORK.
THIS WAS A SERVICE THEY COULD PROVIDE PROFESSIONALLY.
LIKE THE AROMA OF COFFEE,
THE FRISSON OF RECENT SEXUAL ACTIVITY
COULD BE A POWERFUL SUBLIMINAL SELLING TECHNIQUE,
AND VALERIE MADE A MENTAL NOTE TO SUGGEST IT TO A PROPERTY CONSULTANT.

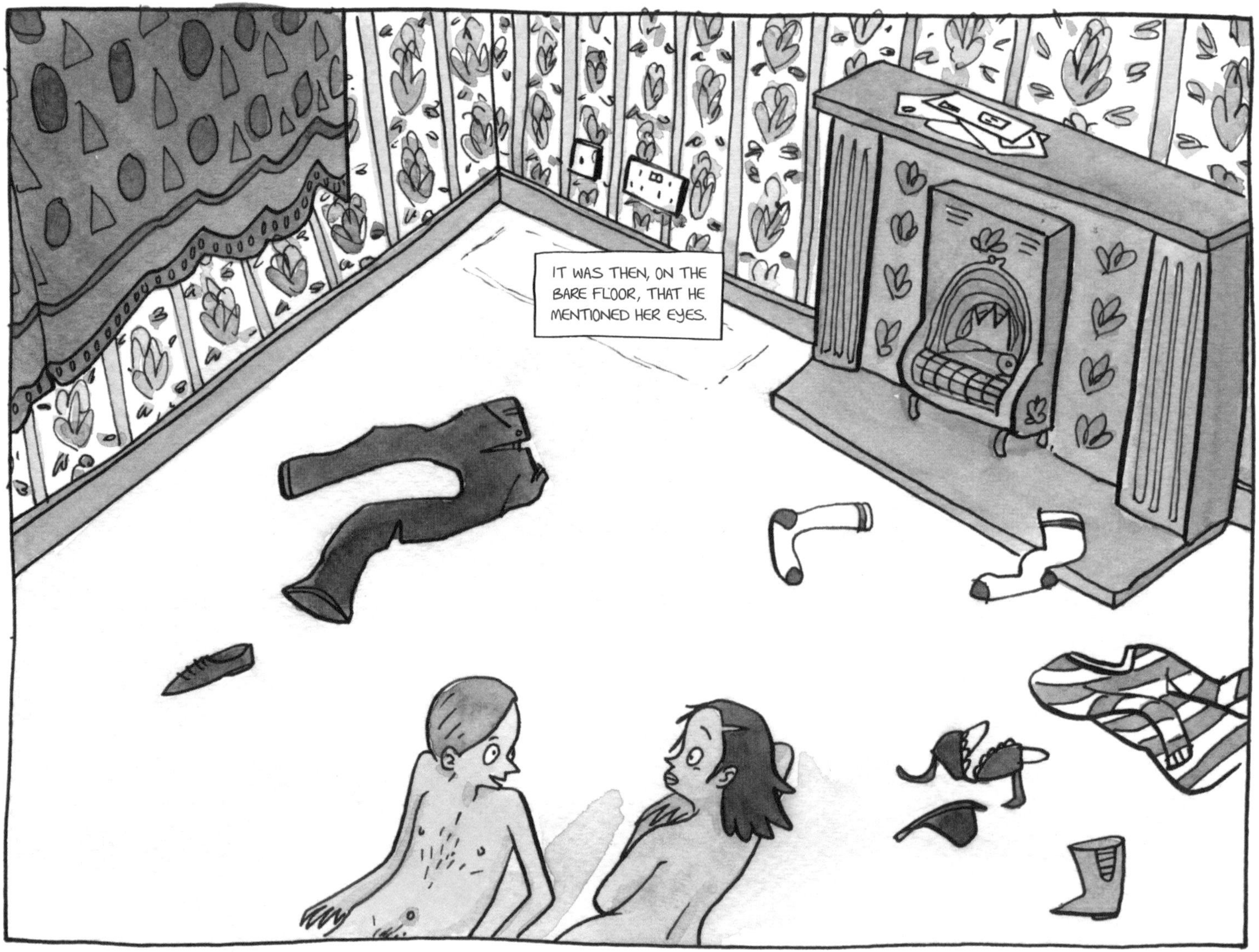
IT WAS THEN, ON THE BARE FLOOR, THAT HE MENTIONED HER EYES.

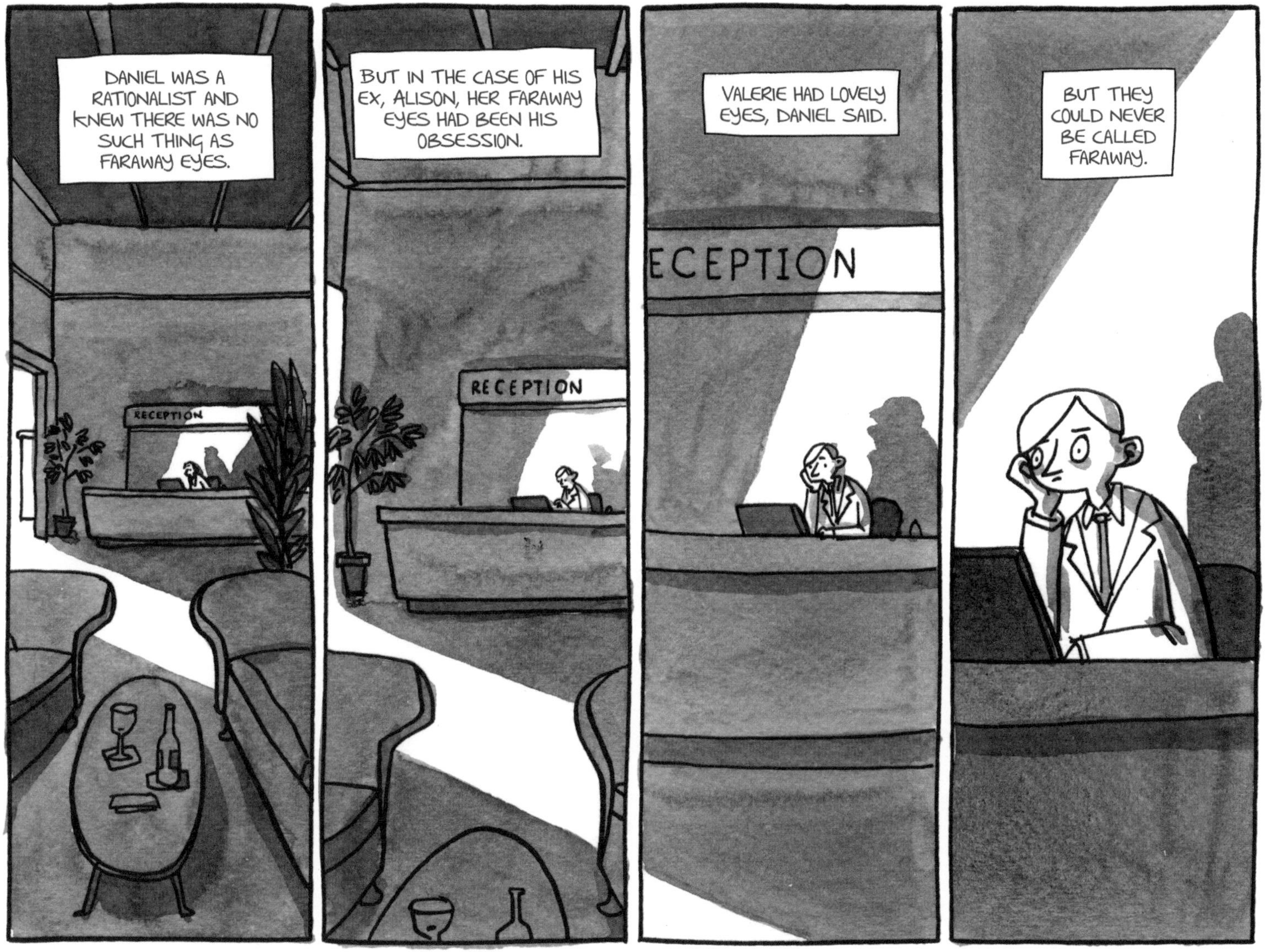
DANIEL WAS A RATIONALIST AND KNEW THERE WAS NO SUCH THING AS FARAWAY EYES.
RECEPTION
BUT IN THE CASE OF HIS EX, ALISON, HER FARAWAY EYES HAD BEEN HIS OBSESSION.
RECEPTION
VALERIE HAD LOVELY EYES, DANIEL SAID.
ECEPTION
BUT THEY COULD NEVER BE CALLED FARAWAY.

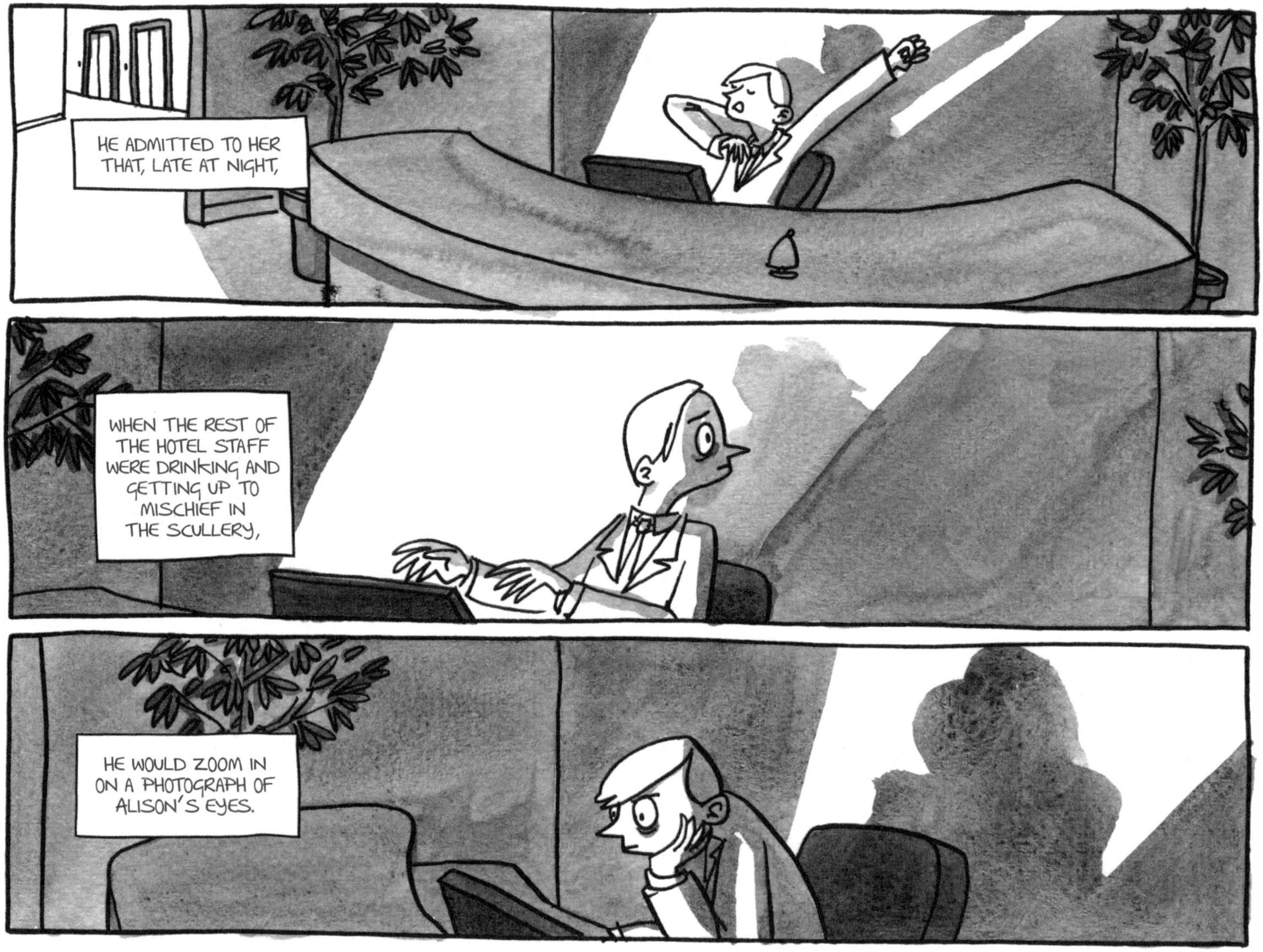
HE ADMITTED TO HER THAT, LATE AT NIGHT,
WHEN THE REST OF THE HOTEL STAFF WERE DRINKING AND GETTING UP TO MISCHIEF IN THE SCULLERY,
HE WOULD ZOOM IN ON A PHOTOGRAPH OF ALISON'S EYES.

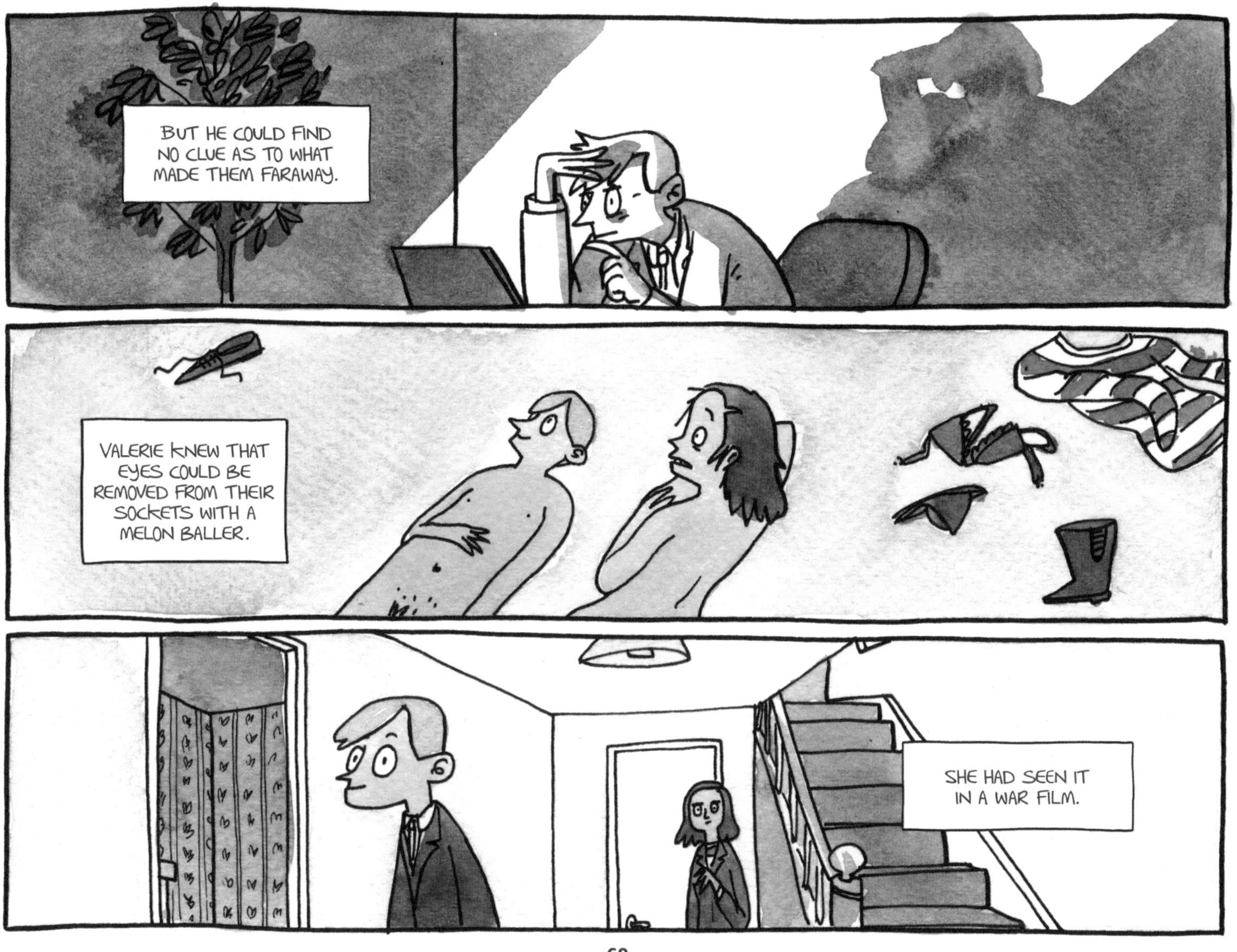
BUT HE COULD FIND NO CLUE AS TO WHAT MADE THEM FARAWAY.
VALERIE KNEW THAT EYES COULD BE REMOVED FROM THEIR SOCKETS WITH A MELON BALLER.
SHE HAD SEEN IT IN A WAR FILM.

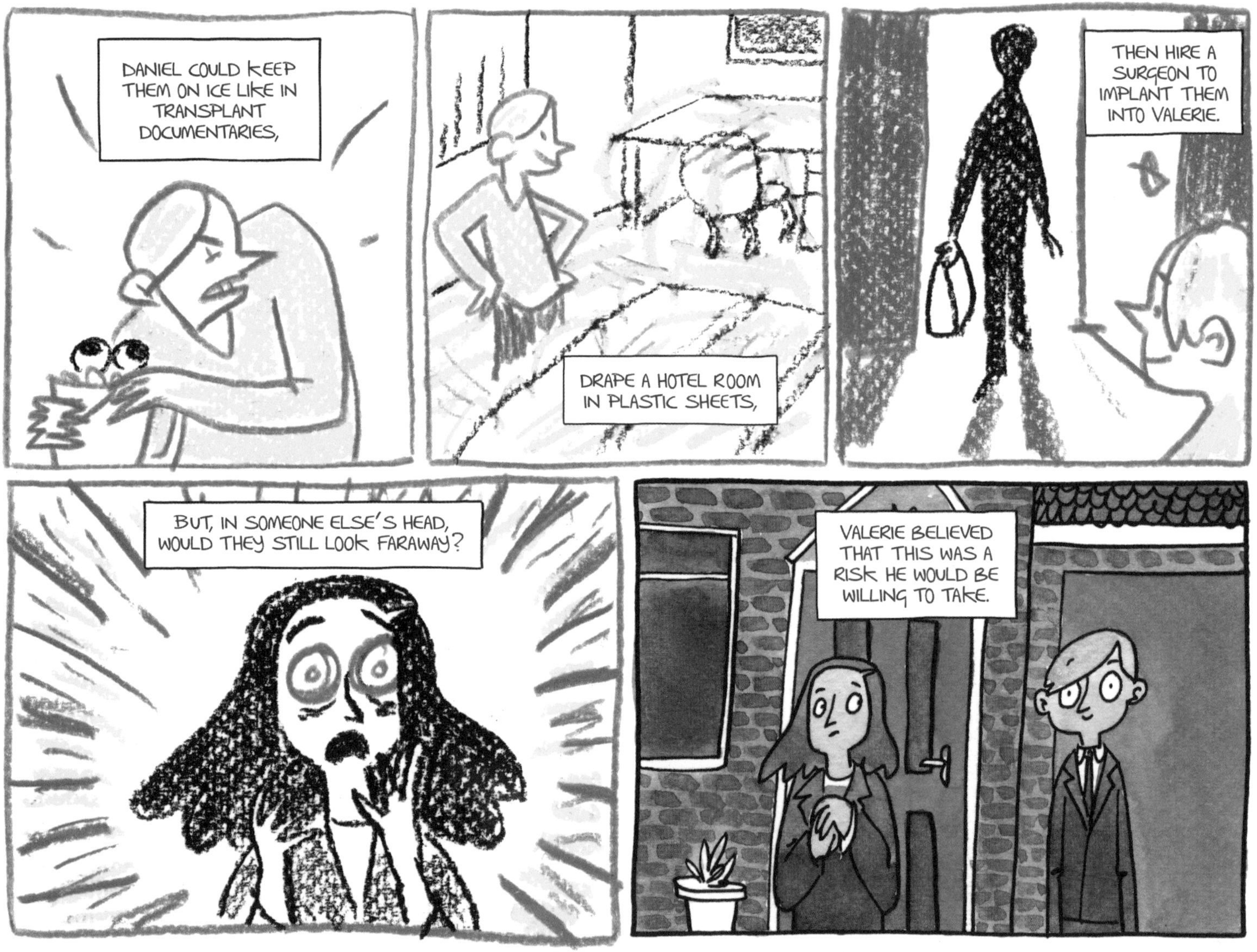
DANIEL COULD KEEP THEM ON ICE LIKE IN TRANSPLANT DOCUMENTARIES,
DRAPE A HOTEL ROOM IN PLASTIC SHEETS,
THEN HIRE A SURGEON TO IMPLANT THEM INTO VALERIE.
BUT, IN SOMEONE ELSE'S HEAD, WOULD THEY STILL LOOK FARAWAY?
VALERIE BELIEVED THAT THIS WAS A RISK HE WOULD BE WILLING TO TAKE.

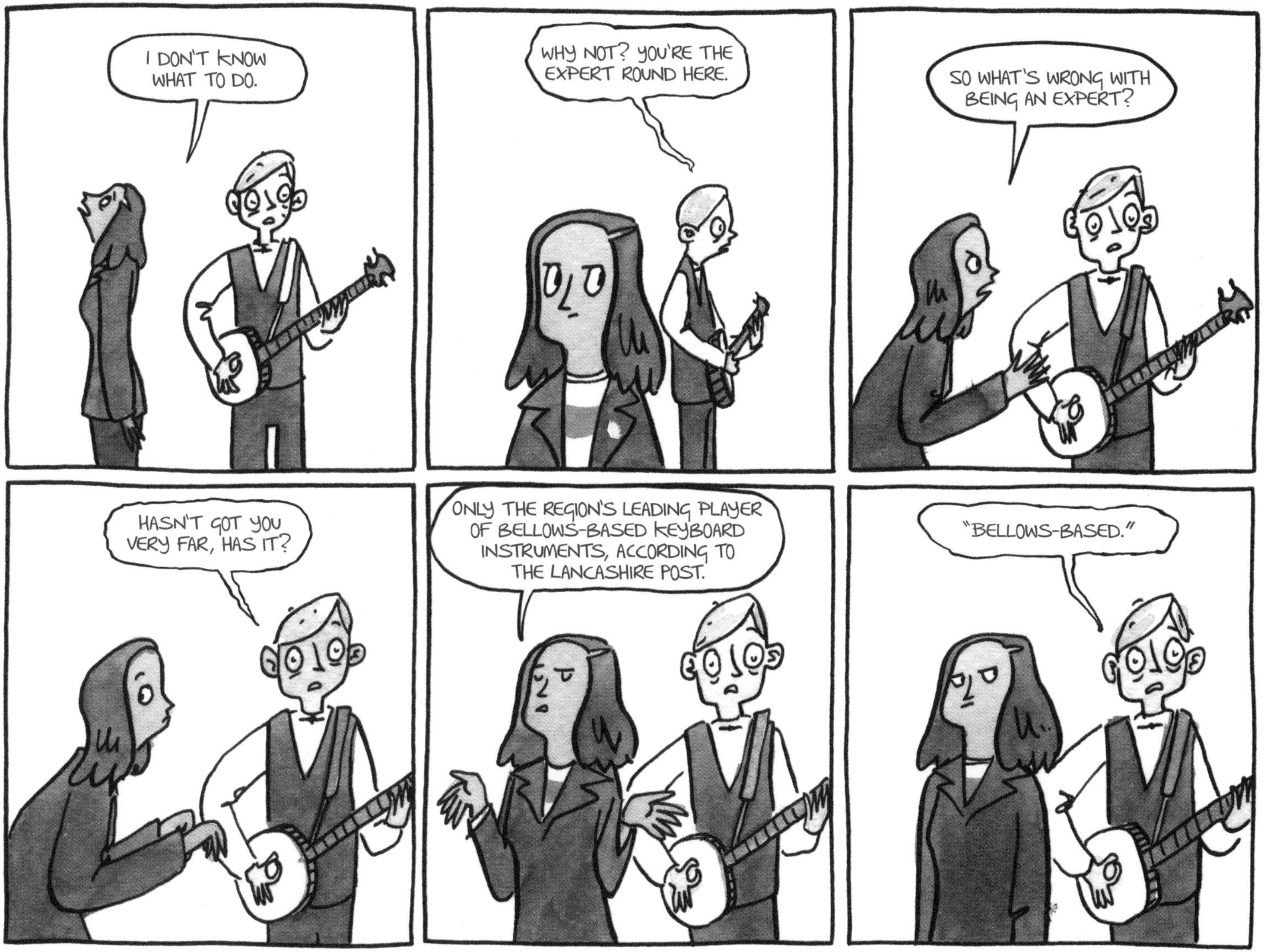
I DON'T KNOW WHAT TO DO.
WHY NOT? YOU'RE THE EXPERT ROUND HERE.
SO WHAT'S WRONG WITH BEING AN EXPERT?
HASN'T GOT YOU VERY FAR, HAS IT?
ONLY THE REGION'S LEADING PLAYER OF BELLOWS-BASED KEYBOARD INSTRUMENTS, ACCORDING TO THE LANCASHIRE POST.
"BELLOWS-BASED."

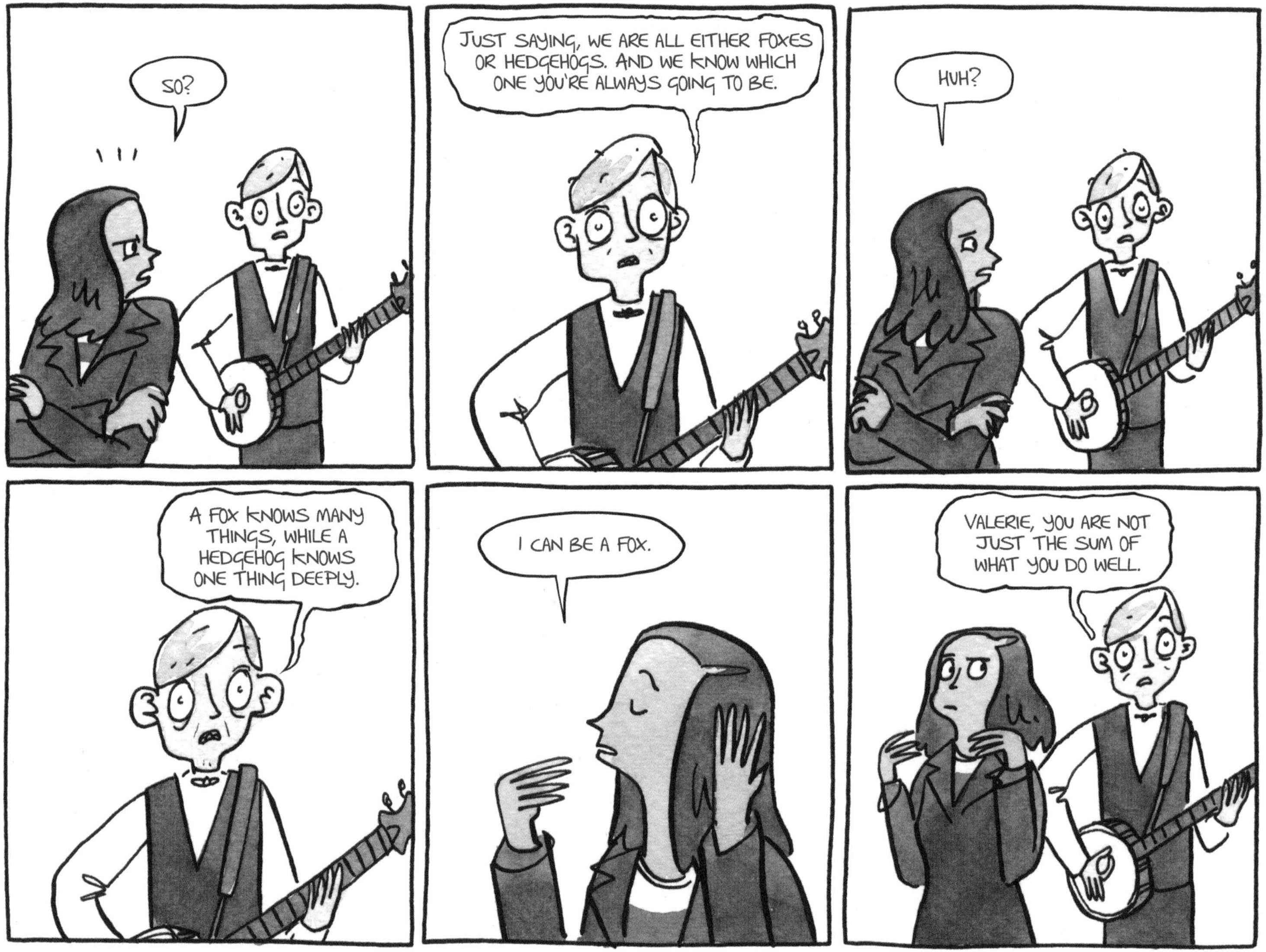
SO?
JUST SAYING, WE ARE ALL EITHER FOXES OR HEDGEHOGS. AND WE KNOW WHICH ONE YOU'RE ALWAYS GOING TO BE.
HUH?
A FOX KNOWS MANY THINGS, WHILE A HEDGEHOG KNOWS ONE THING DEEPLY.
I CAN BE A FOX.
VALERIE, YOU ARE NOT JUST THE SUM OF WHAT YOU DO WELL.

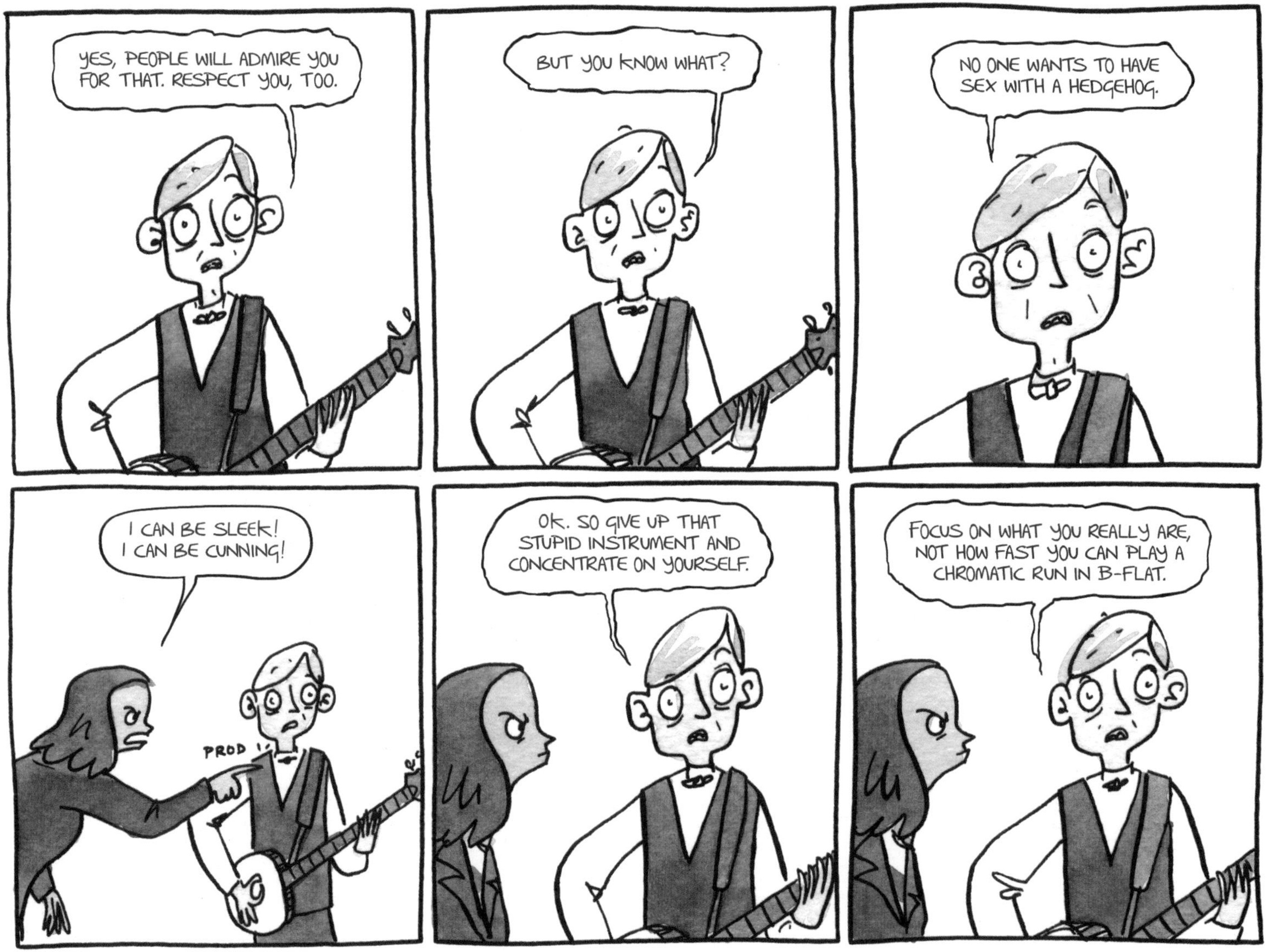
YES, PEOPLE WILL ADMIRE YOU FOR THAT. RESPECT YOU, TOO.
BUT YOU KNOW WHAT?
NO ONE WANTS TO HAVE SEX WITH A HEDGEHOG.
I CAN BE SLEEK! I CAN BE CUNNING!
PROD !
OK. SO GIVE UP THAT STUPID INSTRUMENT AND CONCENTRATE ON YOURSELF.
FOCUS ON WHAT YOU REALLY ARE, NOT HOW FAST YOU CAN PLAY A CHROMATIC RUN IN B-FLAT.

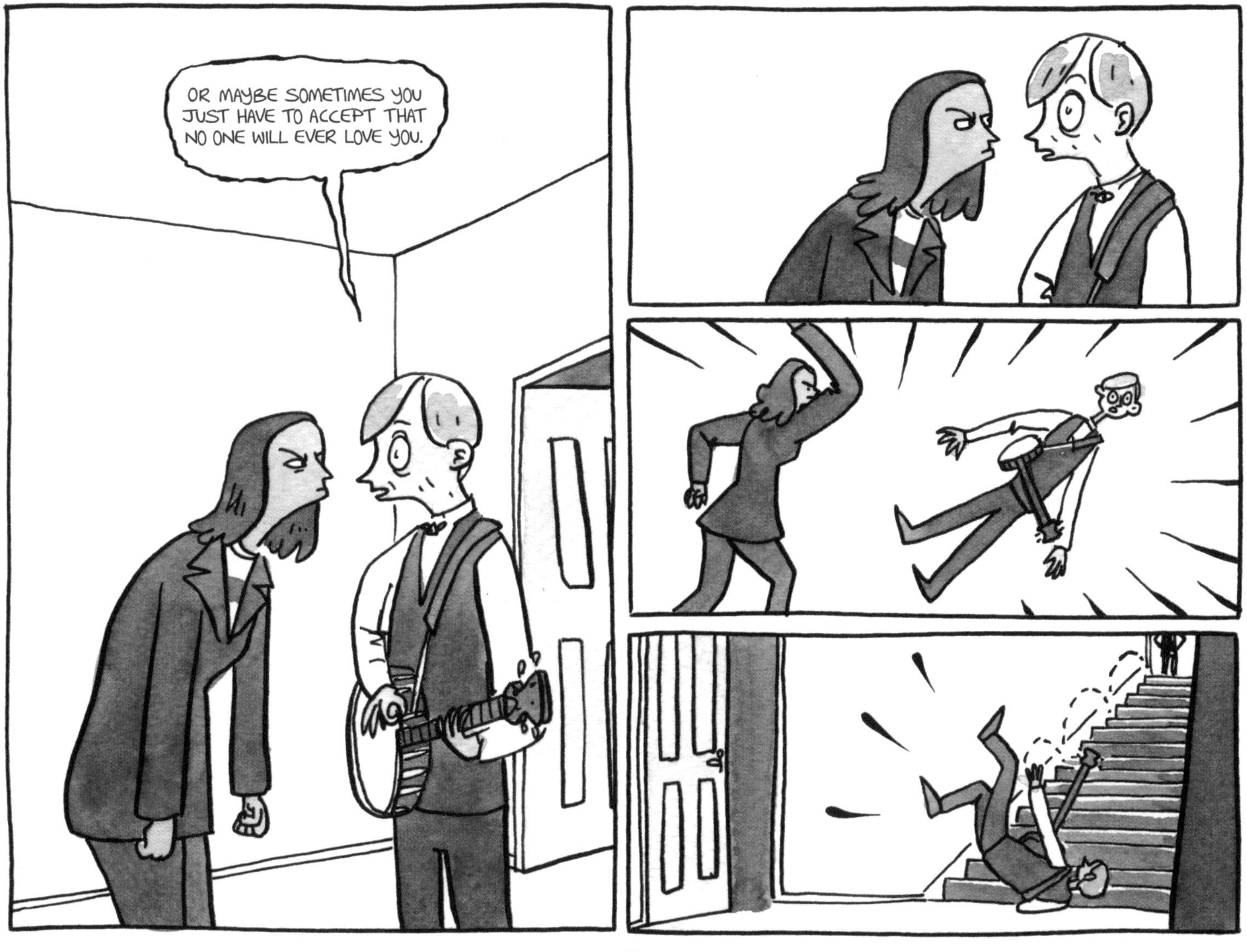
OR MAYBE SOMETIMES YOU JUST HAVE TO ACCEPT THAT NO ONE WILL EVER LOVE YOU.

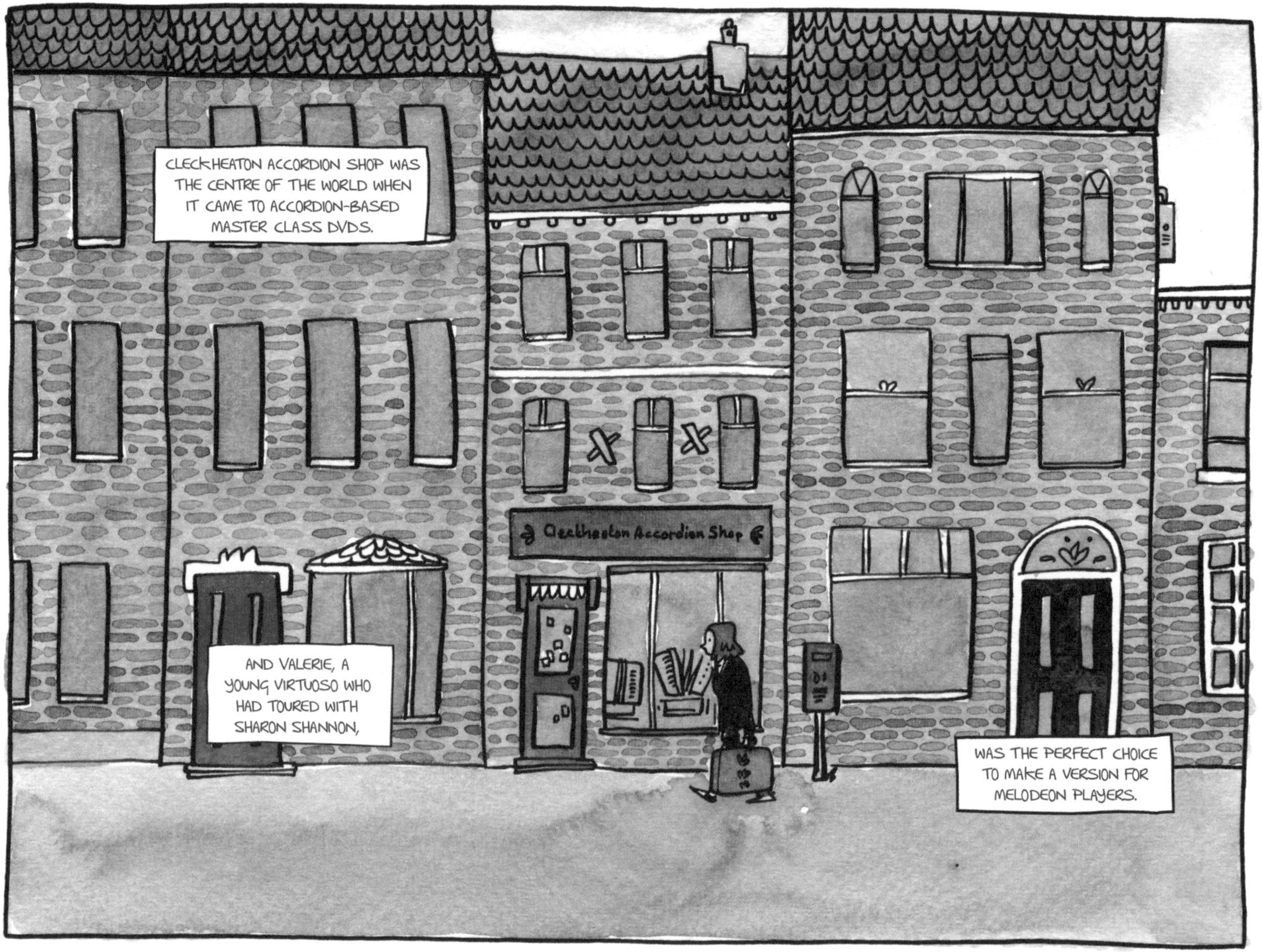
CLECKHEATON ACCORDION SHOP WAS THE CENTRE OF THE WORLD WHEN IT CAME TO ACCORDION-BASED MASTER CLASS DVDS.
Cleckheaton Accordion Shop
AND VALERIE, A YOUNG VIRTUOSO WHO HAD TOURED WITH SHARON SHANNON,
WAS THE PERFECT CHOICE TO MAKE A VERSION FOR MELODEON PLAYERS.

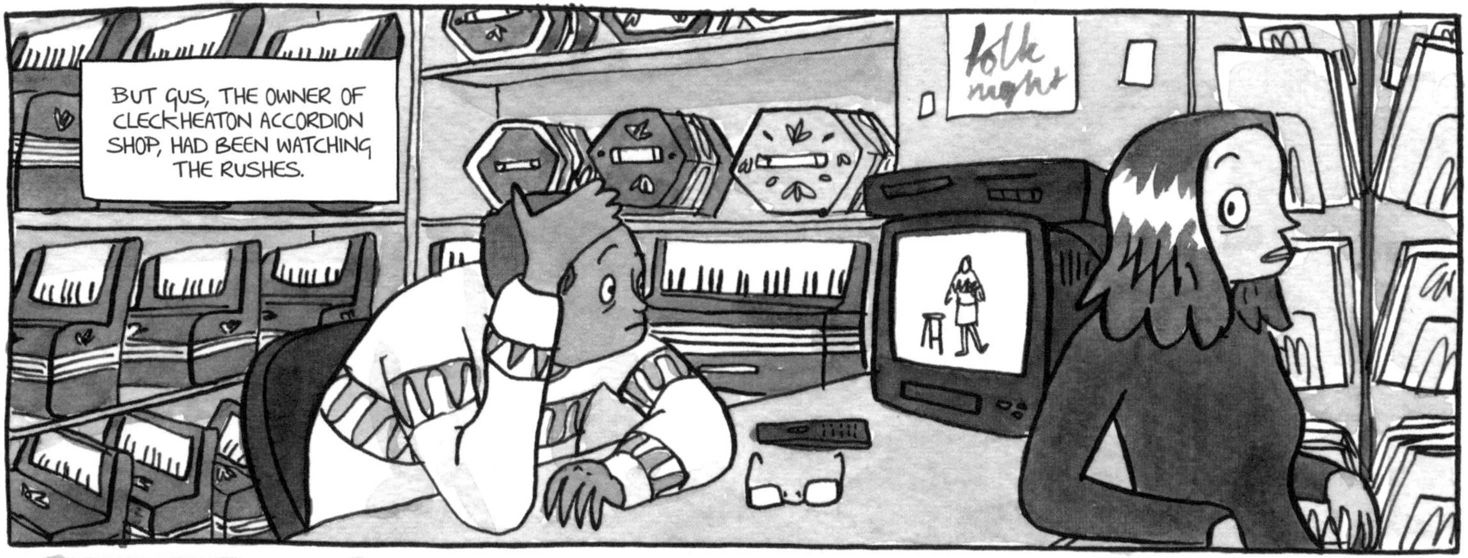
BUT GUS, THE OWNER OF CLECKHEATON ACCORDION SHOP, HAD BEEN WATCHING THE RUSHES.
folk night

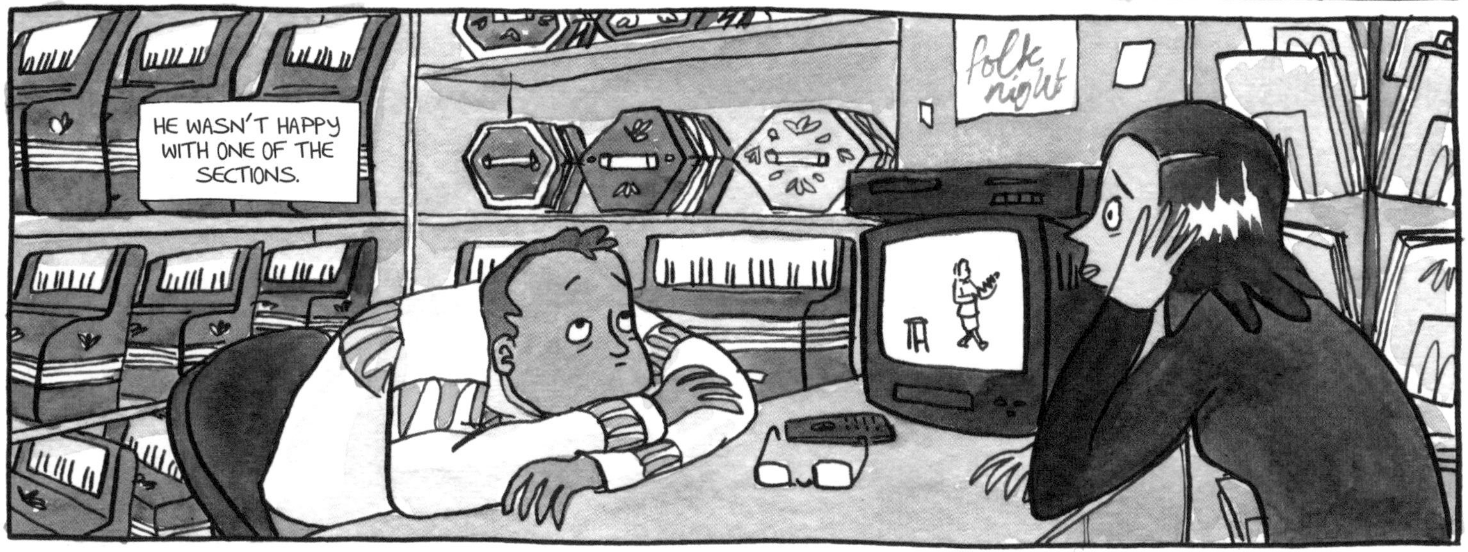
HE WASN'T HAPPY WITH ONE OF THE SECTIONS.
folk night

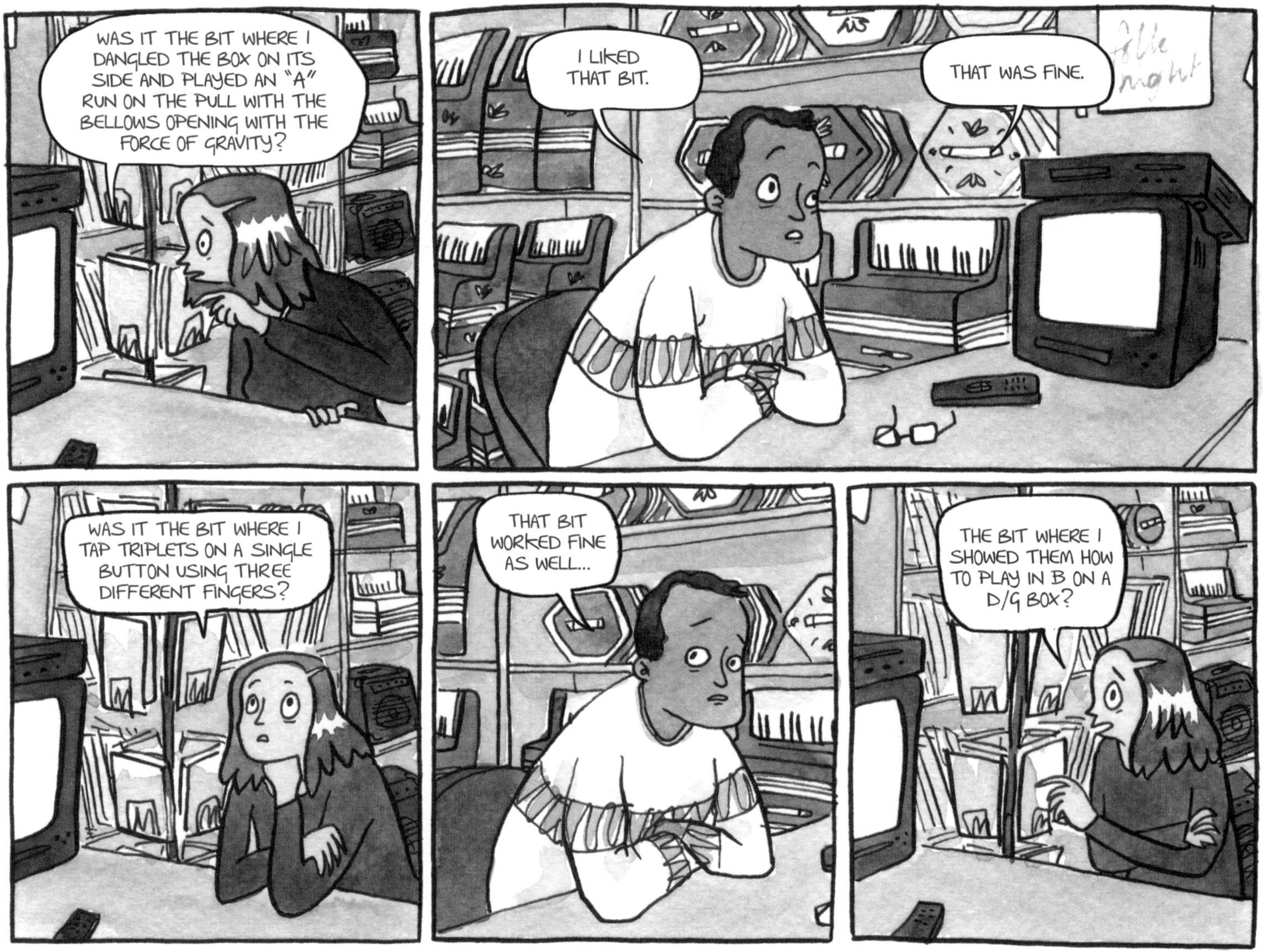
WAS IT THE BIT WHERE I DANGLED THE BOX ON ITS SIDE AND PLAYED AN "A" RUN ON THE PULL WITH THE BELLOWS OPENING WITH THE FORCE OF GRAVITY?
I LIKED THAT BIT.
THAT WAS FINE.
WAS IT THE BIT WHERE I TAP TRIPLETS ON A SINGLE BUTTON USING THREE DIFFERENT FINGERS?
THAT BIT WORKED FINE AS WELL...
THE BIT WHERE I SHOWED THEM HOW TO PLAY IN B ON A D/G BOX?

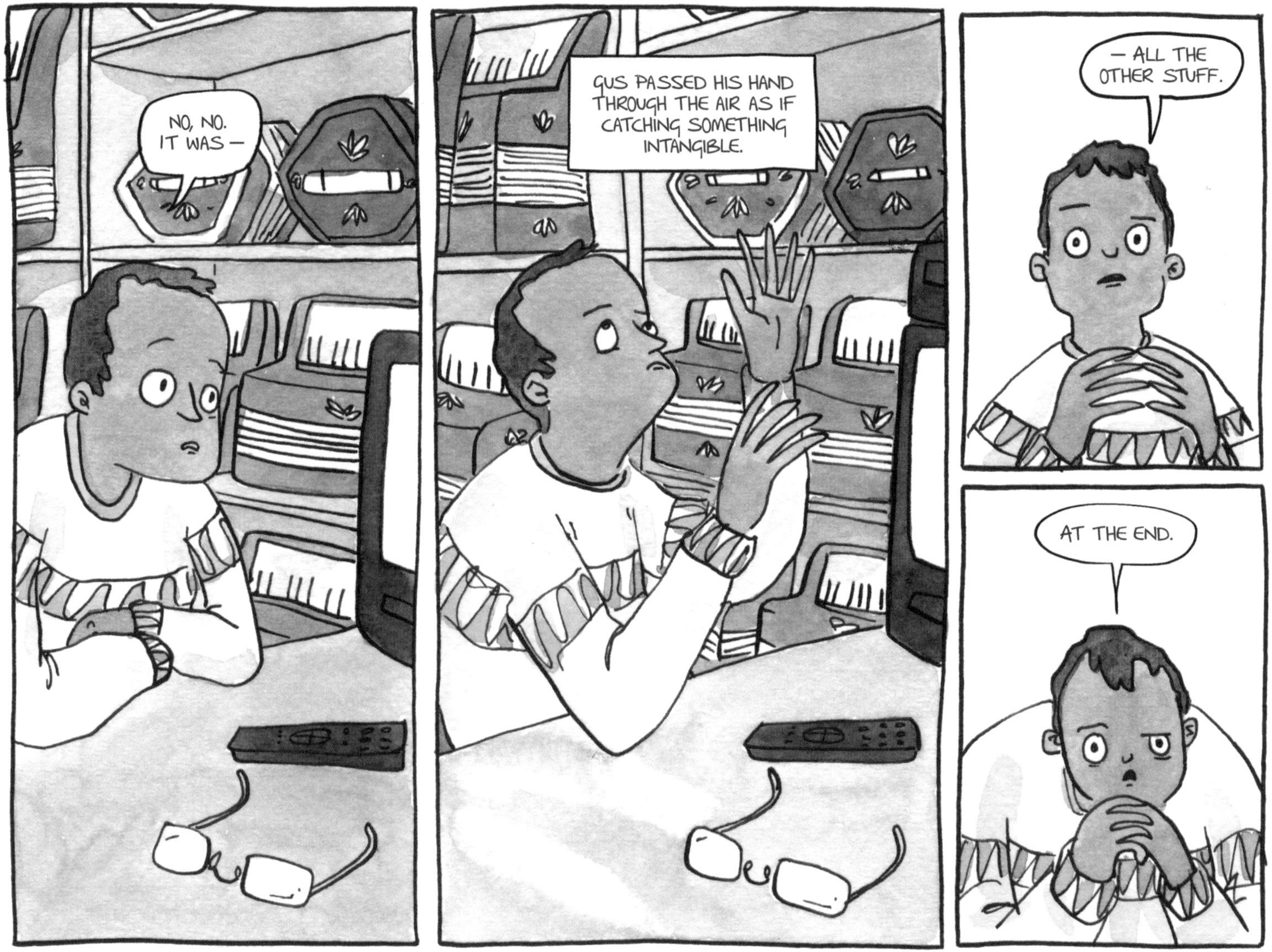
NO, NO. IT WAS—
GUS PASSED HIS HAND THROUGH THE AIR AS IF CATCHING SOMETHING INTANGIBLE.
—ALL THE OTHER STUFF.
AT THE END.

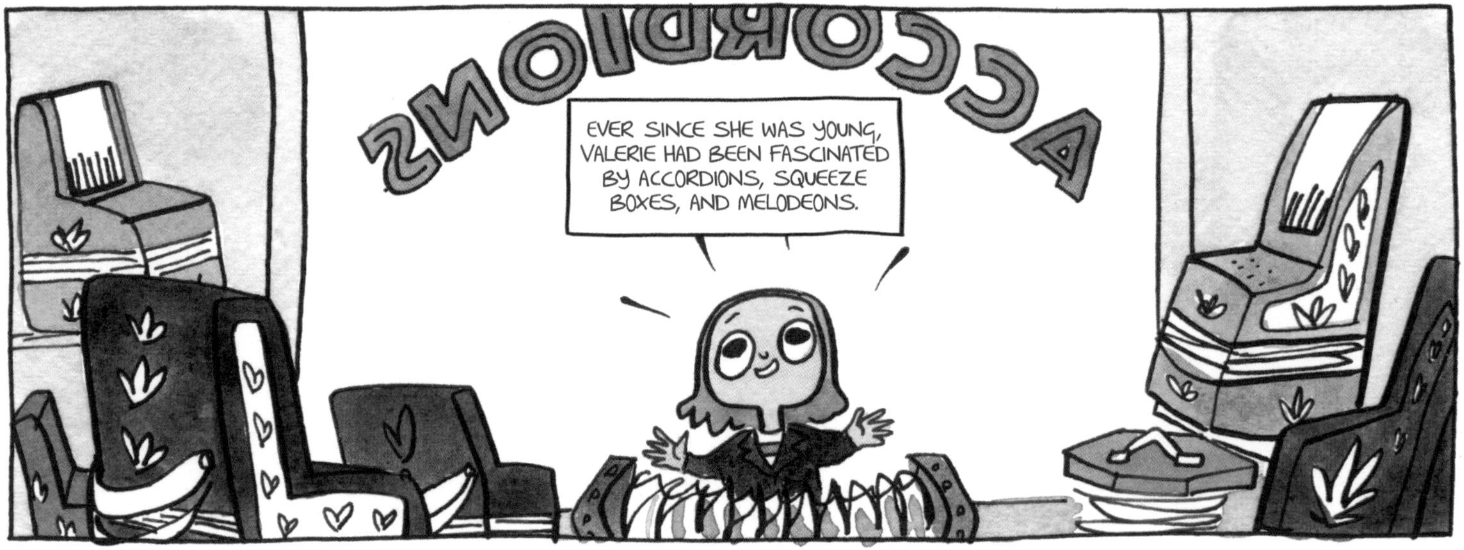
ACCORDIONS
EVER SINCE SHE WAS YOUNG, VALERIE HAD BEEN FASCINATED BY ACCORDIONS, SQUEEZE BOXES, AND MELODEONS.

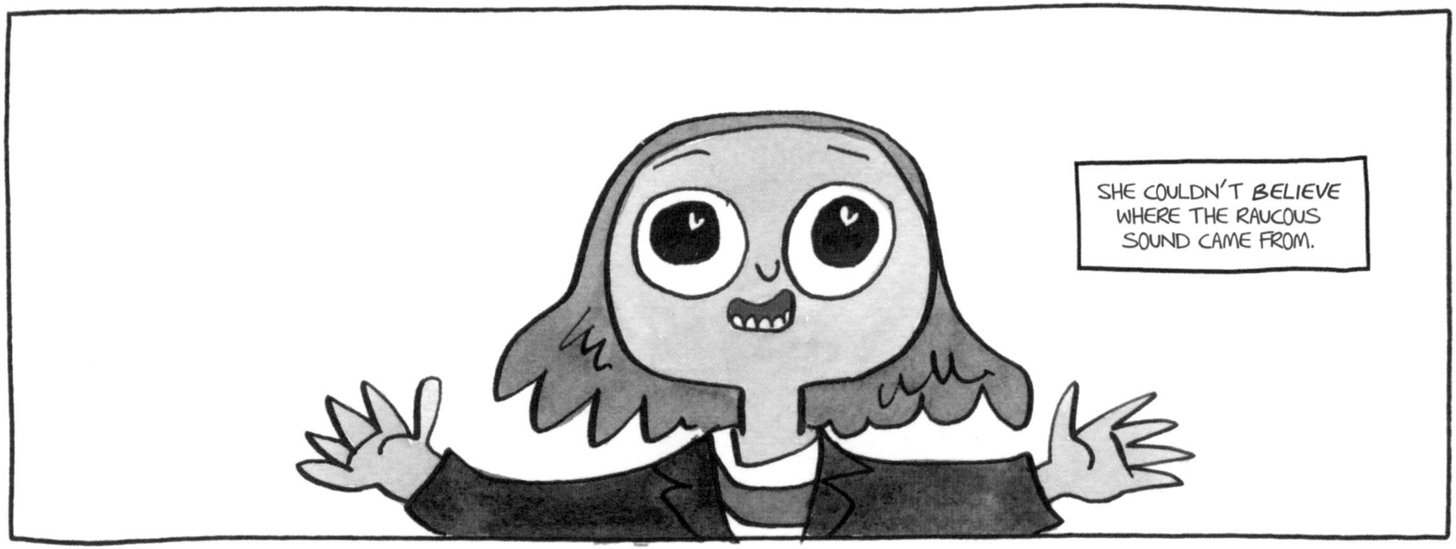
SHE COULDN'T *BELIEVE* WHERE THE RAUCOUS SOUND CAME FROM.

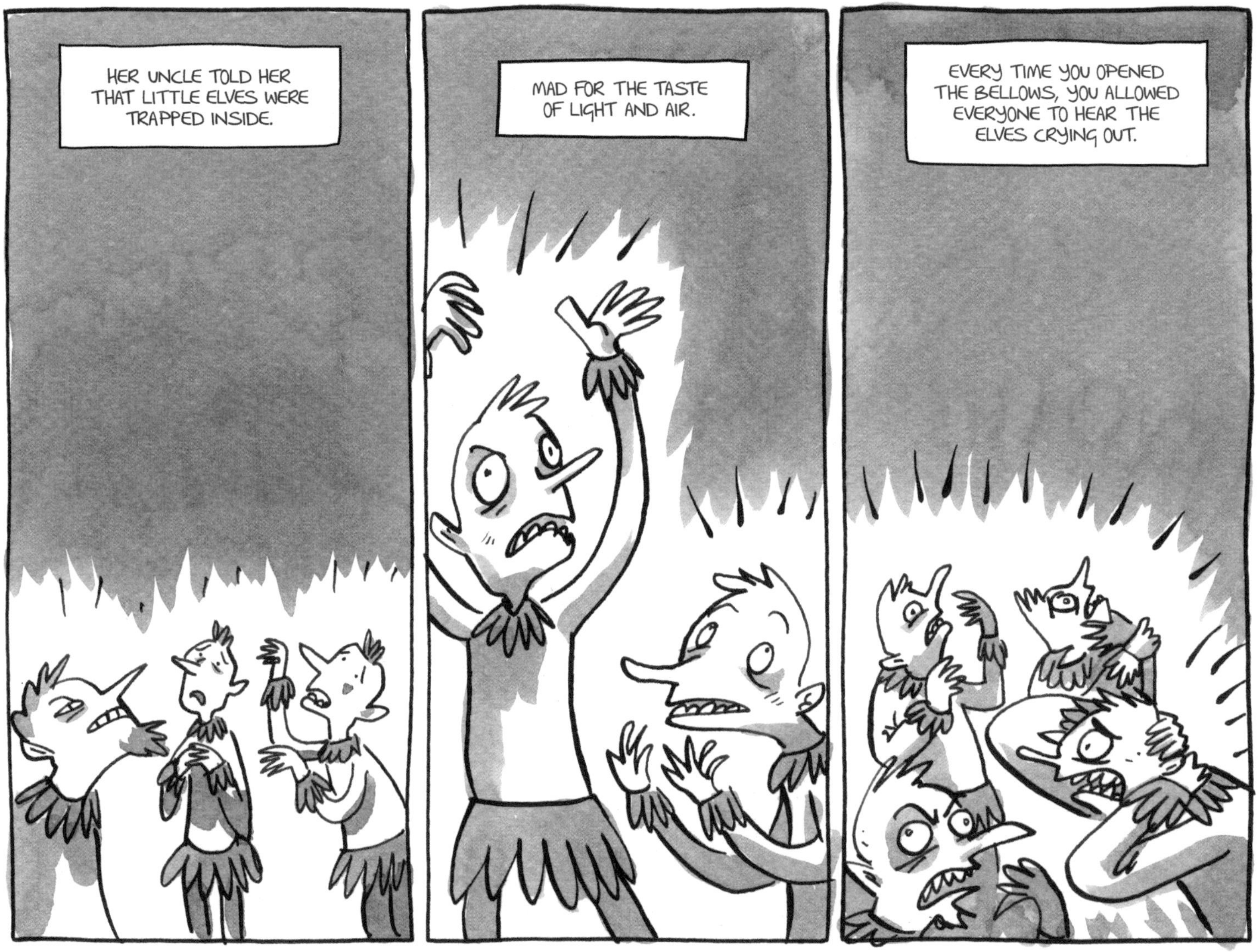
HER UNCLE TOLD HER THAT LITTLE ELVES WERE TRAPPED INSIDE.
MAD FOR THE TASTE OF LIGHT AND AIR.
EVERY TIME YOU OPENED THE BELLOWS, YOU ALLOWED EVERYONE TO HEAR THE ELVES CRYING OUT.

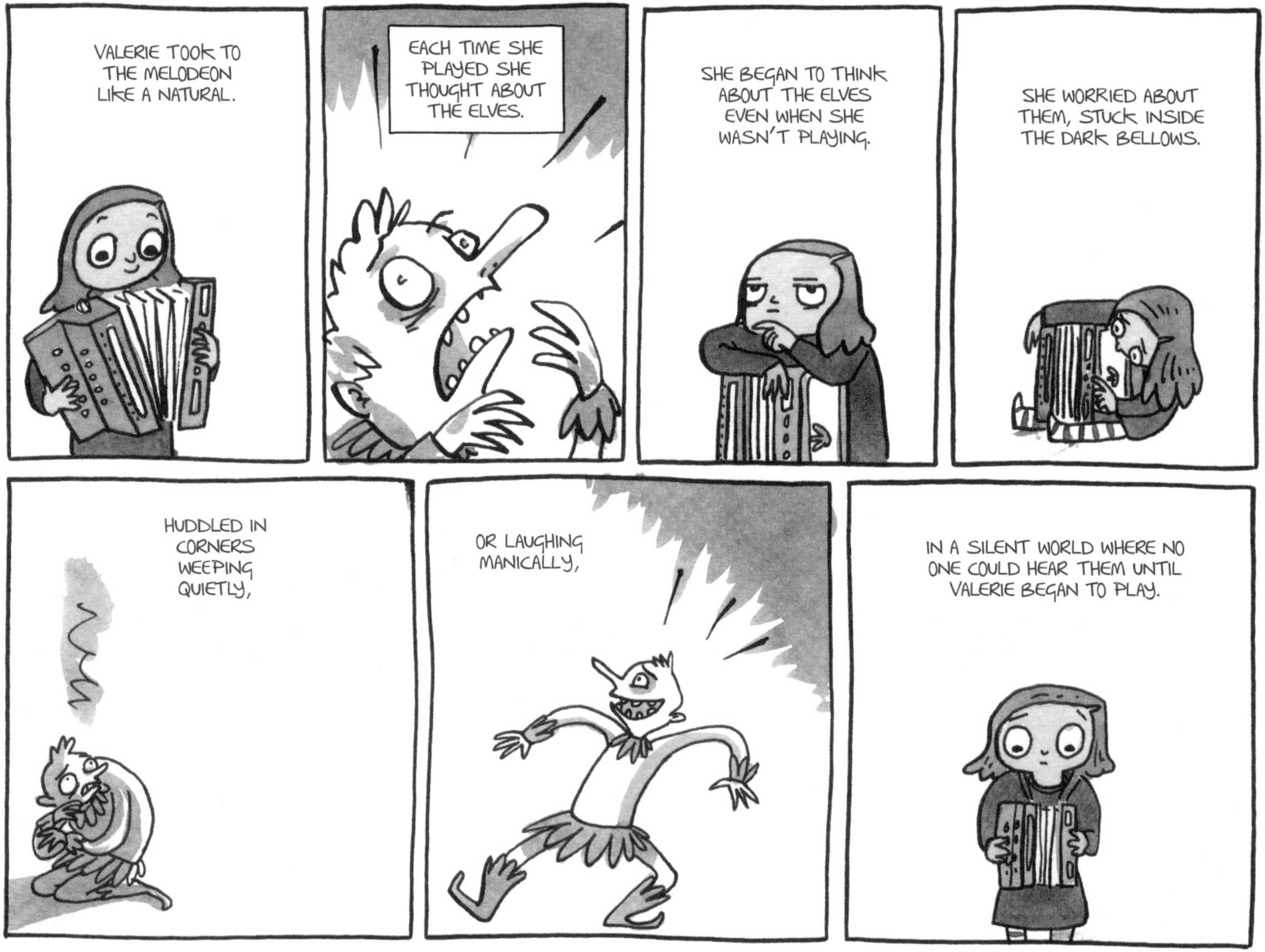
VALERIE TOOK TO THE MELODEON LIKE A NATURAL.
EACH TIME SHE PLAYED SHE THOUGHT ABOUT THE ELVES.
SHE BEGAN TO THINK ABOUT THE ELVES EVEN WHEN SHE WASN'T PLAYING.
SHE WORRIED ABOUT THEM, STUCK INSIDE THE DARK BELLOWS.
HUDDLED IN CORNERS WEEPING QUIETLY,
OR LAUGHING MANICALLY,
IN A SILENT WORLD WHERE NO ONE COULD HEAR THEM UNTIL VALERIE BEGAN TO PLAY.

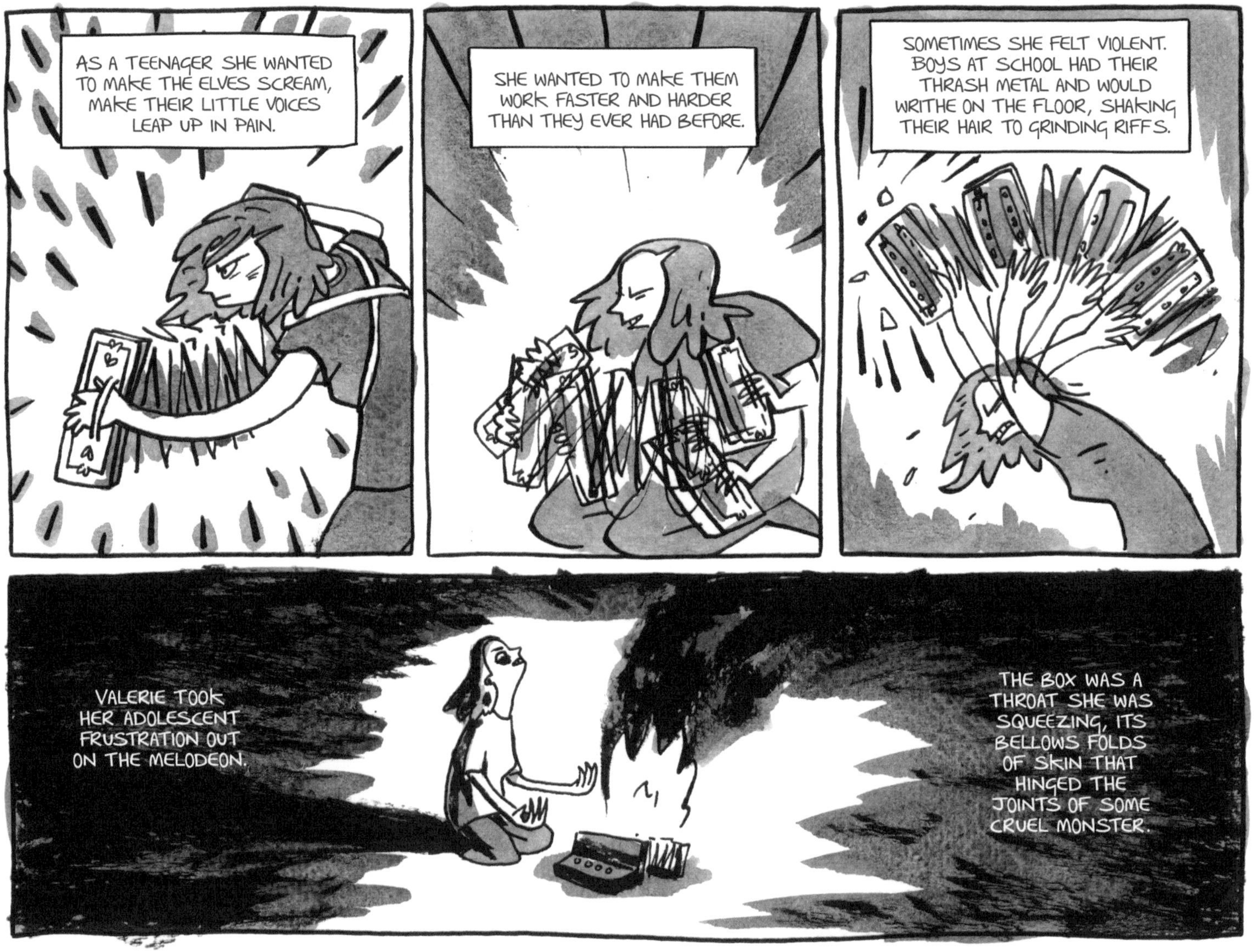
AS A TEENAGER SHE WANTED TO MAKE THE ELVES SCREAM, MAKE THEIR LITTLE VOICES LEAP UP IN PAIN.
SHE WANTED TO MAKE THEM WORK FASTER AND HARDER THAN THEY EVER HAD BEFORE.
SOMETIMES SHE FELT VIOLENT. BOYS AT SCHOOL HAD THEIR THRASH METAL AND WOULD WRITHE ON THE FLOOR, SHAKING THEIR HAIR TO GRINDING RIFFS.
VALERIE TOOK HER ADOLESCENT FRUSTRATION OUT ON THE MELODEON.
THE BOX WAS A THROAT SHE WAS SQUEEZING, ITS BELLOWS FOLDS OF SKIN THAT HINGED THE JOINTS OF SOME CRUEL MONSTER.

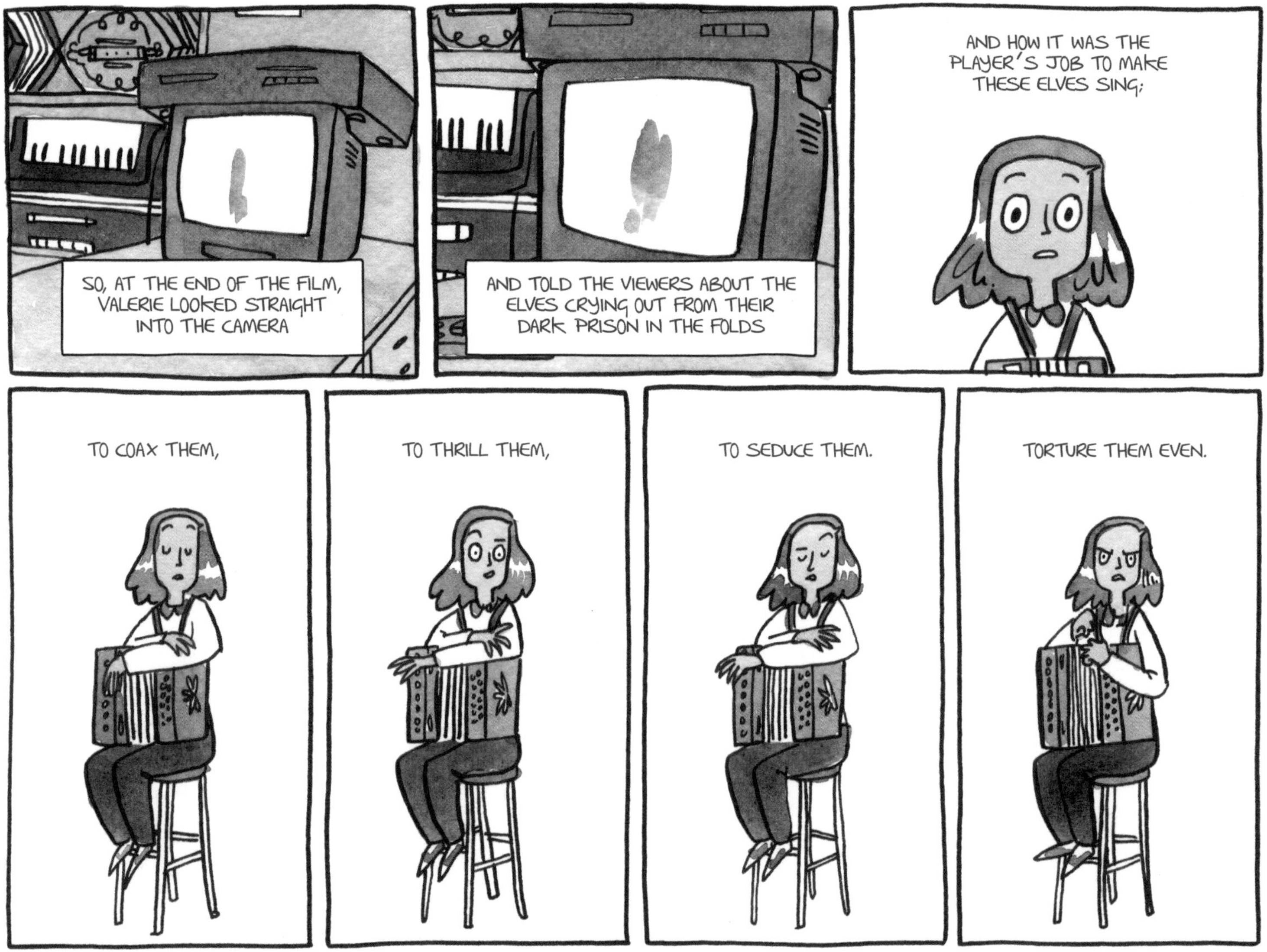
SO, AT THE END OF THE FILM, VALERIE LOOKED STRAIGHT INTO THE CAMERA
AND TOLD THE VIEWERS ABOUT THE ELVES CRYING OUT FROM THEIR DARK PRISON IN THE FOLDS
AND HOW IT WAS THE PLAYER'S JOB TO MAKE THESE ELVES SING;
TO COAX THEM,
TO THRILL THEM,
TO SEDUCE THEM.
TORTURE THEM EVEN.

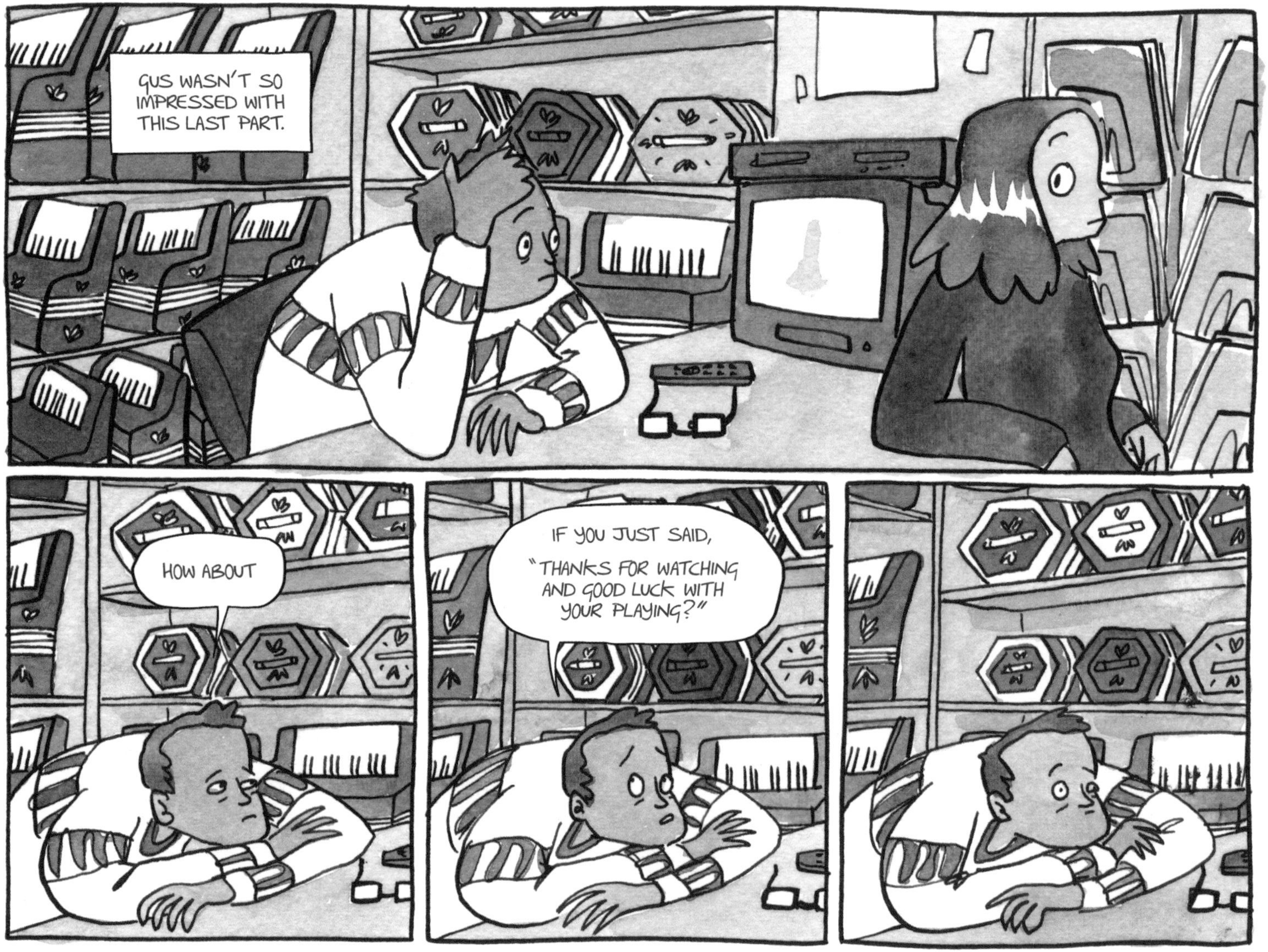
GUS WASN'T SO IMPRESSED WITH THIS LAST PART.
HOW ABOUT
IF YOU JUST SAID,
"THANKS FOR WATCHING AND GOOD LUCK WITH YOUR PLAYING?"

GUS LEFT THE ACCORDION SHOP SOON AFTER I MET HIM AND WENT TO WORK AT PHOTOQUICK.

HE HAD WORKED THERE FOR MONTHS BEFORE I DISCOVERED HIS SECRET:

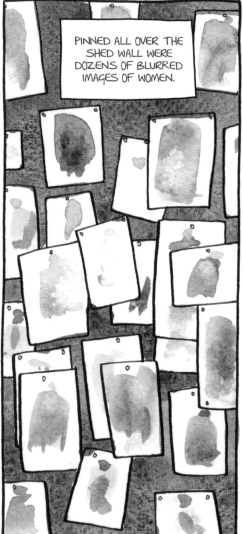

PINNED ALL OVER THE SHED WALL WERE DOZENS OF BLURRED IMAGES OF WOMEN.

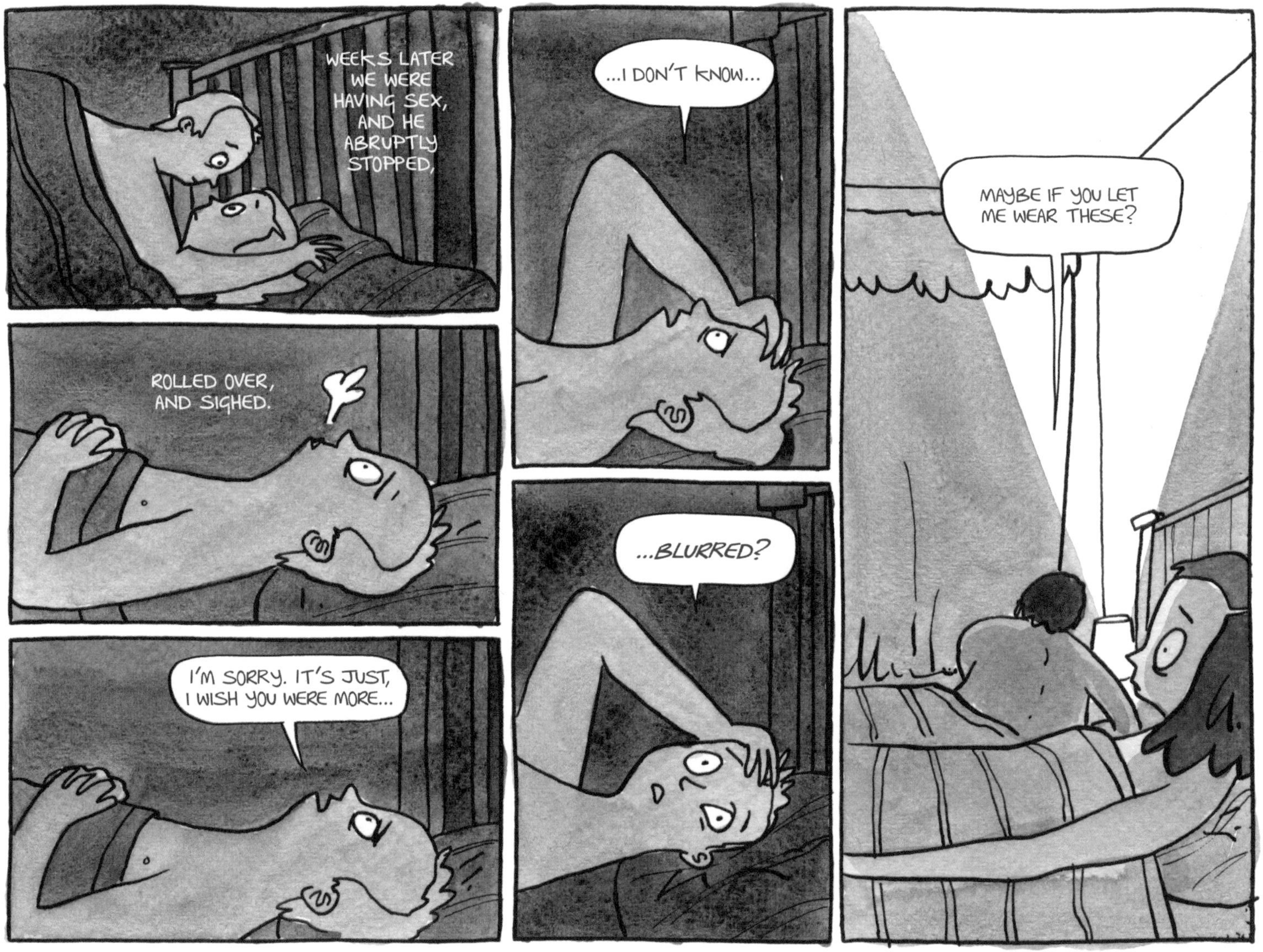
WEEKS LATER WE WERE HAVING SEX, AND HE ABRUPTLY STOPPED,
ROLLED OVER, AND SIGHED.
I'M SORRY. IT'S JUST, I WISH YOU WERE MORE...
...I DON'T KNOW...
...BLURRED?
MAYBE IF YOU LET ME WEAR THESE?

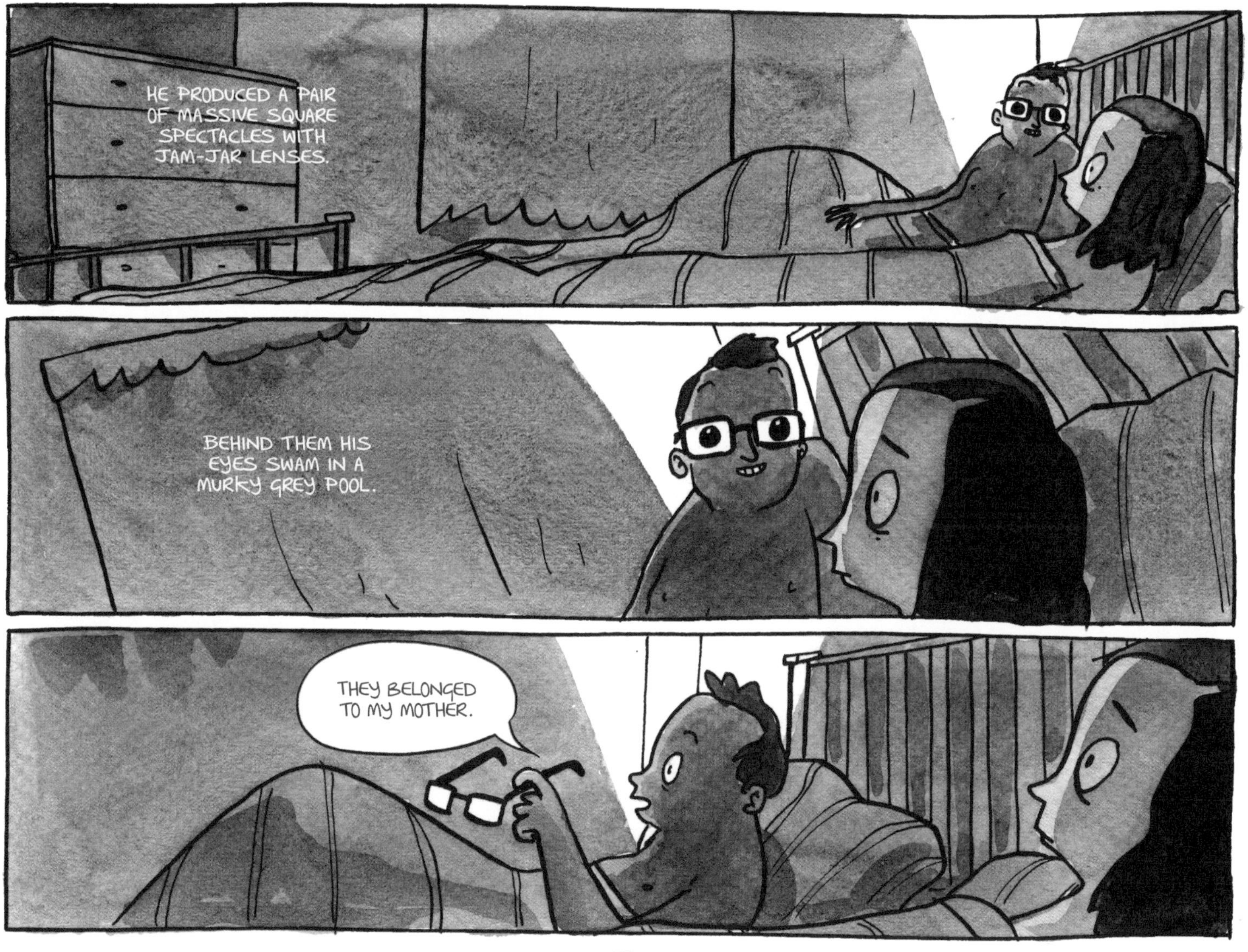
HE PRODUCED A PAIR OF MASSIVE SQUARE SPECTACLES WITH JAM-JAR LENSES.
BEHIND THEM HIS EYES SWAM IN A MURKY GREY POOL.
THEY BELONGED TO MY MOTHER.

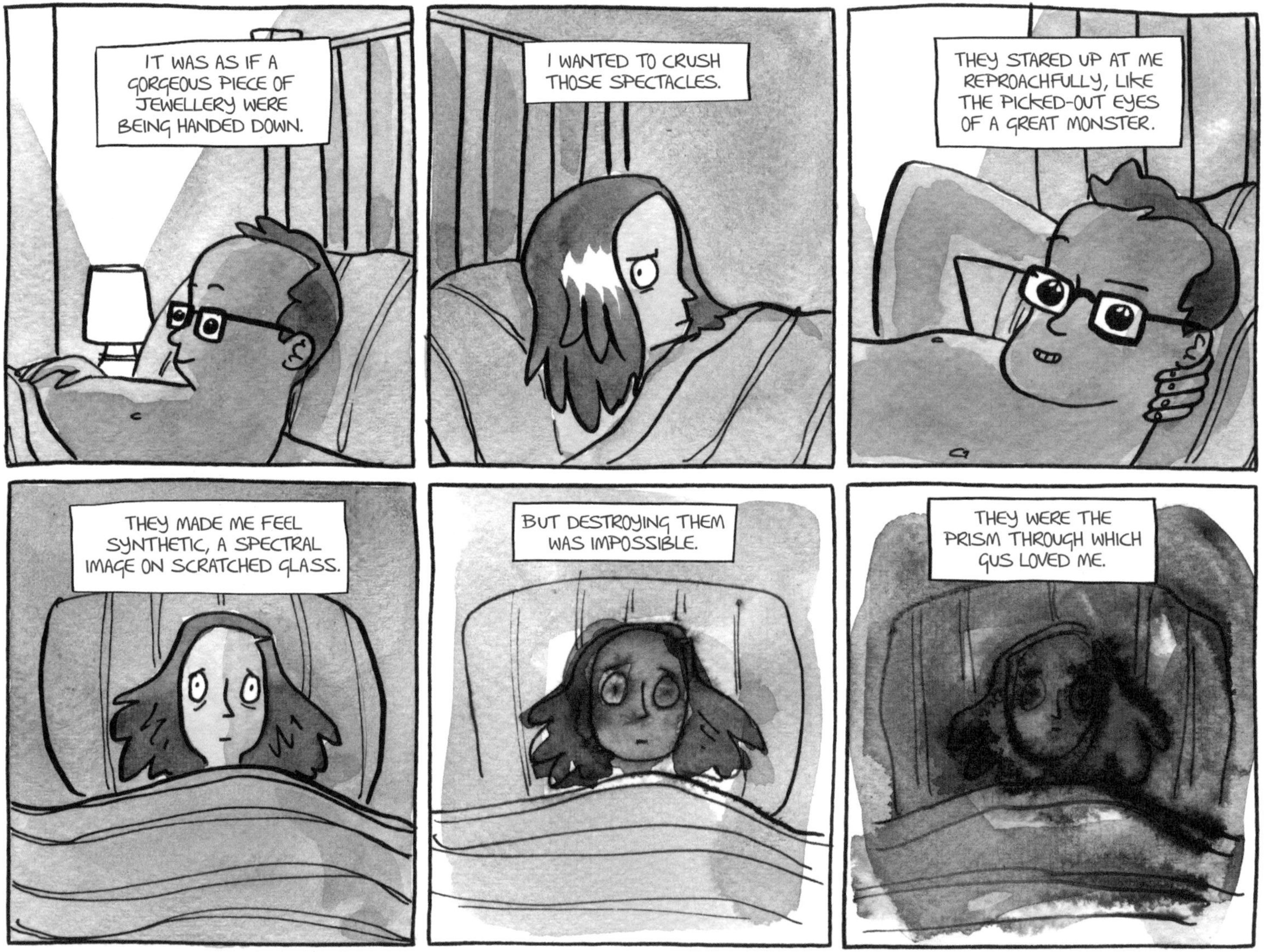
IT WAS AS IF A GORGEOUS PIECE OF JEWELLERY WERE BEING HANDED DOWN.
I WANTED TO CRUSH THOSE SPECTACLES.
THEY STARED UP AT ME REPROACHFULLY, LIKE THE PICKED-OUT EYES OF A GREAT MONSTER.
THEY MADE ME FEEL SYNTHETIC, A SPECTRAL IMAGE ON SCRATCHED GLASS.
BUT DESTROYING THEM WAS IMPOSSIBLE.
THEY WERE THE PRISM THROUGH WHICH GUS LOVED ME.

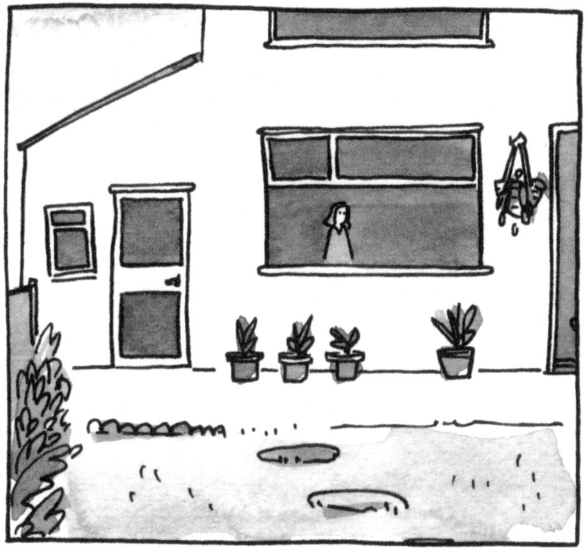

I TRIED TO ACCOMMODATE HIS WISHES, BUT OVER TIME HIS OBSESSION GREW TOO DIFFICULT TO BEAR.

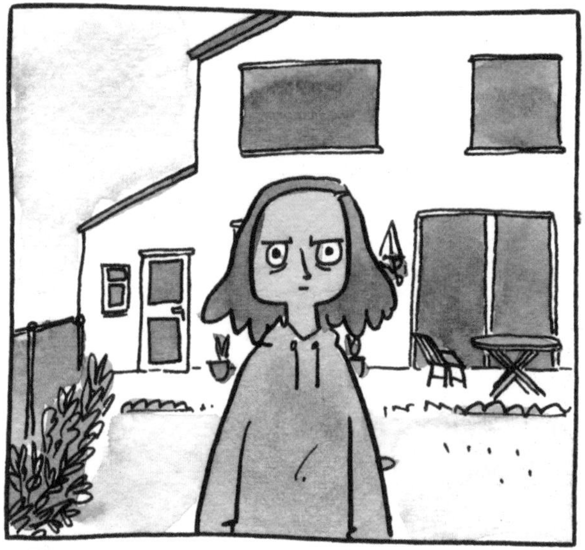

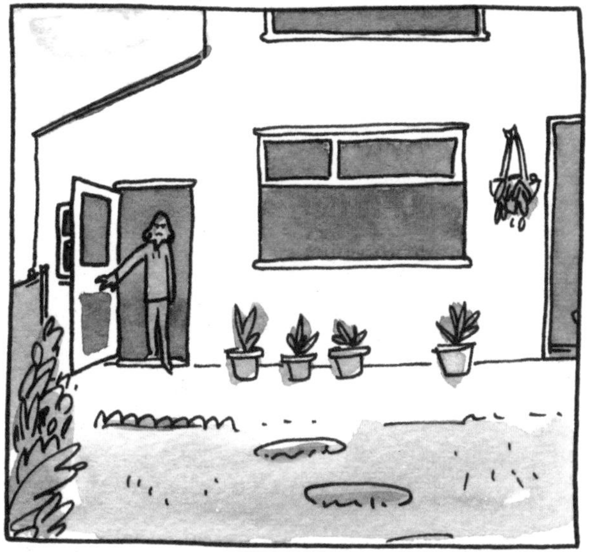

IN THE SHED THE COLLECTION HAD GROWN. A DIM AQUARIUM OF BLURRED GIRLS, ALL INNOCENT OF THEIR PLACE IN HIS SICK MUSEUM.

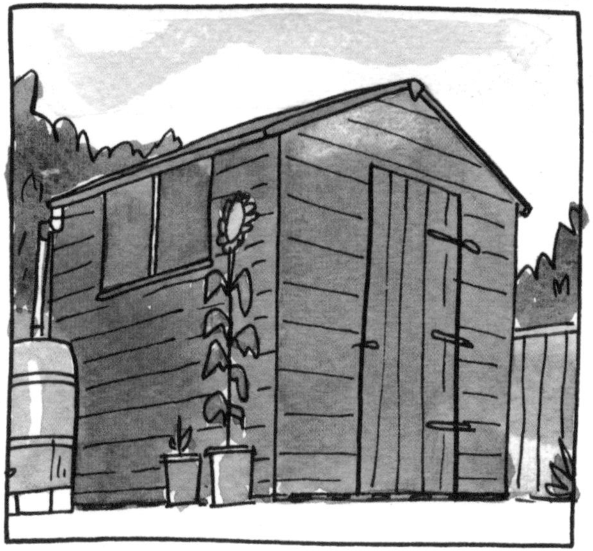

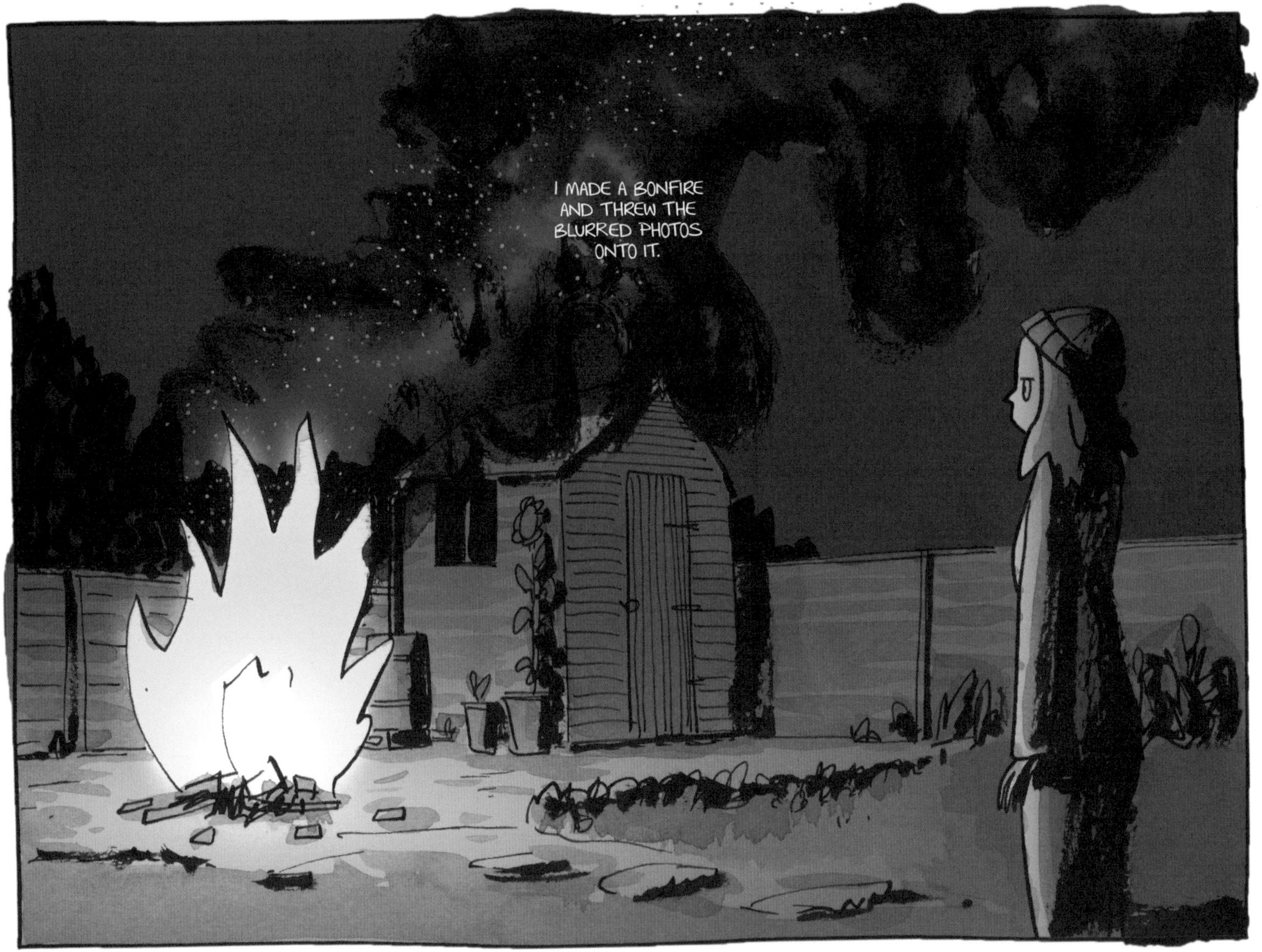
I MADE A BONFIRE AND THREW THE BLURRED PHOTOS ONTO IT.

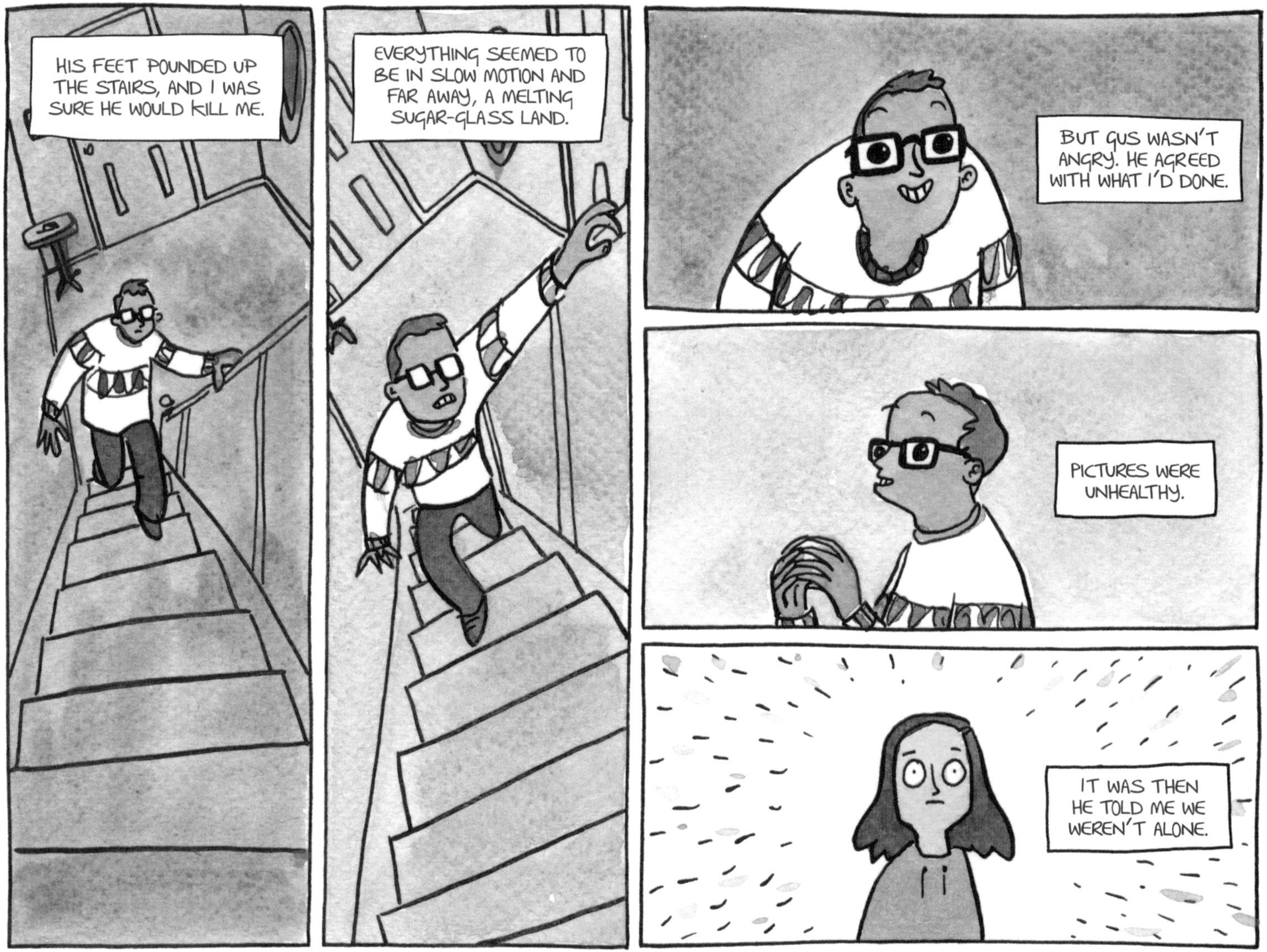
HIS FEET POUNDED UP THE STAIRS, AND I WAS SURE HE WOULD KILL ME.
EVERYTHING SEEMED TO BE IN SLOW MOTION AND FAR AWAY, A MELTING SUGAR-GLASS LAND.
BUT GUS WASN'T ANGRY. HE AGREED WITH WHAT I'D DONE.
PICTURES WERE UNHEALTHY.
IT WAS THEN HE TOLD ME WE WEREN'T ALONE.

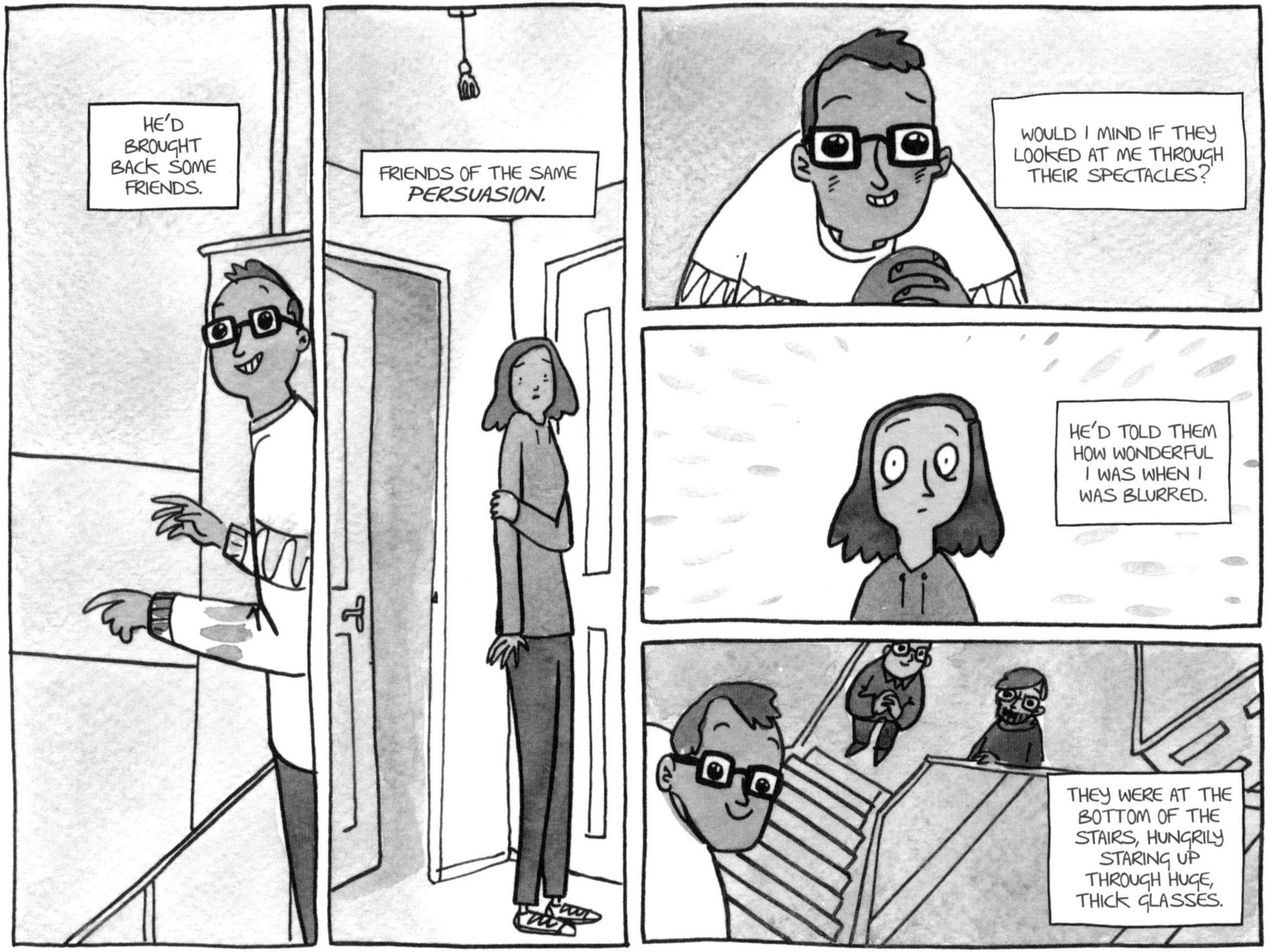
HE'D BROUGHT BACK SOME FRIENDS.
FRIENDS OF THE SAME *PERSUASION.*
WOULD I MIND IF THEY LOOKED AT ME THROUGH THEIR SPECTACLES?
HE'D TOLD THEM HOW WONDERFUL I WAS WHEN I WAS BLURRED.
THEY WERE AT THE BOTTOM OF THE STAIRS, HUNGRILY STARING UP THROUGH HUGE, THICK GLASSES.

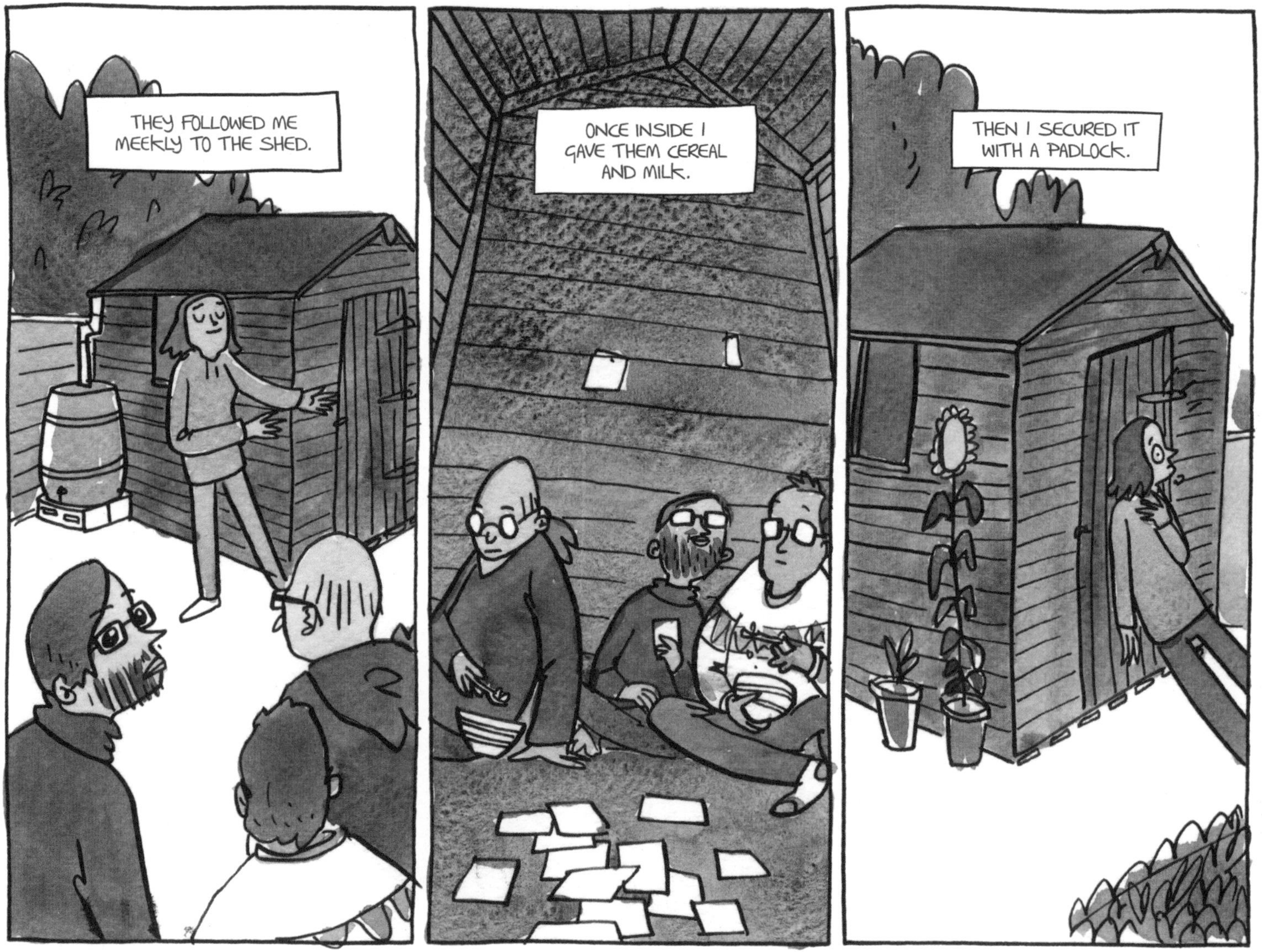
THEY FOLLOWED ME MEEKLY TO THE SHED.
ONCE INSIDE I GAVE THEM CEREAL AND MILK.
THEN I SECURED IT WITH A PADLOCK.

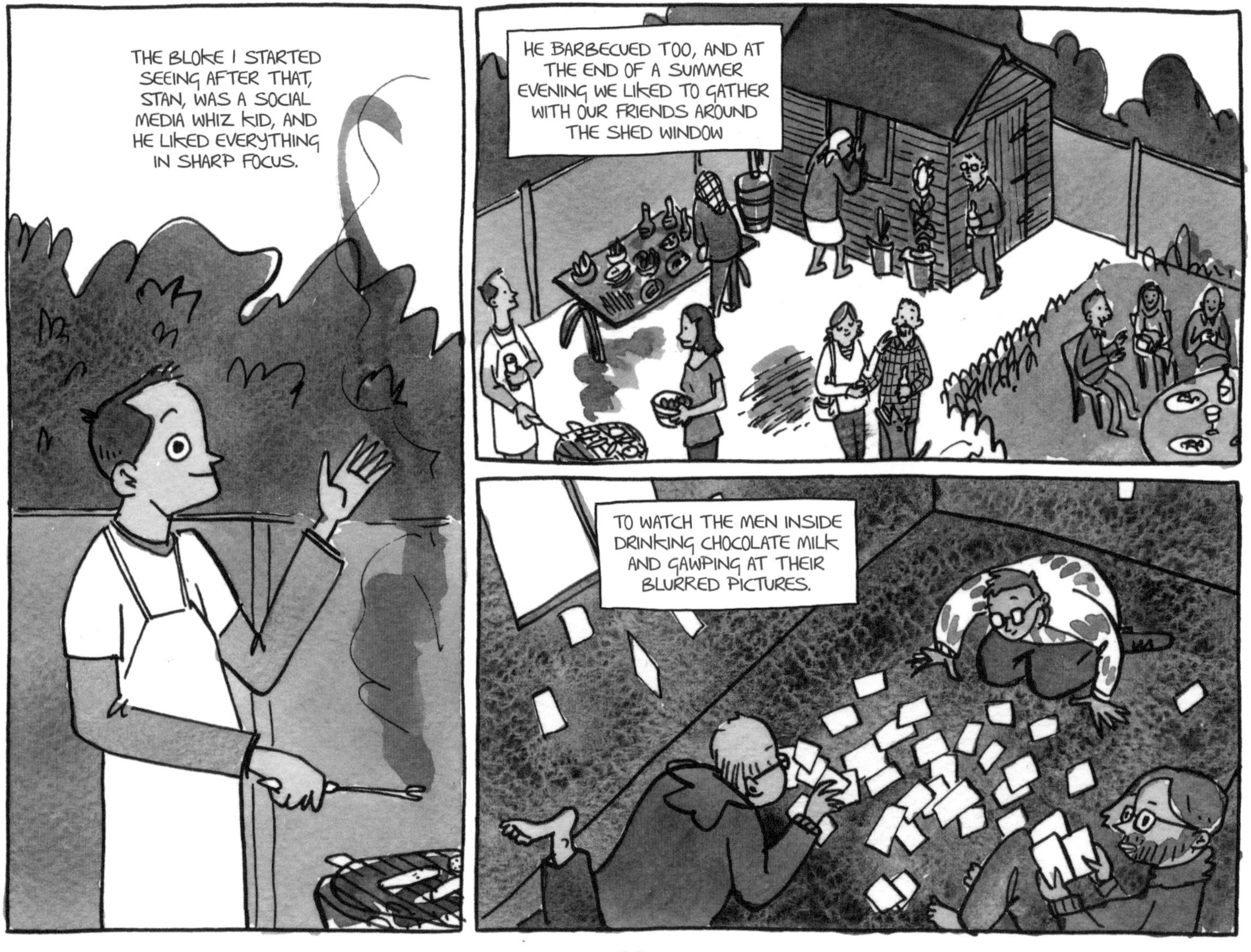
THE BLOKE I STARTED SEEING AFTER THAT, STAN, WAS A SOCIAL MEDIA WHIZ KID, AND HE LIKED EVERYTHING IN SHARP FOCUS.
HE BARBECUED TOO, AND AT THE END OF A SUMMER EVENING WE LIKED TO GATHER WITH OUR FRIENDS AROUND THE SHED WINDOW
TO WATCH THE MEN INSIDE DRINKING CHOCOLATE MILK AND GAWPING AT THEIR BLURRED PICTURES.

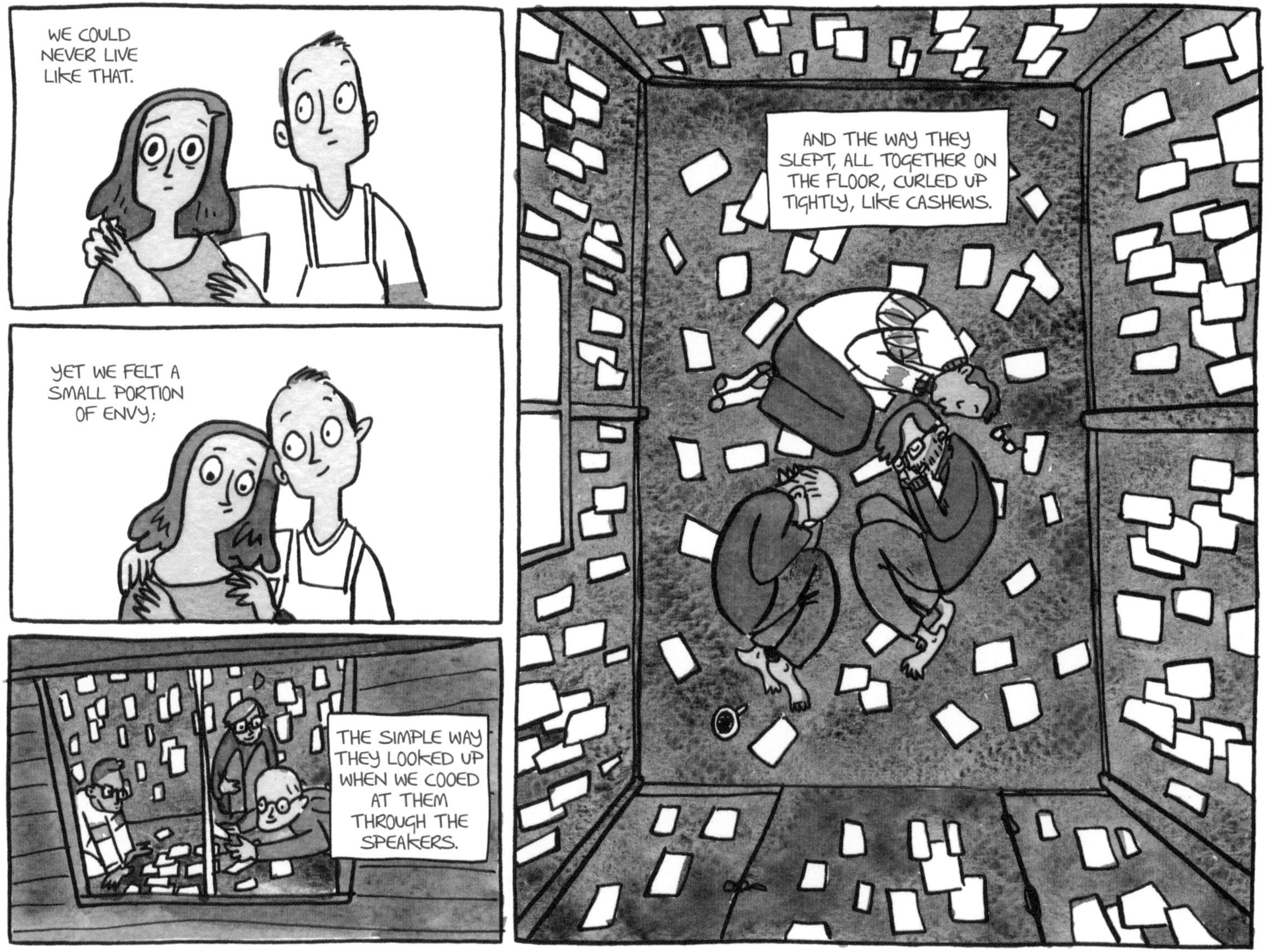
WE COULD NEVER LIVE LIKE THAT.
YET WE FELT A SMALL PORTION OF ENVY;
THE SIMPLE WAY THEY LOOKED UP WHEN WE COOED AT THEM THROUGH THE SPEAKERS.
AND THE WAY THEY SLEPT, ALL TOGETHER ON THE FLOOR, CURLED UP TIGHTLY, LIKE CASHEWS.

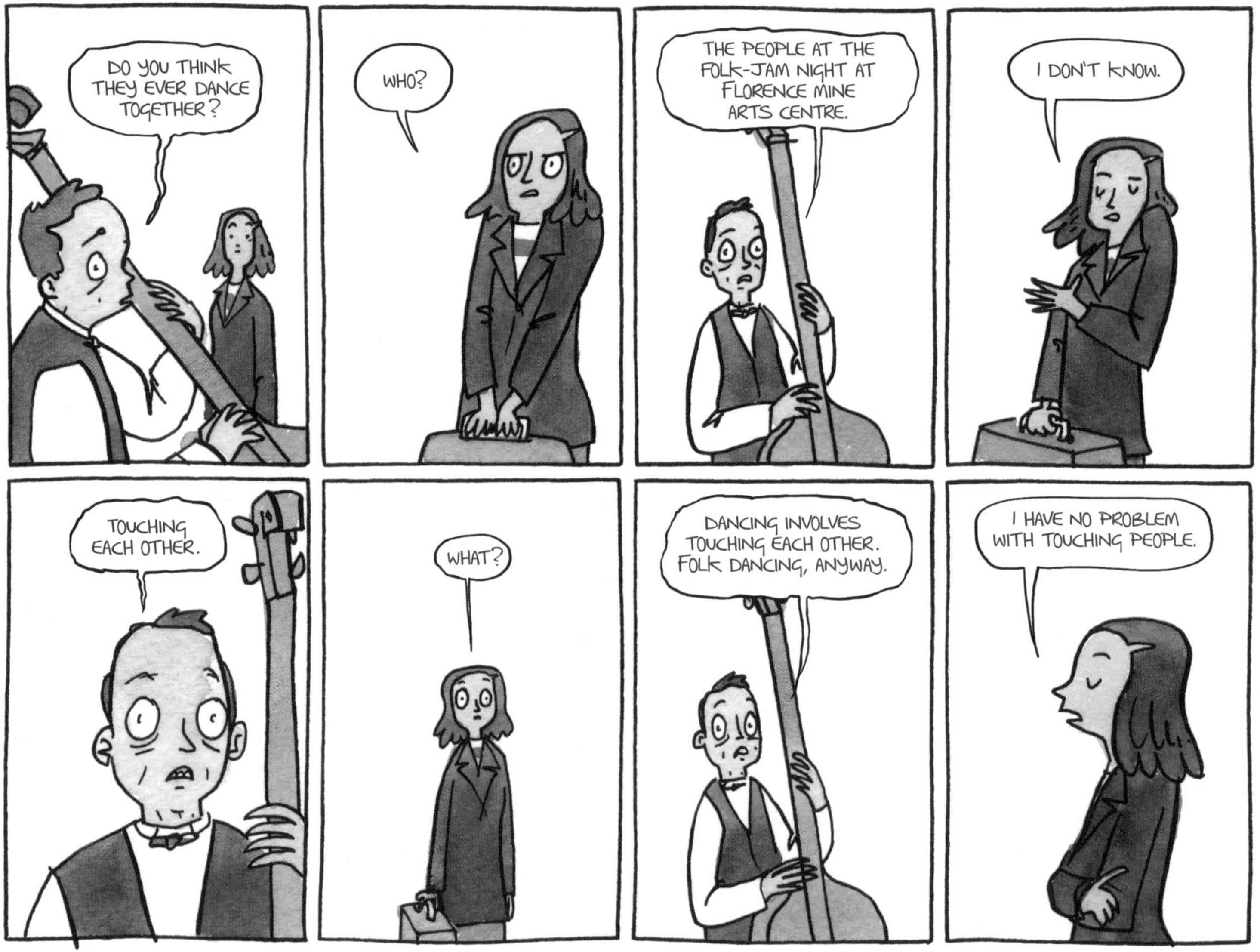
DO YOU THINK THEY EVER DANCE TOGETHER?
WHO?
THE PEOPLE AT THE FOLK-JAM NIGHT AT FLORENCE MINE ARTS CENTRE.
I DON'T KNOW.
TOUCHING EACH OTHER.
WHAT?
DANCING INVOLVES TOUCHING EACH OTHER. FOLK DANCING, ANYWAY.
I HAVE NO PROBLEM WITH TOUCHING PEOPLE.

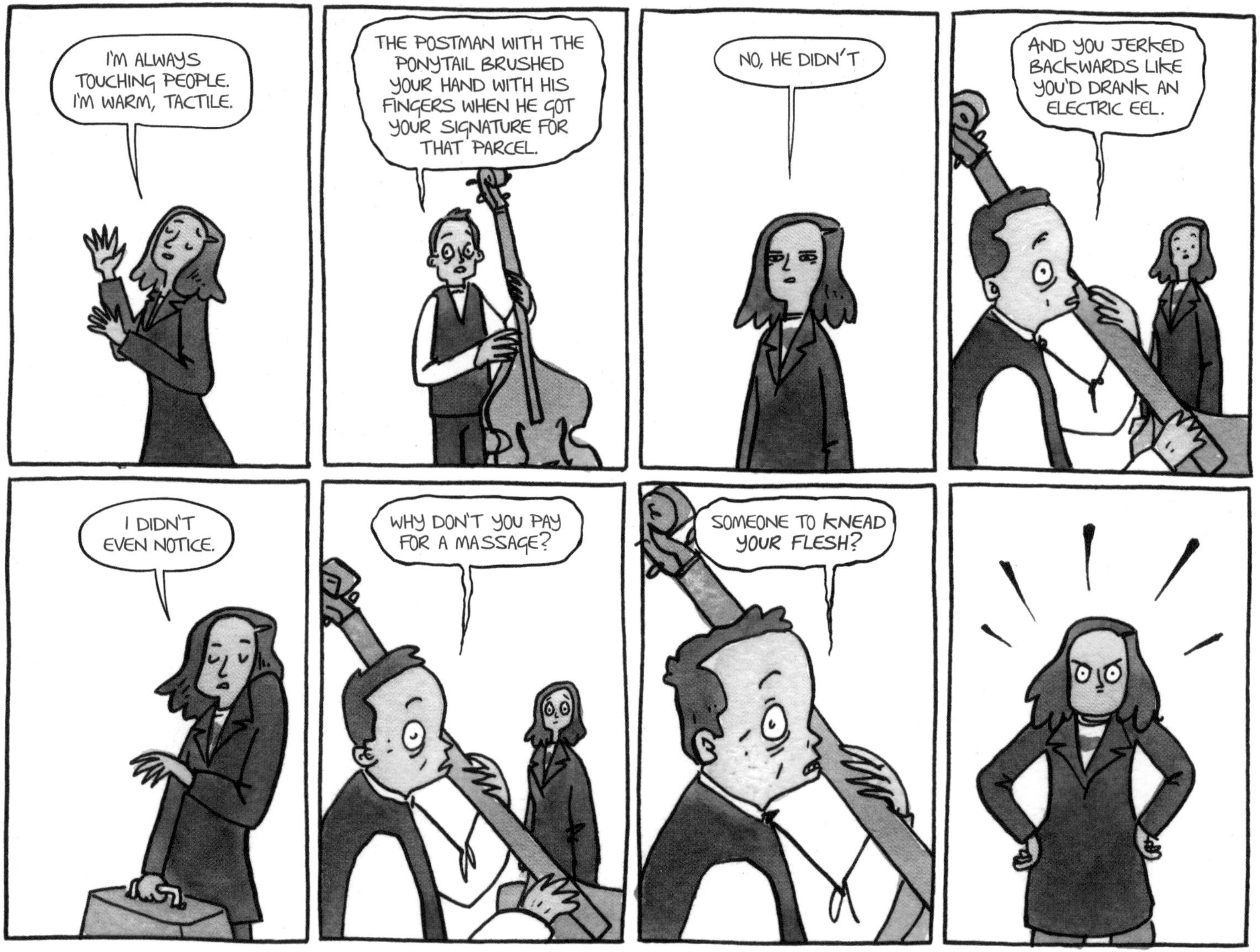
I'M ALWAYS TOUCHING PEOPLE. I'M WARM, TACTILE.
THE POSTMAN WITH THE PONYTAIL BRUSHED YOUR HAND WITH HIS FINGERS WHEN HE GOT YOUR SIGNATURE FOR THAT PARCEL.
NO, HE DIDN'T
AND YOU JERKED BACKWARDS LIKE YOU'D DRANK AN ELECTRIC EEL.
I DIDN'T EVEN NOTICE.
WHY DON'T YOU PAY FOR A MASSAGE?
SOMEONE TO KNEAD YOUR FLESH?

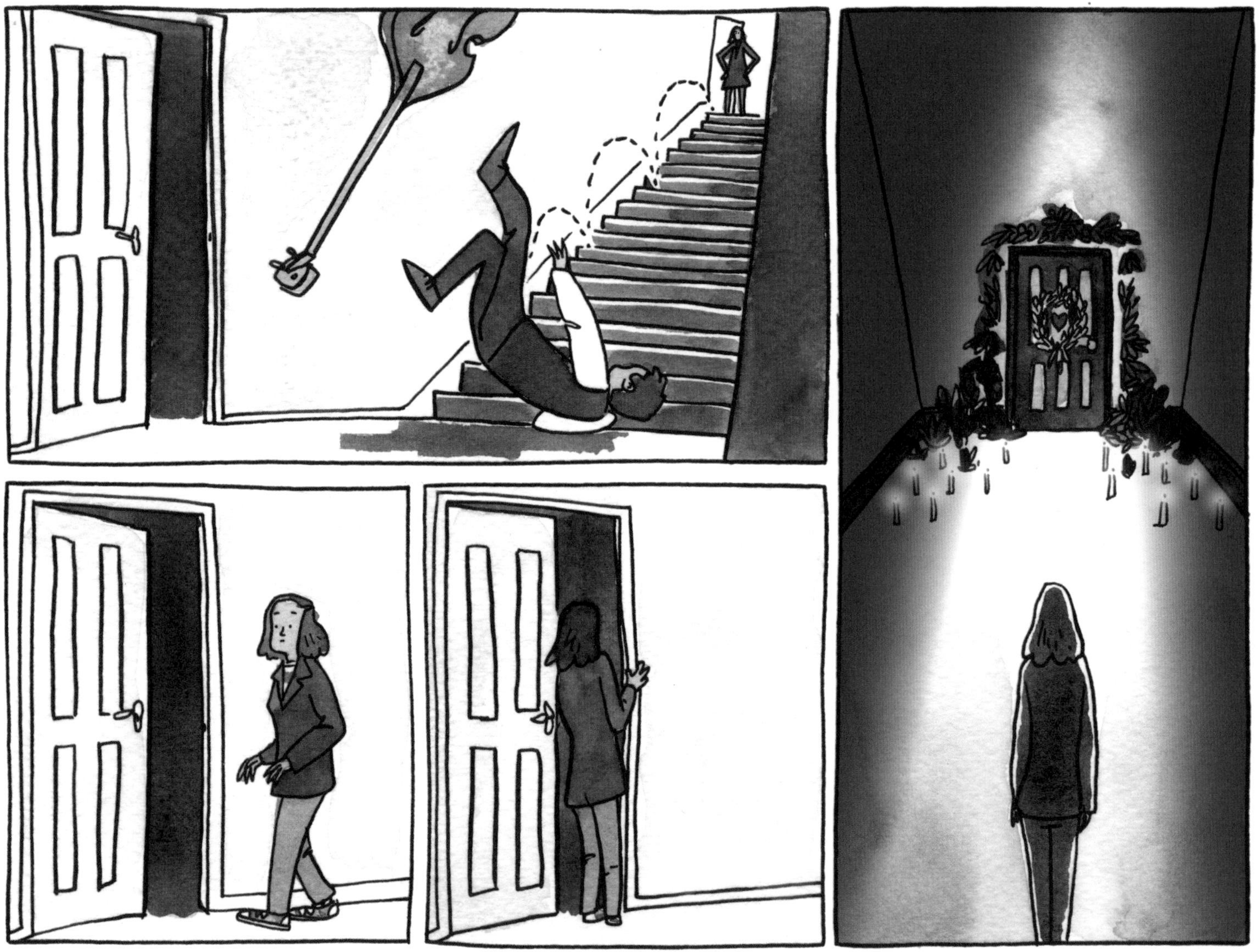

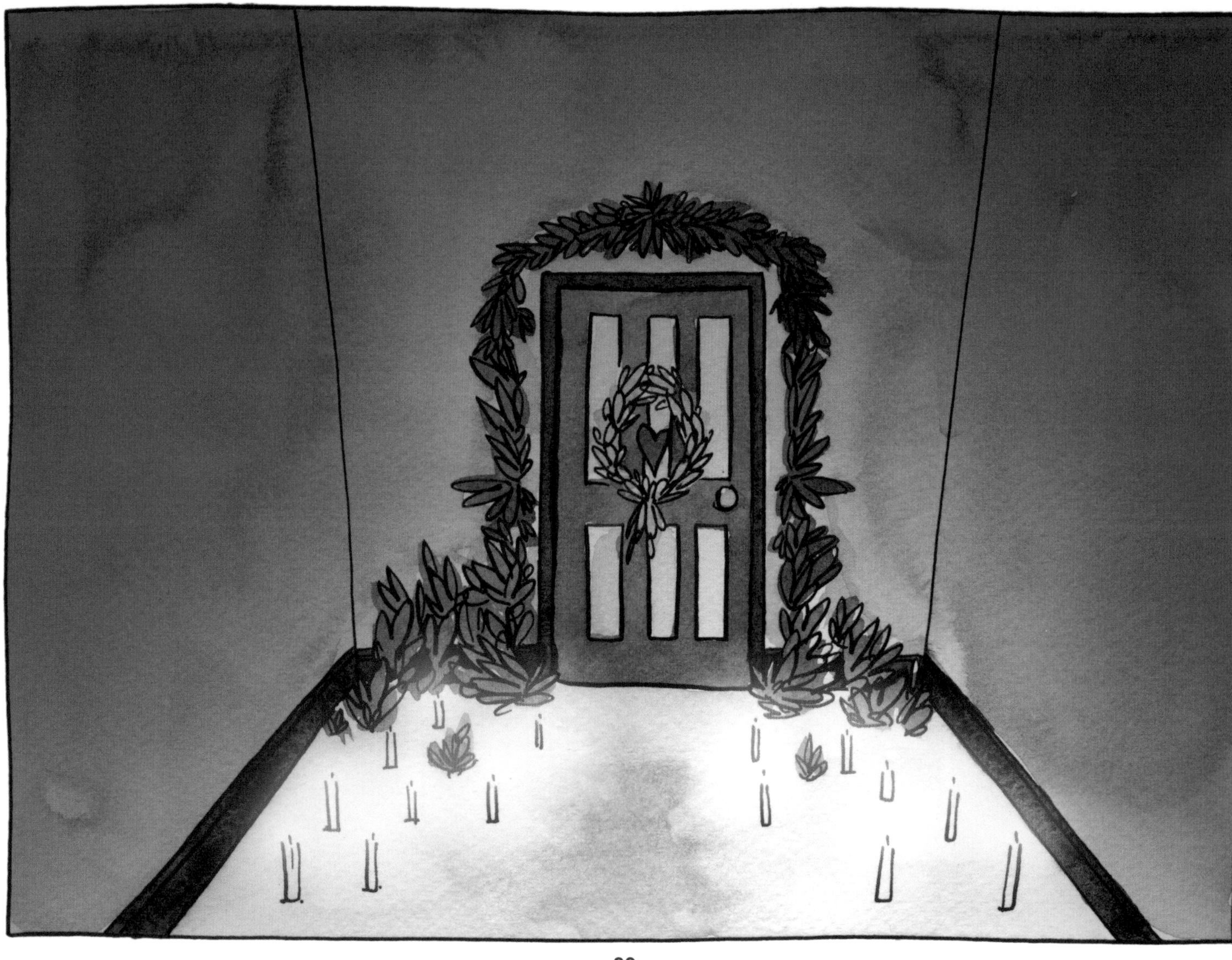

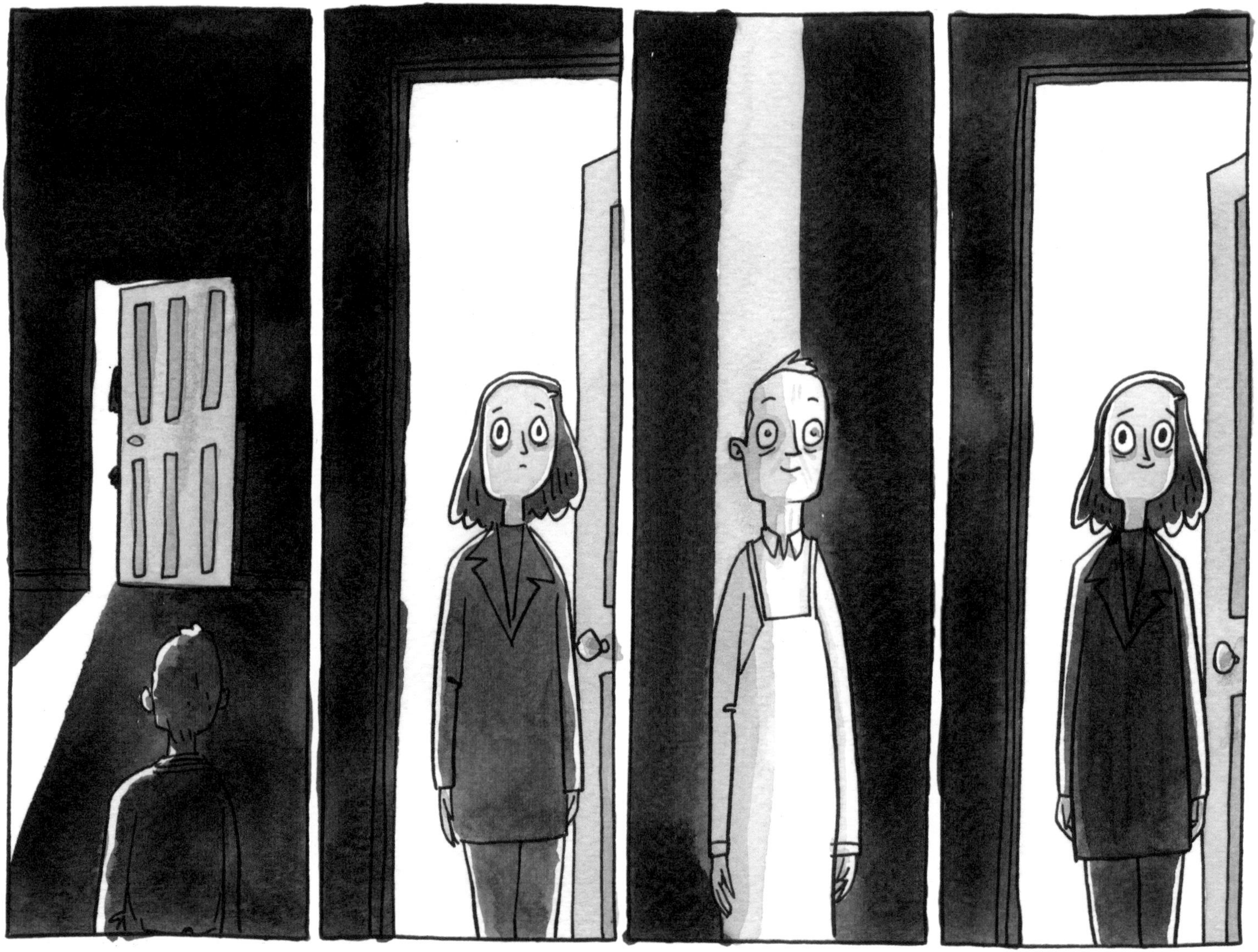

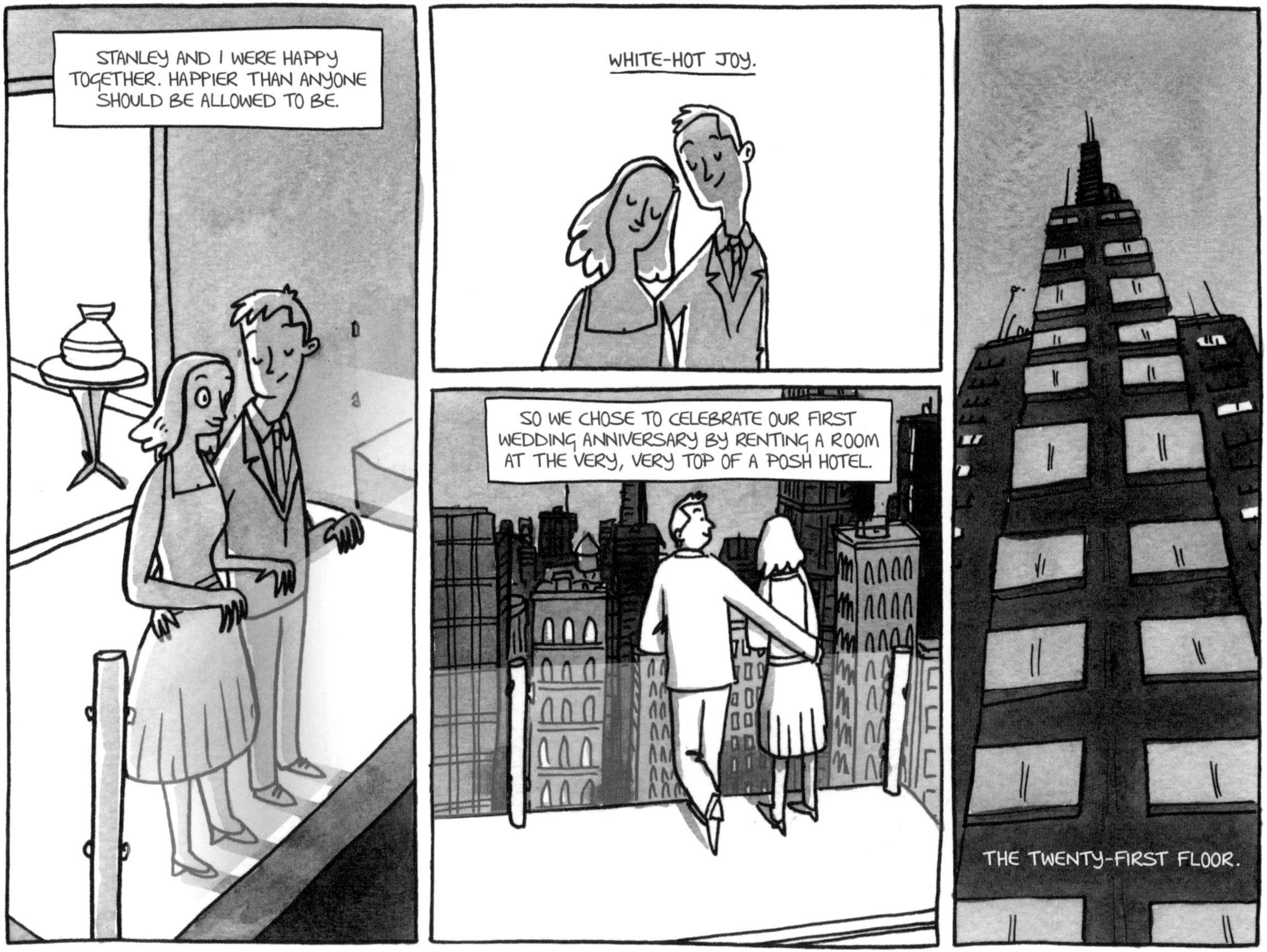
STANLEY AND I WERE HAPPY TOGETHER. HAPPIER THAN ANYONE SHOULD BE ALLOWED TO BE.
WHITE-HOT JOY.
SO WE CHOSE TO CELEBRATE OUR FIRST WEDDING ANNIVERSARY BY RENTING A ROOM AT THE VERY, VERY TOP OF A POSH HOTEL.
THE TWENTY-FIRST FLOOR.

IT WAS AMAZING, BEING ELEVATED LIKE THAT, WAY ABOVE THE NOISE OF THE CITY. WE FELT SO REMOTE, SO SPECIAL.

MAYBE EACH YEAR WE'LL STAY IN A ROOM AT A HIGHER LEVEL.

WE'LL END UP SOMEWHERE LIKE DUBAI.

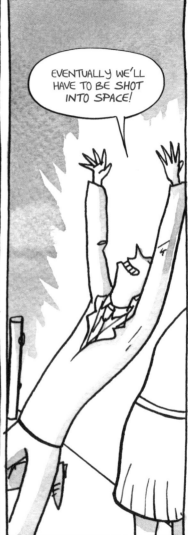

EVENTUALLY WE'LL HAVE TO BE SHOT INTO SPACE!

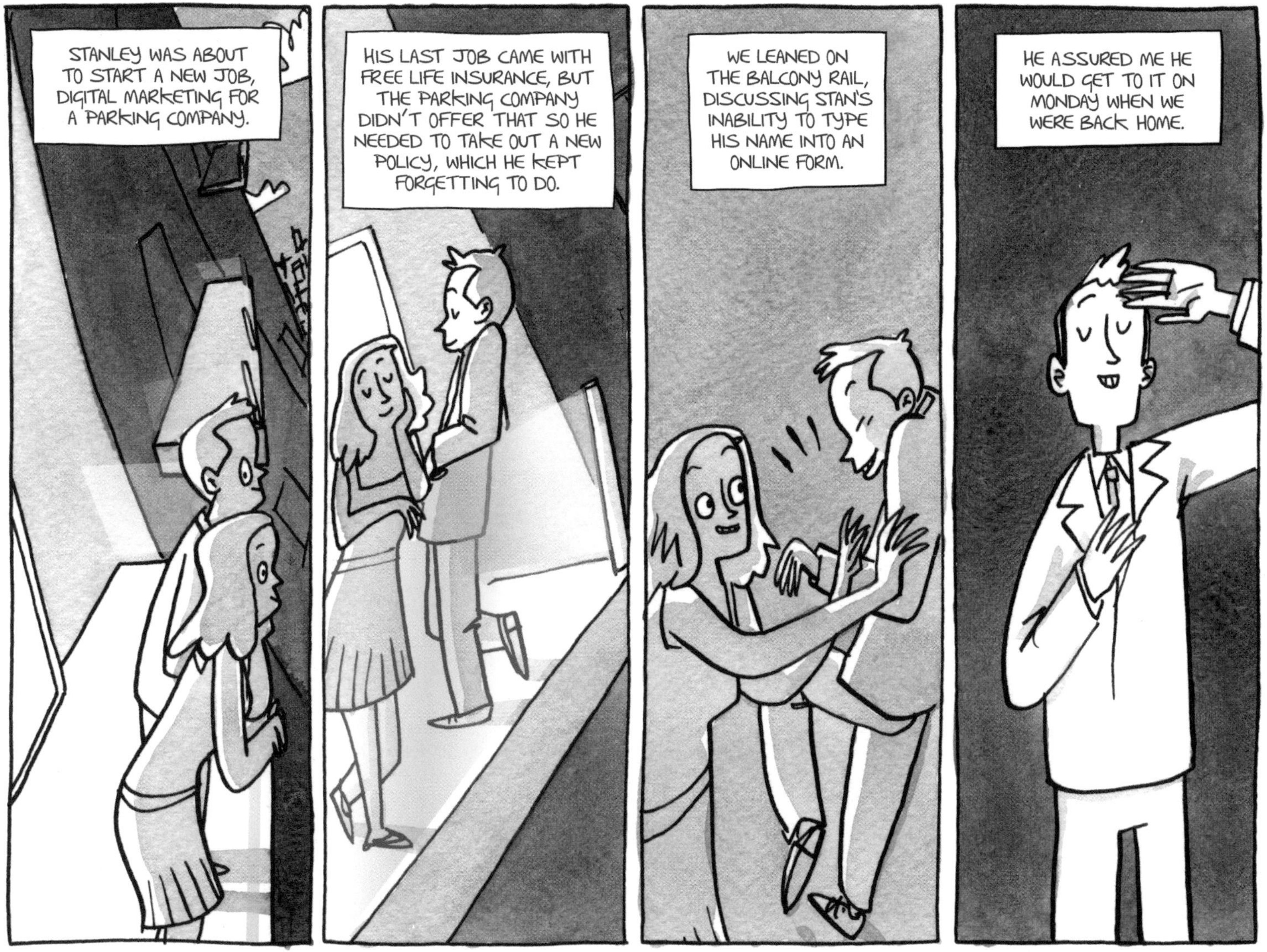
STANLEY WAS ABOUT TO START A NEW JOB, DIGITAL MARKETING FOR A PARKING COMPANY.
HIS LAST JOB CAME WITH FREE LIFE INSURANCE, BUT THE PARKING COMPANY DIDN'T OFFER THAT SO HE NEEDED TO TAKE OUT A NEW POLICY, WHICH HE KEPT FORGETTING TO DO.
WE LEANED ON THE BALCONY RAIL, DISCUSSING STAN'S INABILITY TO TYPE HIS NAME INTO AN ONLINE FORM.
HE ASSURED ME HE WOULD GET TO IT ON MONDAY WHEN WE WERE BACK HOME.

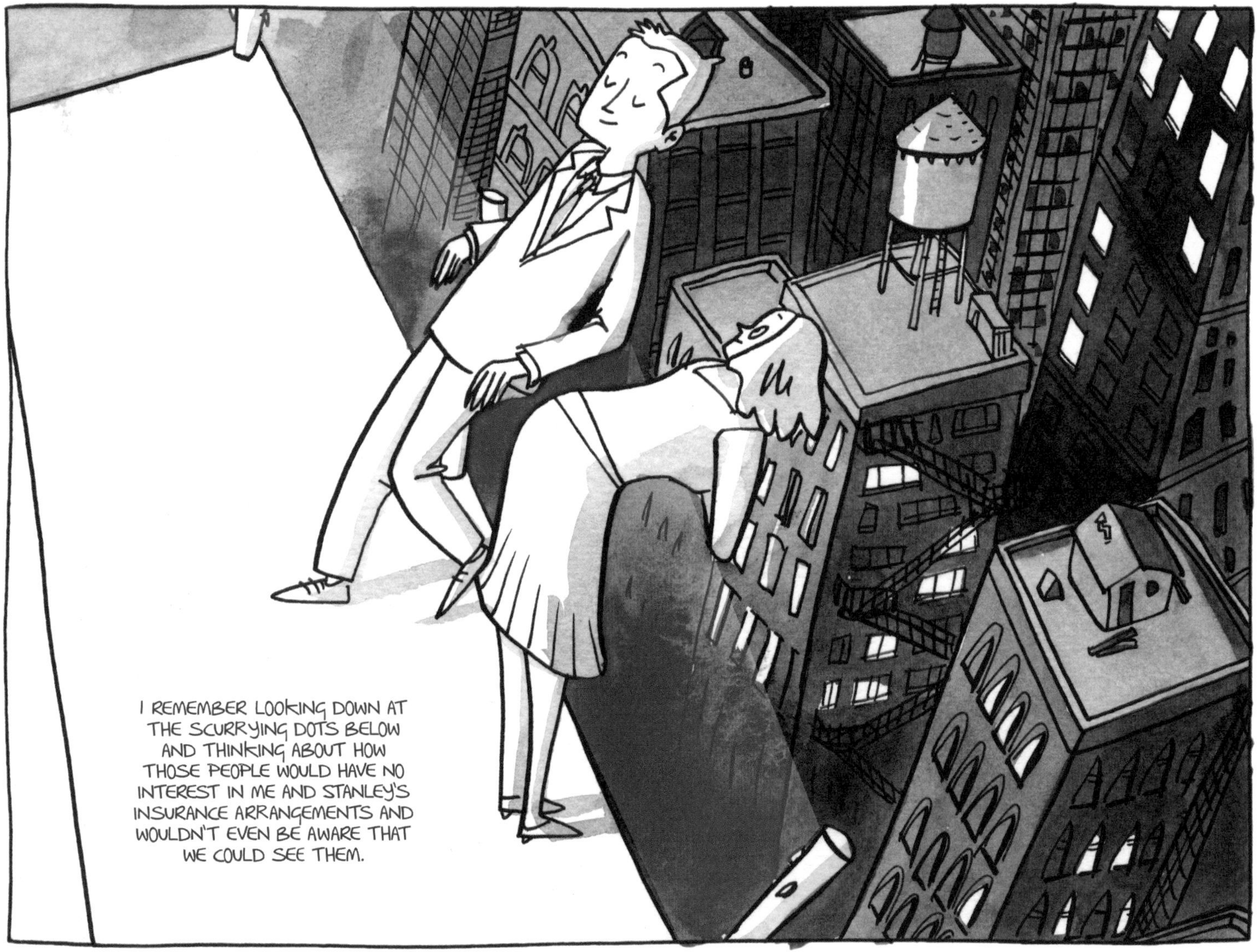
I REMEMBER LOOKING DOWN AT THE SCURRYING DOTS BELOW AND THINKING ABOUT HOW THOSE PEOPLE WOULD HAVE NO INTEREST IN ME AND STANLEY'S INSURANCE ARRANGEMENTS AND WOULDN'T EVEN BE AWARE THAT WE COULD SEE THEM.

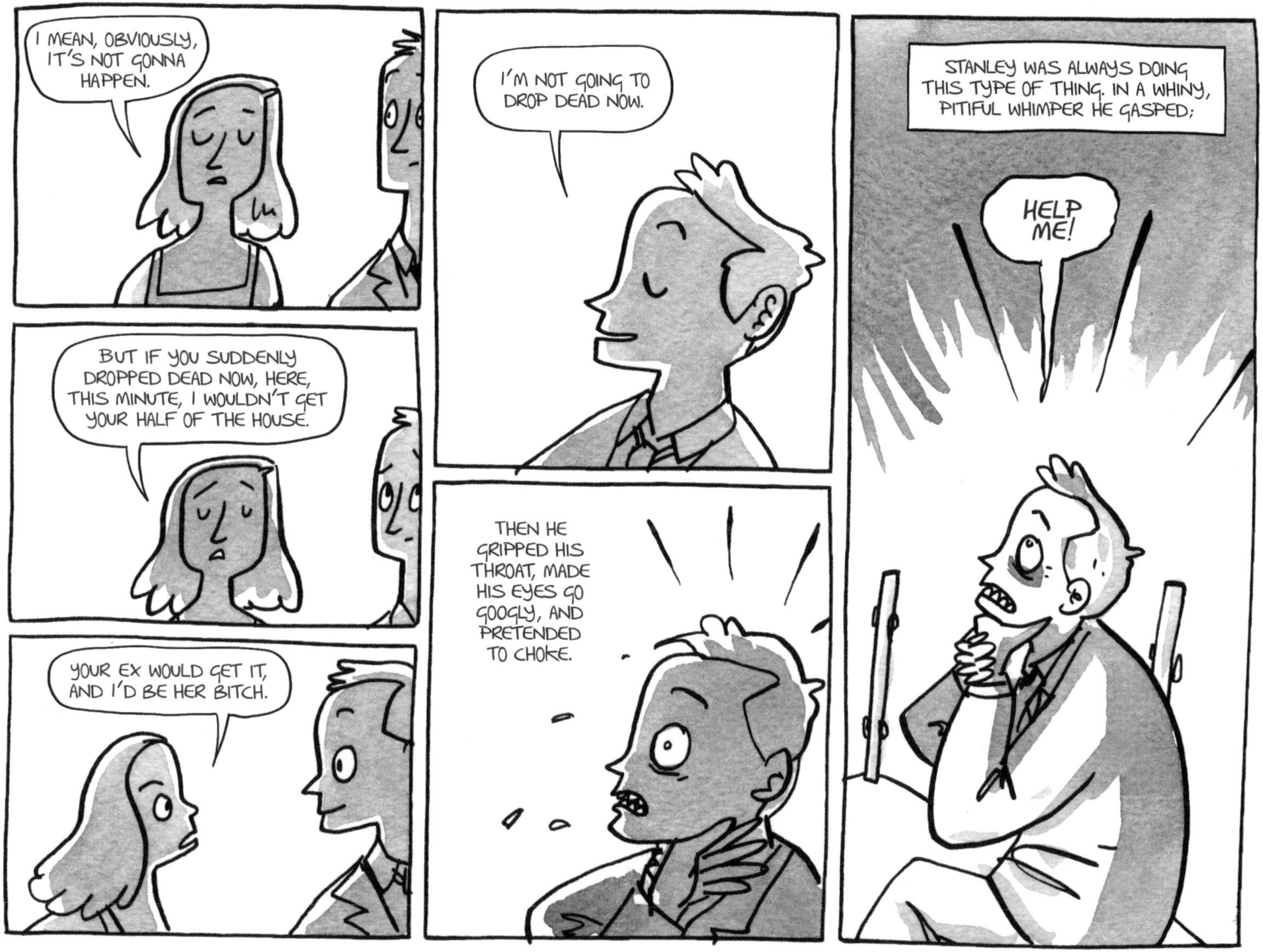

I MEAN, OBVIOUSLY, IT'S NOT GONNA HAPPEN.
BUT IF YOU SUDDENLY DROPPED DEAD NOW, HERE, THIS MINUTE, I WOULDN'T GET YOUR HALF OF THE HOUSE.
YOUR EX WOULD GET IT, AND I'D BE HER BITCH.
I'M NOT GOING TO DROP DEAD NOW.
THEN HE GRIPPED HIS THROAT, MADE HIS EYES GO GOOGLY, AND PRETENDED TO CHOKE.
STANLEY WAS ALWAYS DOING THIS TYPE OF THING. IN A WHINY, PITIFUL WHIMPER HE GASPED;
HELP ME!

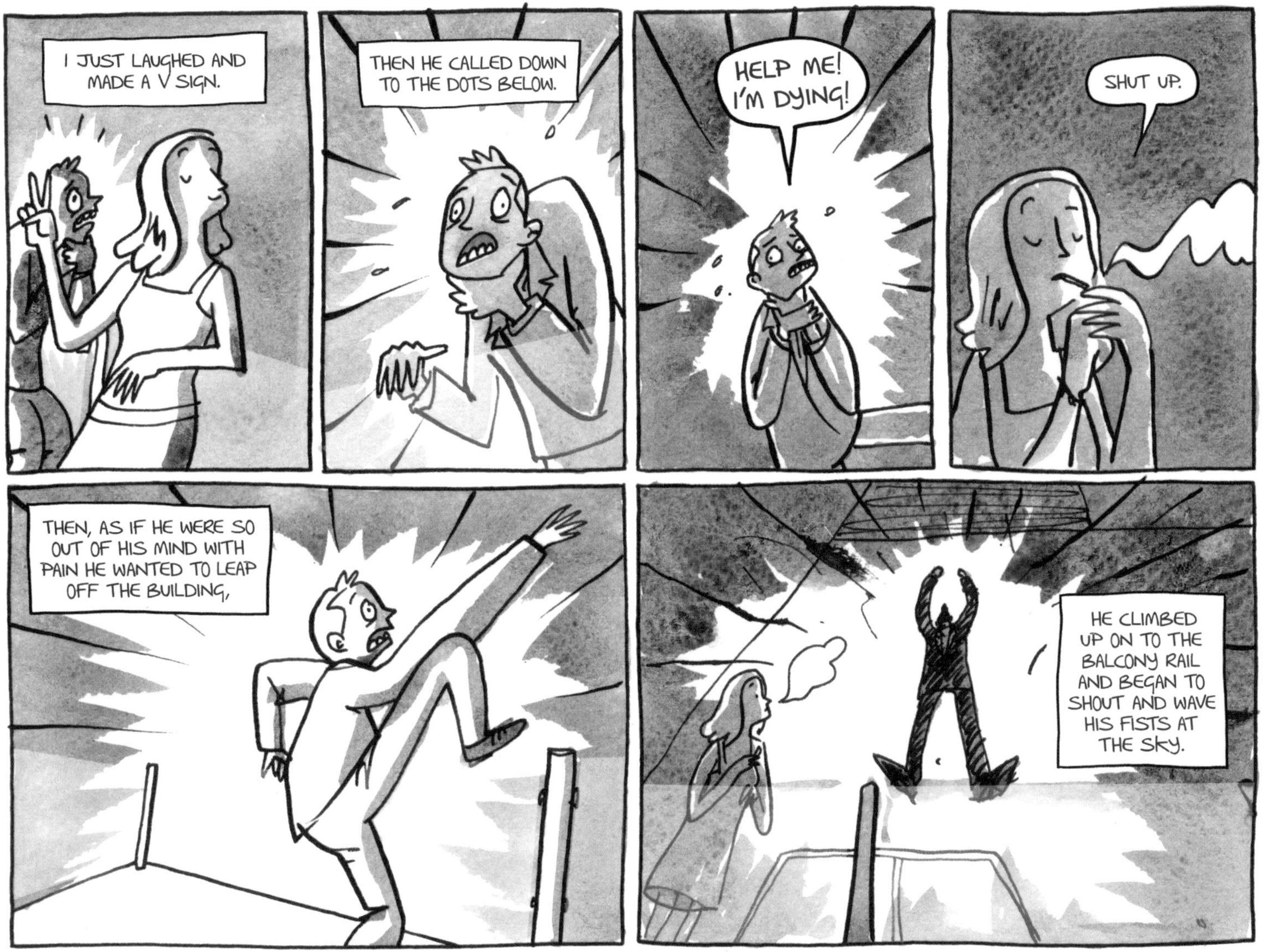
I JUST LAUGHED AND MADE A V SIGN.
THEN HE CALLED DOWN TO THE DOTS BELOW.
HELP ME! I'M DYING!
SHUT UP.
THEN, AS IF HE WERE SO OUT OF HIS MIND WITH PAIN HE WANTED TO LEAP OFF THE BUILDING,
HE CLIMBED UP ON TO THE BALCONY RAIL AND BEGAN TO SHOUT AND WAVE HIS FISTS AT THE SKY.

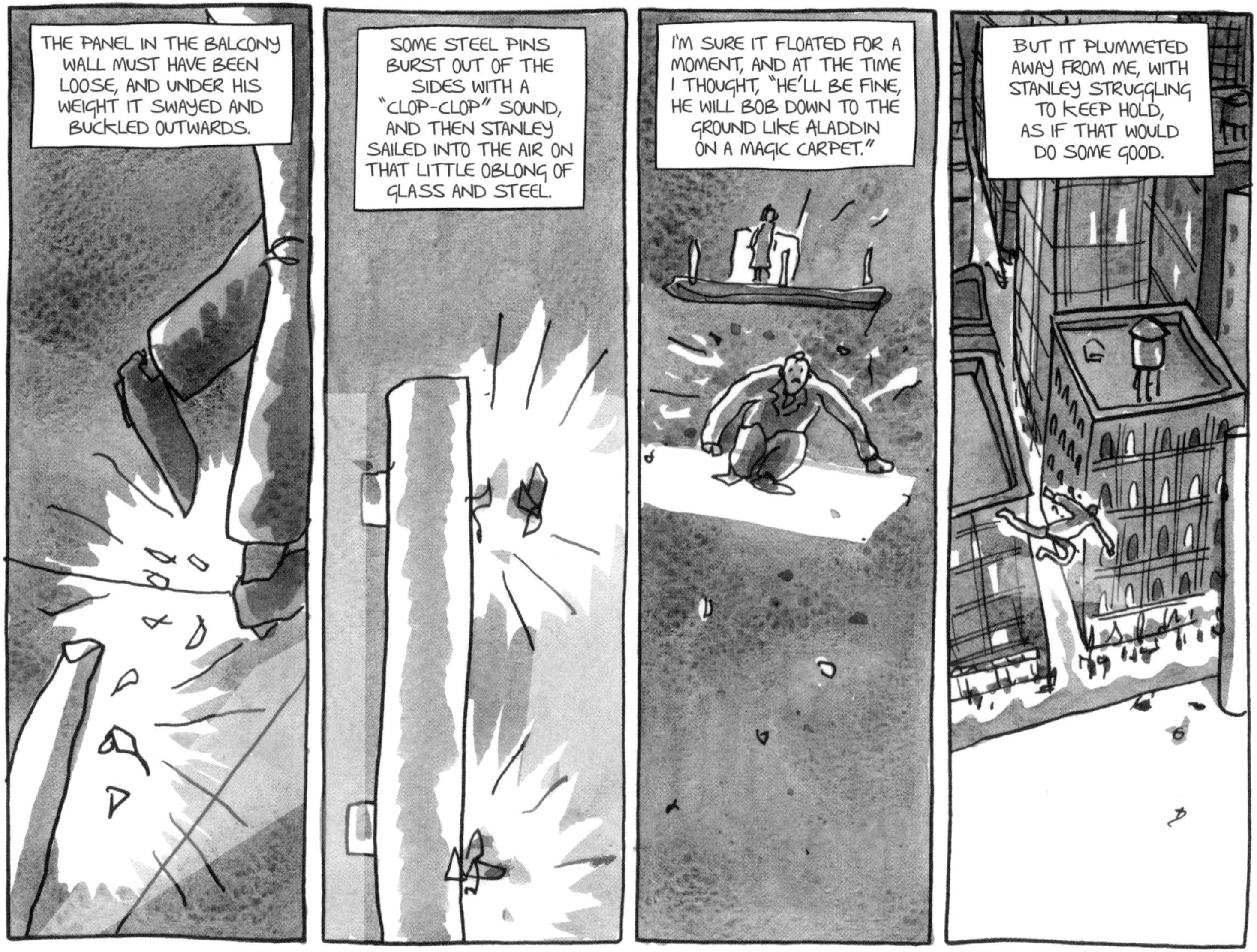
THE PANEL IN THE BALCONY WALL MUST HAVE BEEN LOOSE, AND UNDER HIS WEIGHT IT SWAYED AND BUCKLED OUTWARDS.
SOME STEEL PINS BURST OUT OF THE SIDES WITH A "CLOP-CLOP" SOUND, AND THEN STANLEY SAILED INTO THE AIR ON THAT LITTLE OBLONG OF GLASS AND STEEL.
I'M SURE IT FLOATED FOR A MOMENT, AND AT THE TIME I THOUGHT, "HE'LL BE FINE, HE WILL BOB DOWN TO THE GROUND LIKE ALADDIN ON A MAGIC CARPET."
BUT IT PLUMMETED AWAY FROM ME, WITH STANLEY STRUGGLING TO KEEP HOLD, AS IF THAT WOULD DO SOME GOOD.

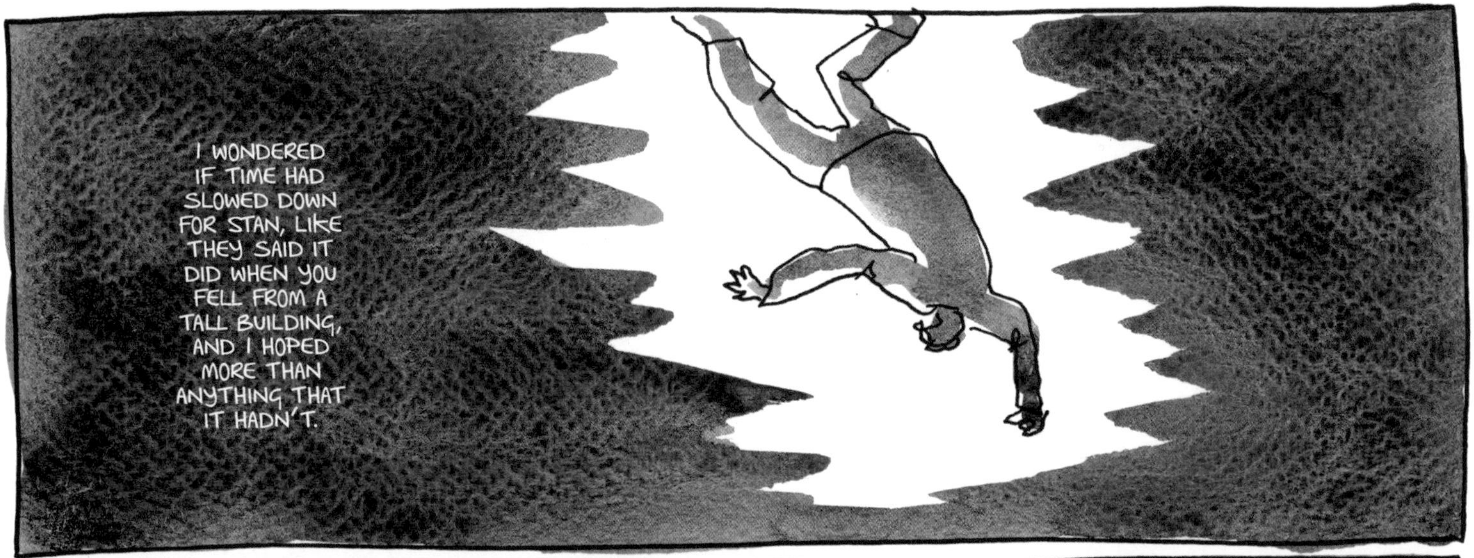
I WONDERED IF TIME HAD SLOWED DOWN FOR STAN, LIKE THEY SAID IT DID WHEN YOU FELL FROM A TALL BUILDING, AND I HOPED MORE THAN ANYTHING THAT IT HADN'T.

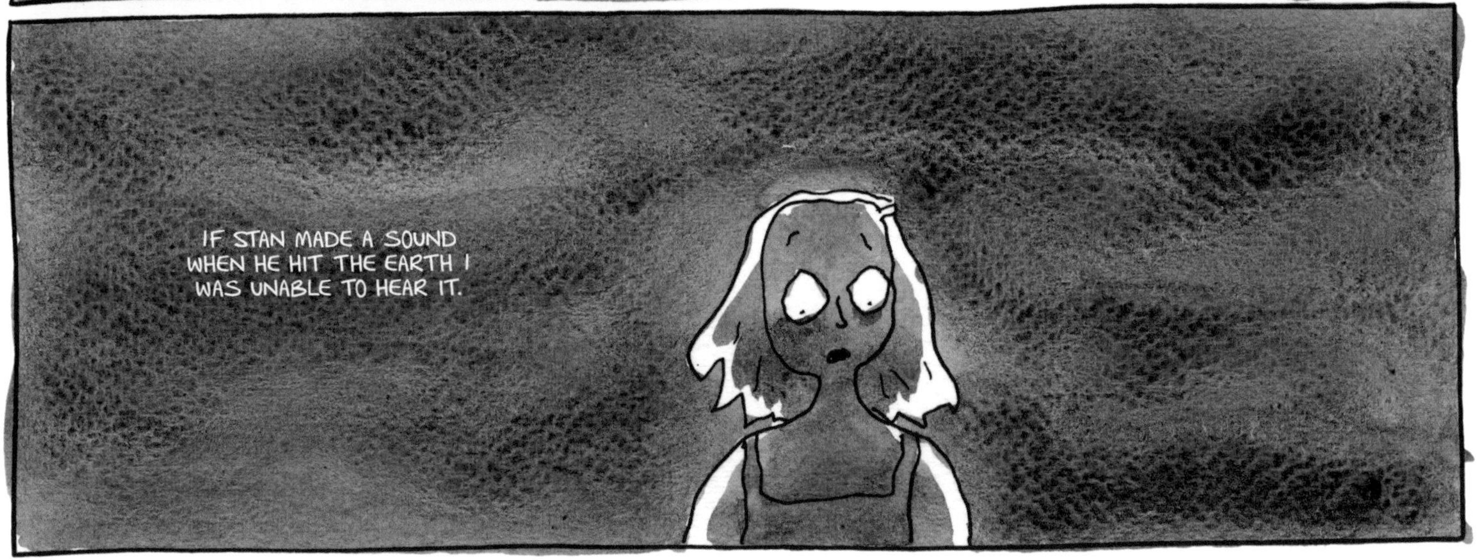
IF STAN MADE A SOUND WHEN HE HIT THE EARTH I WAS UNABLE TO HEAR IT.

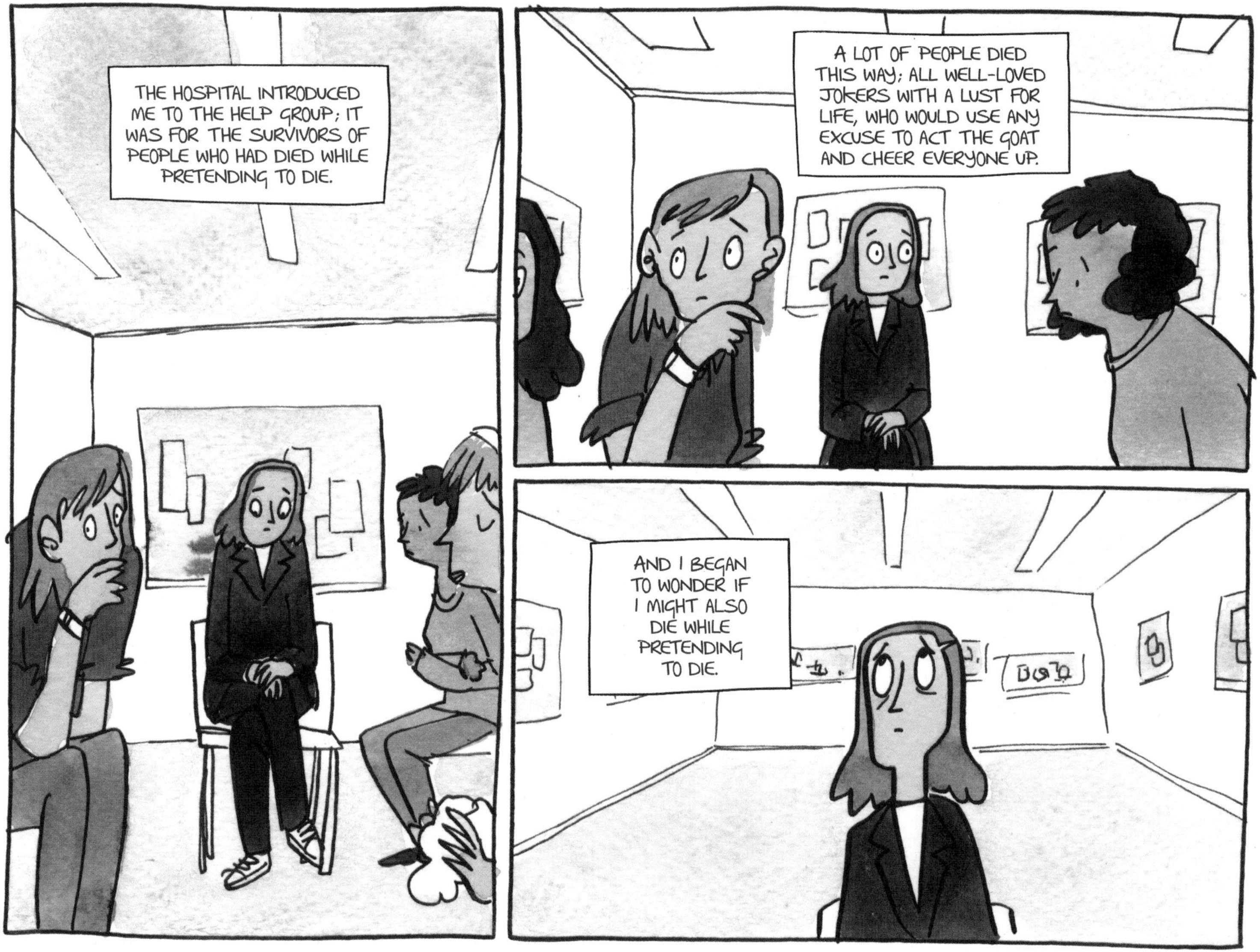
THE HOSPITAL INTRODUCED ME TO THE HELP GROUP; IT WAS FOR THE SURVIVORS OF PEOPLE WHO HAD DIED WHILE PRETENDING TO DIE.
A LOT OF PEOPLE DIED THIS WAY; ALL WELL-LOVED JOKERS WITH A LUST FOR LIFE, WHO WOULD USE ANY EXCUSE TO ACT THE GOAT AND CHEER EVERYONE UP.
AND I BEGAN TO WONDER IF I MIGHT ALSO DIE WHILE PRETENDING TO DIE.

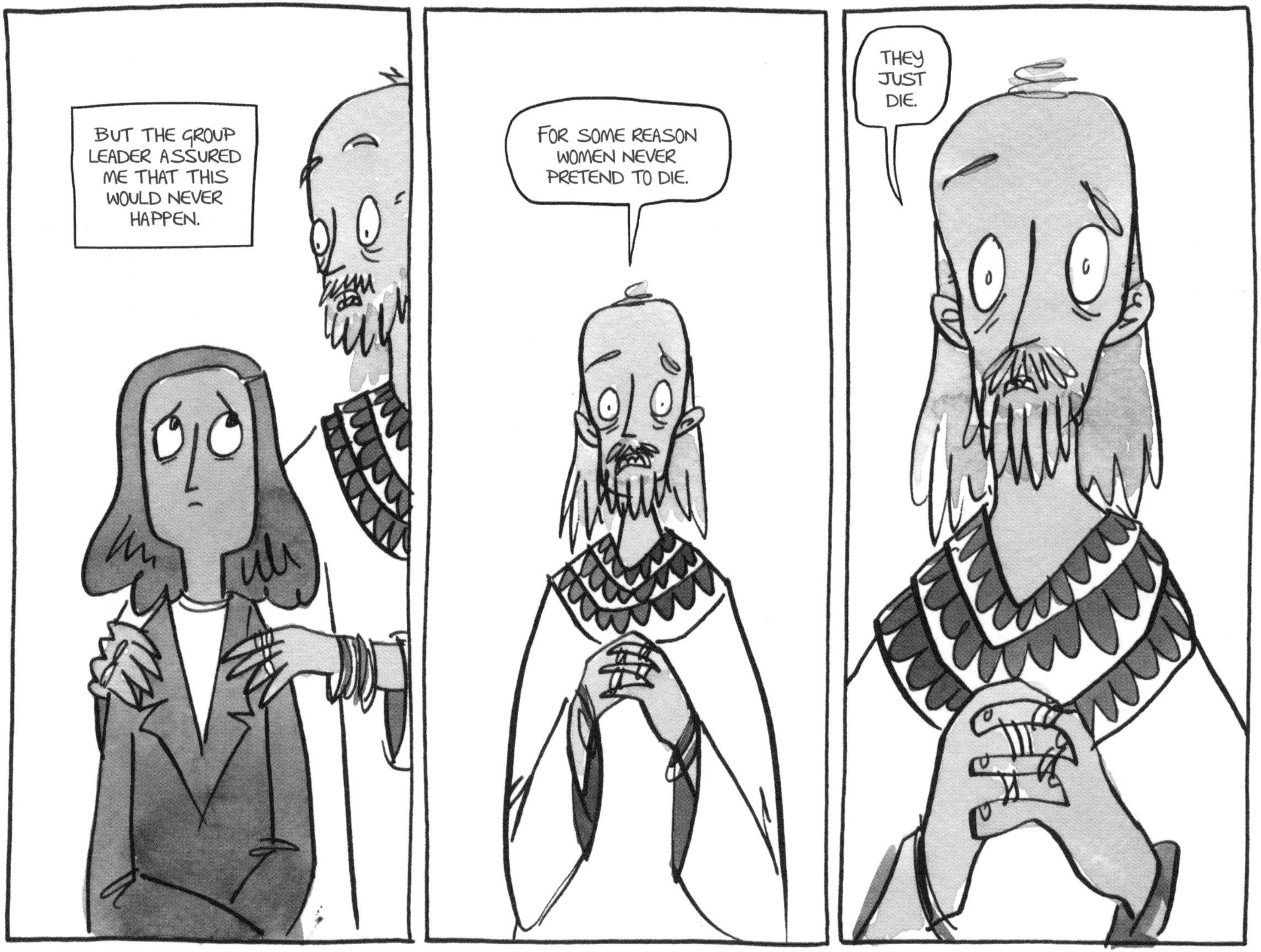
BUT THE GROUP LEADER ASSURED ME THAT THIS WOULD NEVER HAPPEN.
FOR SOME REASON WOMEN NEVER PRETEND TO DIE.
THEY JUST DIE.

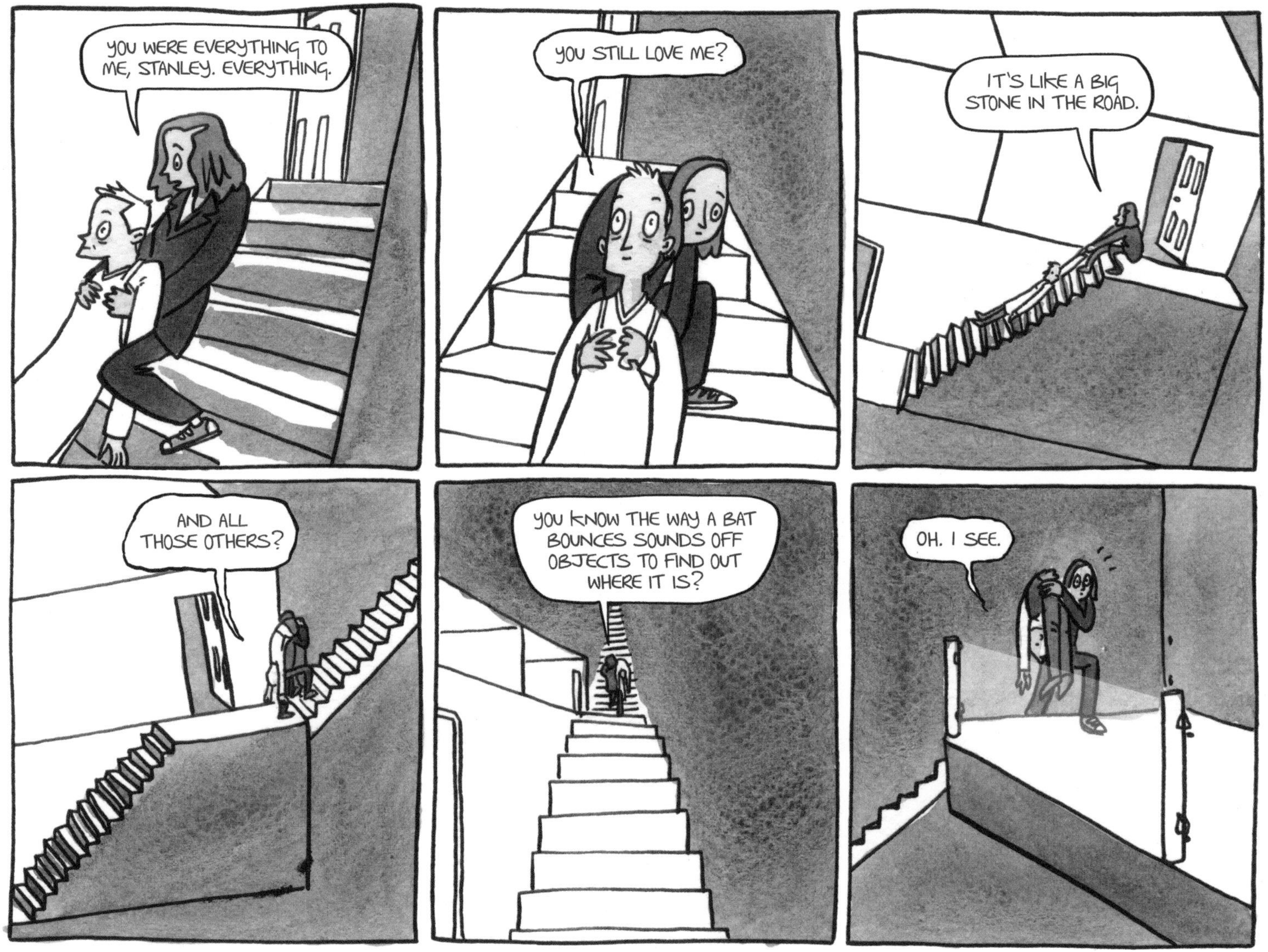
YOU WERE EVERYTHING TO ME, STANLEY. EVERYTHING.
YOU STILL LOVE ME?
IT'S LIKE A BIG STONE IN THE ROAD.
AND ALL THOSE OTHERS?
YOU KNOW THE WAY A BAT BOUNCES SOUNDS OFF OBJECTS TO FIND OUT WHERE IT IS?
OH. I SEE.

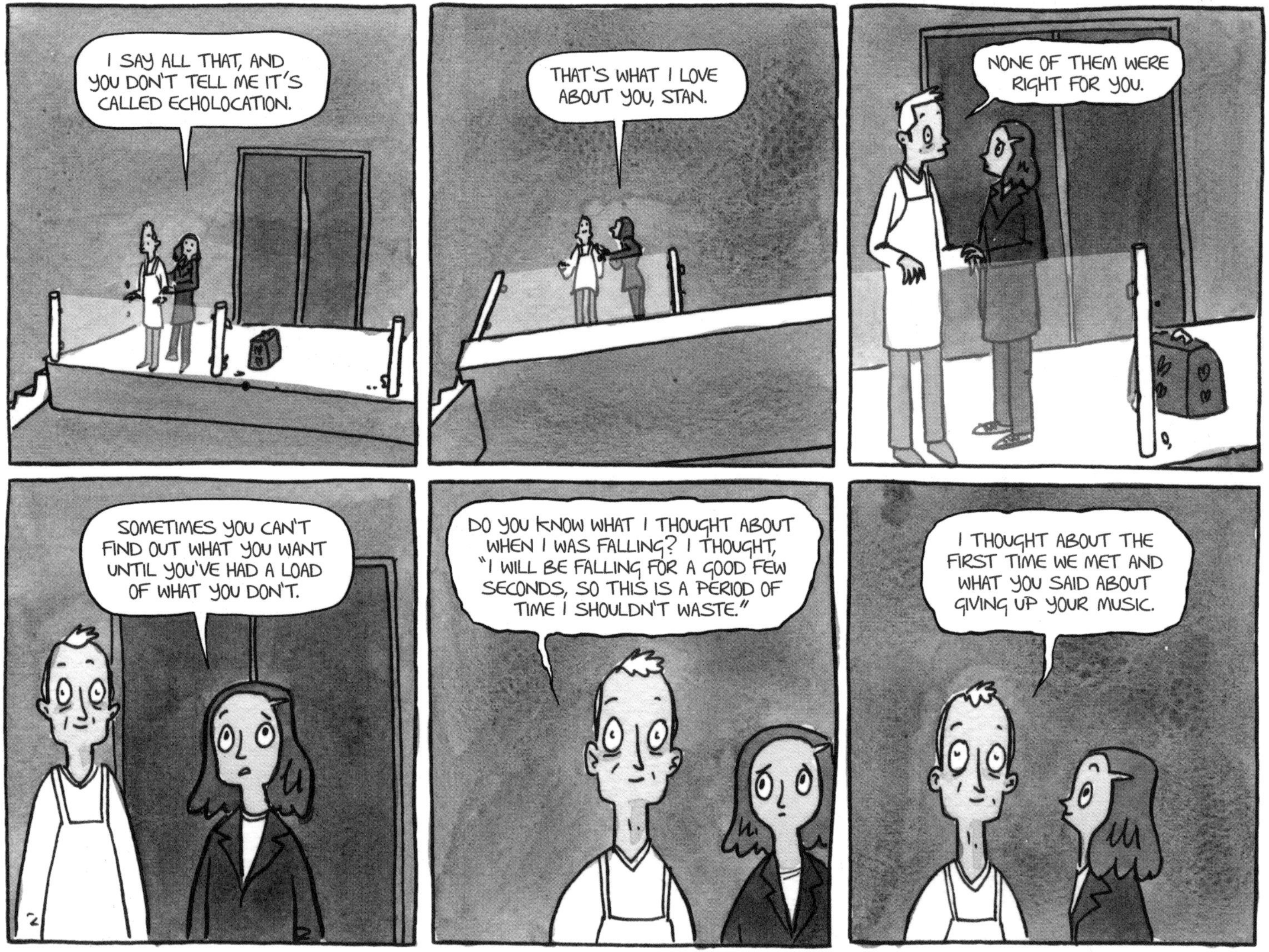
I SAY ALL THAT, AND YOU DON'T TELL ME IT'S CALLED ECHOLOCATION.
THAT'S WHAT I LOVE ABOUT YOU, STAN.
NONE OF THEM WERE RIGHT FOR YOU.
SOMETIMES YOU CAN'T FIND OUT WHAT YOU WANT UNTIL YOU'VE HAD A LOAD OF WHAT YOU DON'T.
DO YOU KNOW WHAT I THOUGHT ABOUT WHEN I WAS FALLING? I THOUGHT, "I WILL BE FALLING FOR A GOOD FEW SECONDS, SO THIS IS A PERIOD OF TIME I SHOULDN'T WASTE."
I THOUGHT ABOUT THE FIRST TIME WE MET AND WHAT YOU SAID ABOUT GIVING UP YOUR MUSIC.

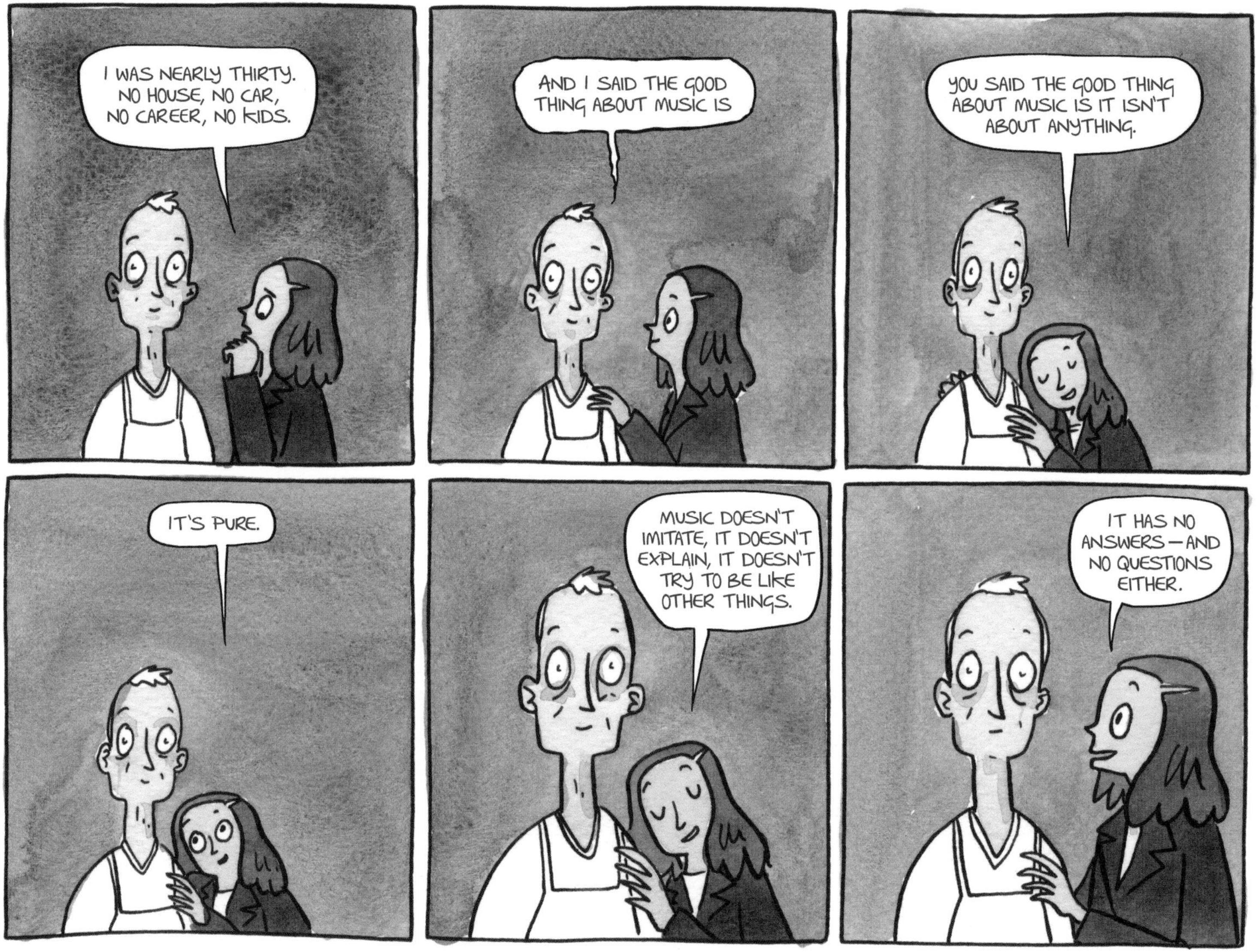
I WAS NEARLY THIRTY. NO HOUSE, NO CAR, NO CAREER, NO KIDS.
AND I SAID THE GOOD THING ABOUT MUSIC IS
YOU SAID THE GOOD THING ABOUT MUSIC IS IT ISN'T ABOUT ANYTHING.
IT'S PURE.
MUSIC DOESN'T IMITATE, IT DOESN'T EXPLAIN, IT DOESN'T TRY TO BE LIKE OTHER THINGS.
IT HAS NO ANSWERS—AND NO QUESTIONS EITHER.

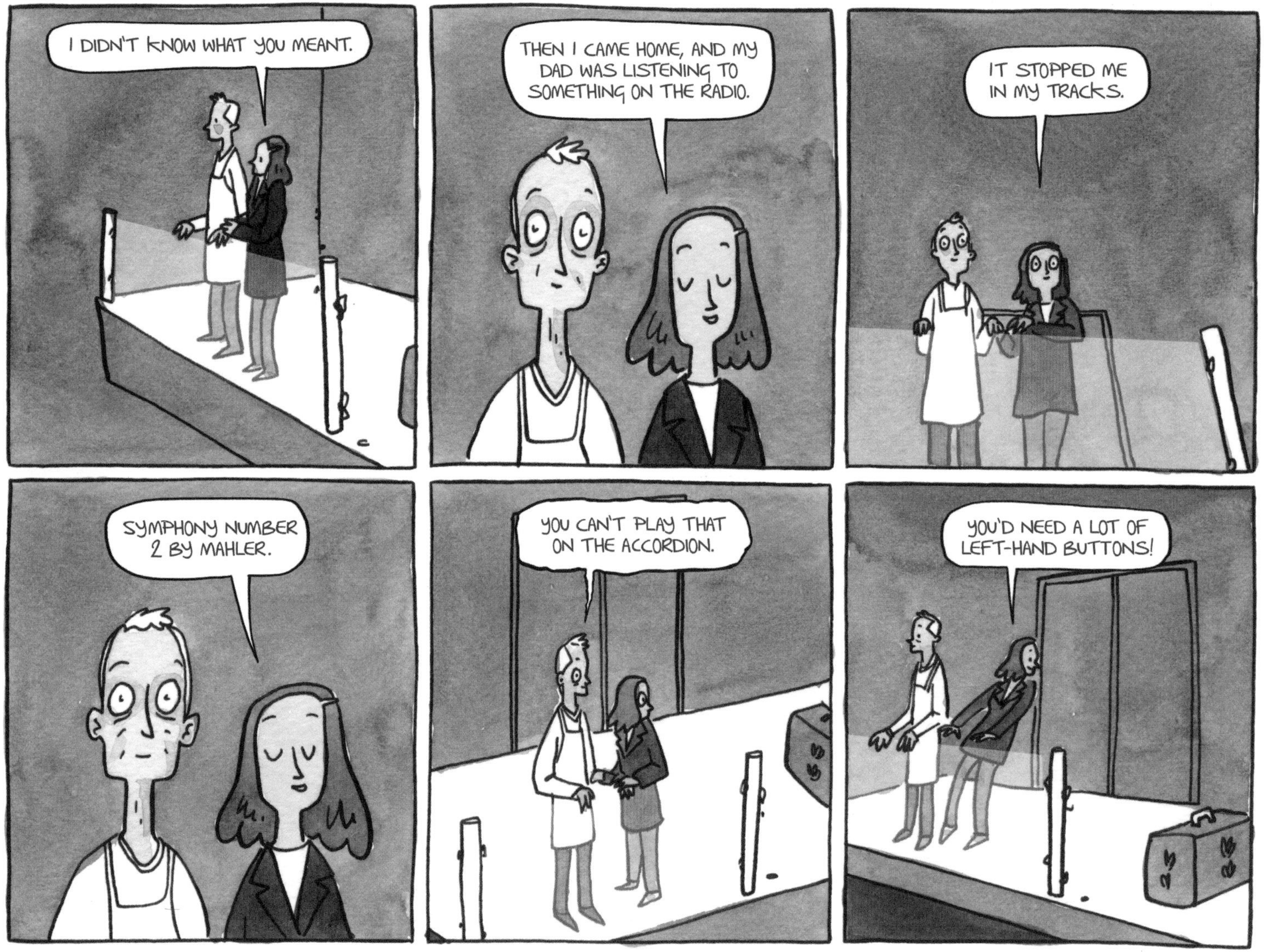
I DIDN'T KNOW WHAT YOU MEANT.
THEN I CAME HOME, AND MY DAD WAS LISTENING TO SOMETHING ON THE RADIO.
IT STOPPED ME IN MY TRACKS.
SYMPHONY NUMBER 2 BY MAHLER.
YOU CAN'T PLAY THAT ON THE ACCORDION.
YOU'D NEED A LOT OF LEFT-HAND BUTTONS!

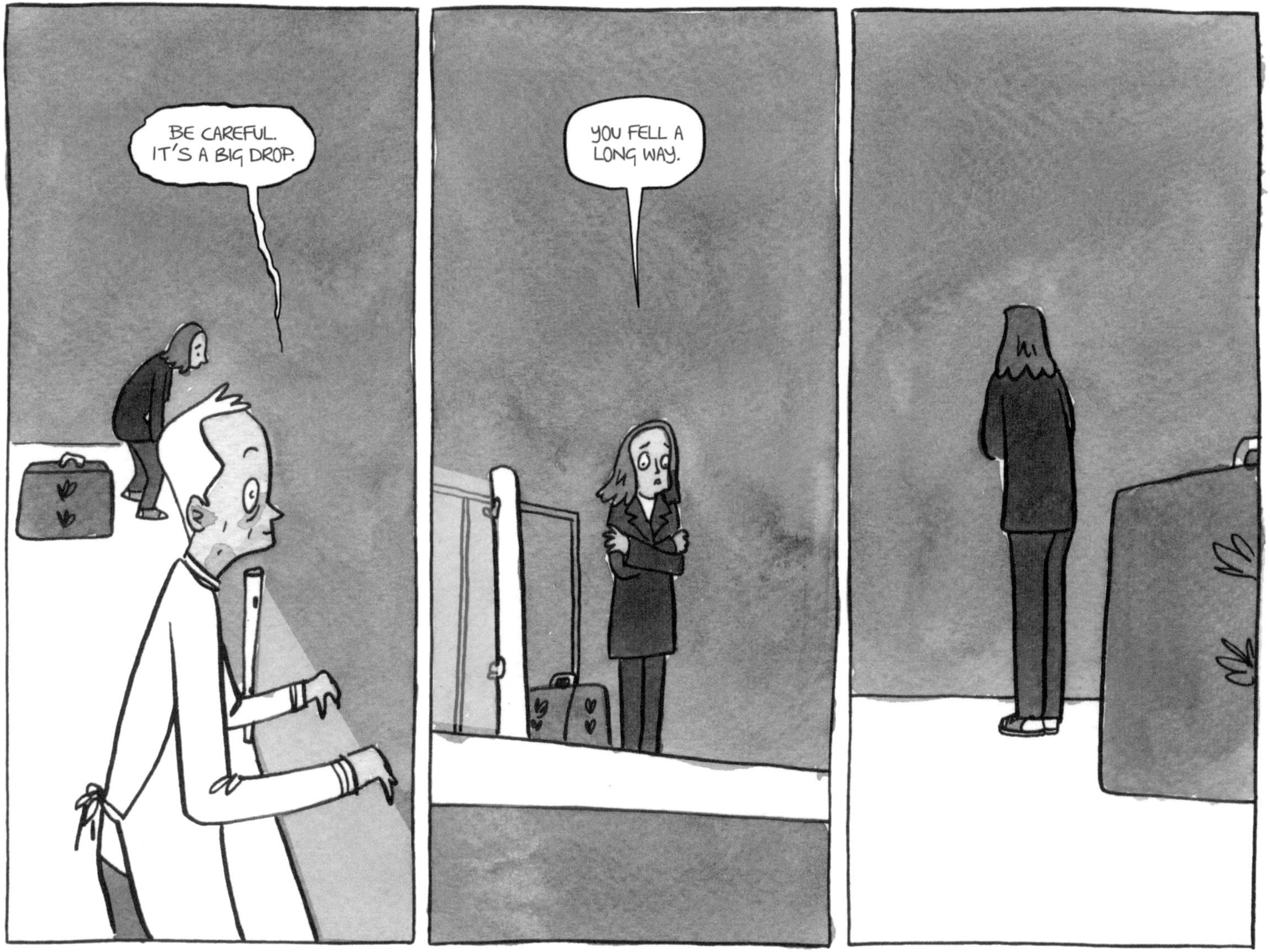
BE CAREFUL. IT'S A BIG DROP.
YOU FELL A LONG WAY.

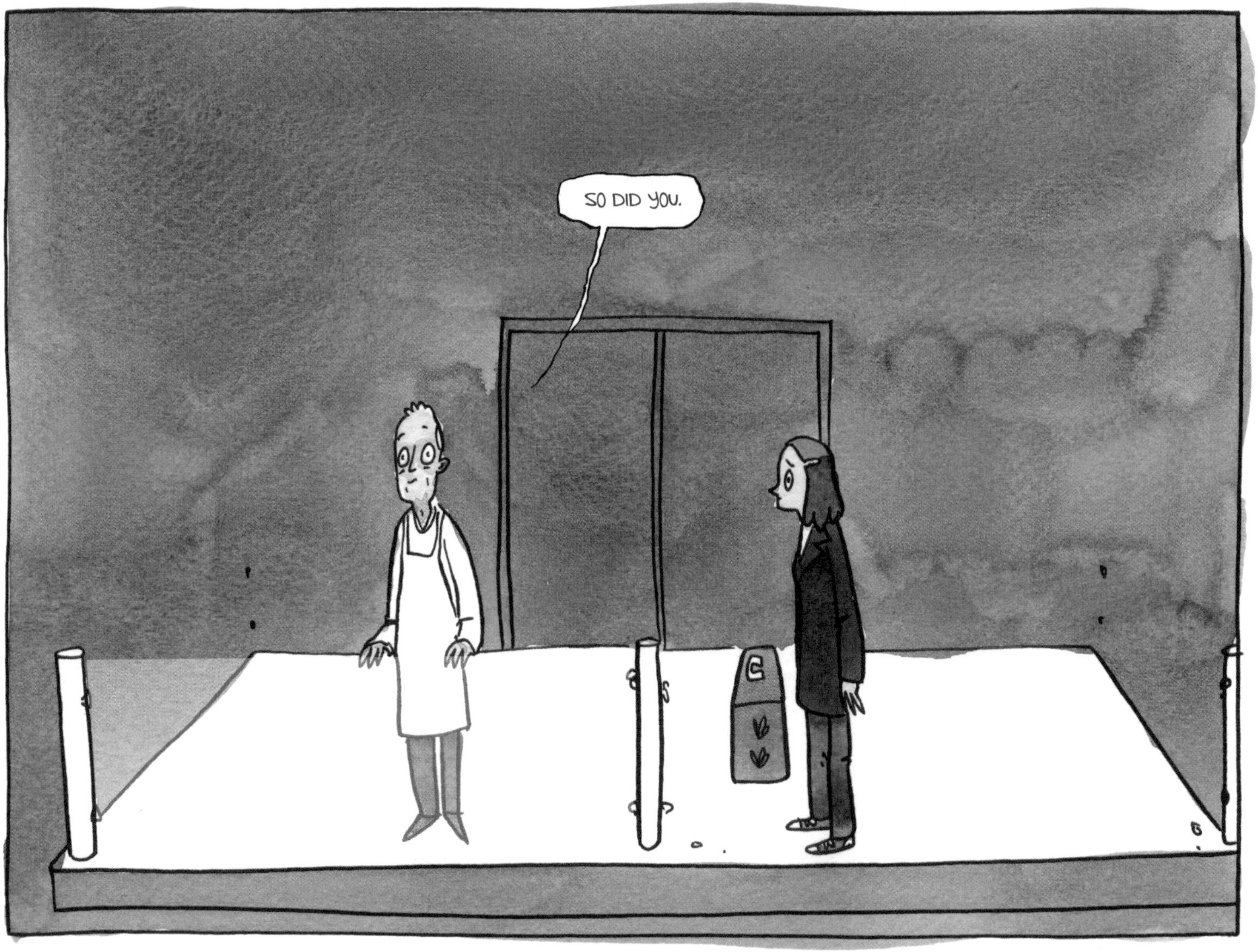
SO DID YOU.

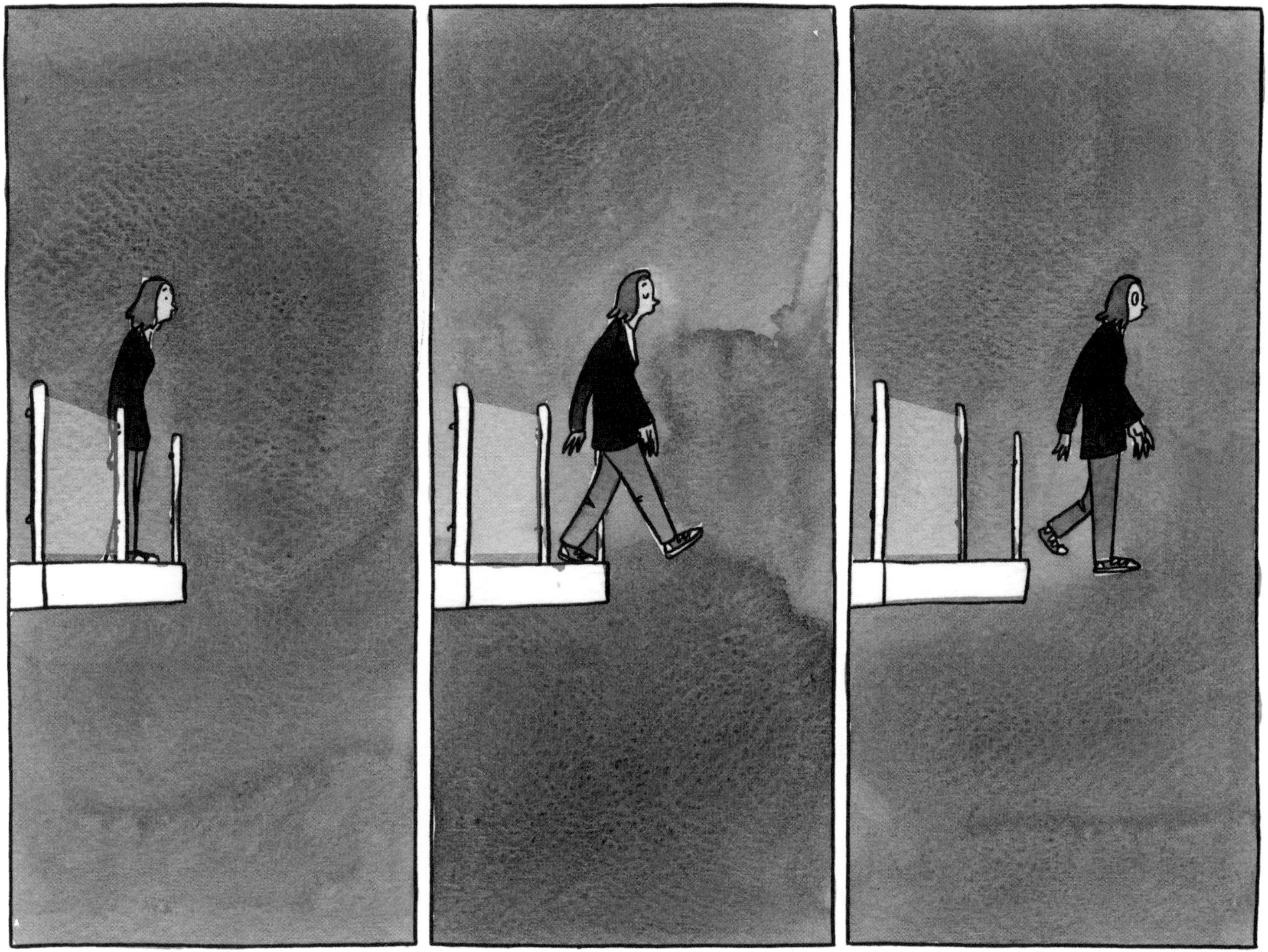

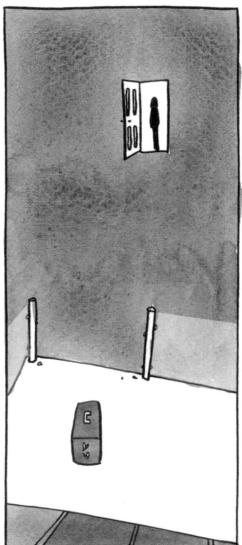

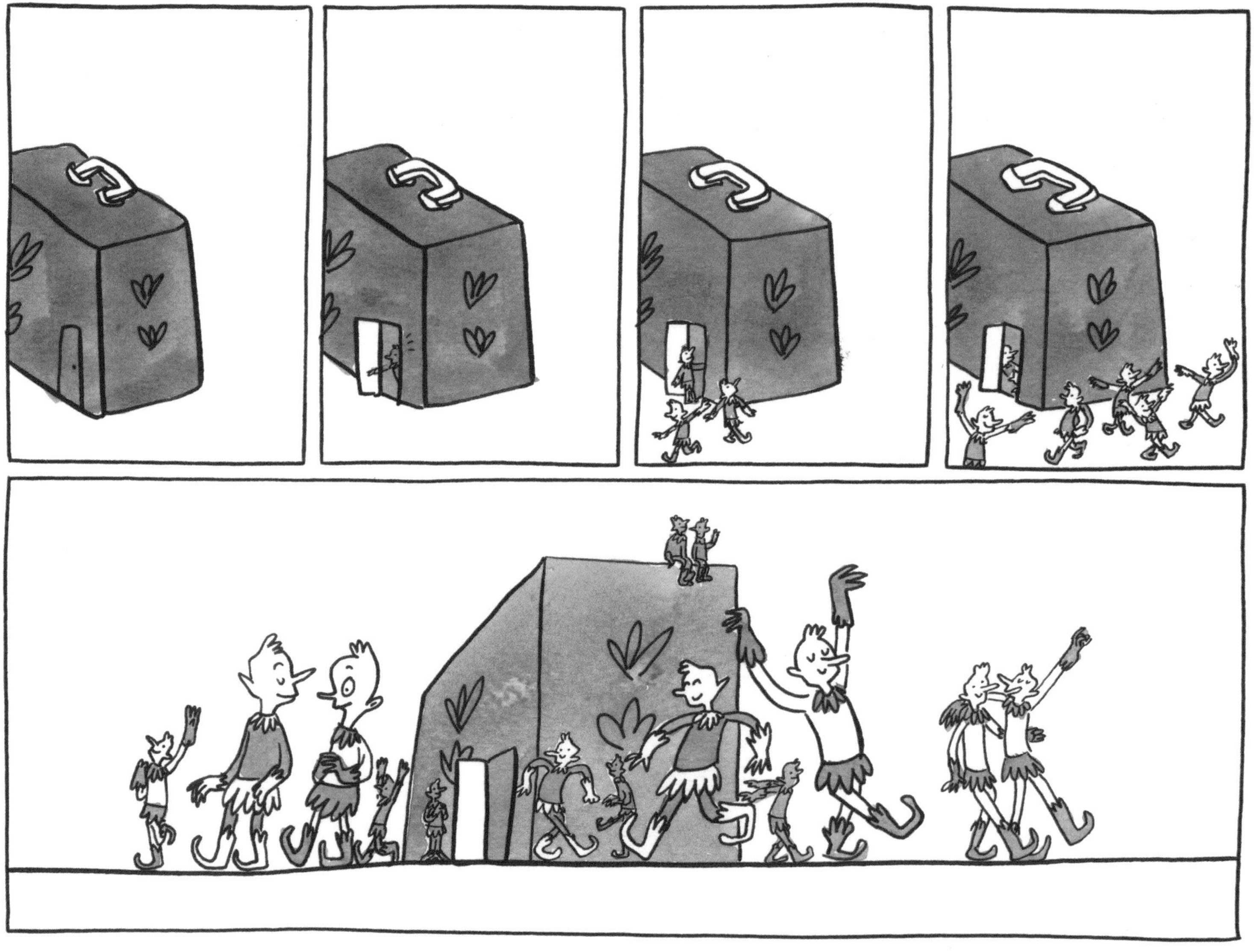

David Gaffney lives in Manchester. He is the author of the novels *Never Never* (2008) and *All the Places I've Ever Lived* (2017), plus the flash-fiction and short-story collections *Sawn-Off Tales* (2006), *Aromabingo* (2007), *The Half-Life of Songs* (2010) and *More Sawn-Off Tales* (2013). *The Guardian* said, "One hundred and fifty words by Gaffney are more worthwhile than novels by a good many others."

davidgaffney.org

Dan Berry is a cartoonist, lecturer, and podcaster from Shrewsbury, England. He is the creator of a number of comic books including *The Suitcase*, *Carry Me*, *Nicholas & Edith*, and *Bear Canyon*. Dan lectures on a degree course in comics at the School of Creative Arts, Wrexham Glyndwr University. He edited the Eisner-nominated anthology *24 by 7*. He is also the host of the popular interview podcast *Make It Then Tell Everybody*.

thingsbydan.co.uk
makeitthentelleverybody.com